22 DAYS AROUND THE WORLD

THE ITINERARY PLANNER

ROGER RAPOPORT
BURL WILLES

John Muir Publications
Santa Fe, New Mexico

For our parents

John Muir Publications, P.O. Box 613, Santa Fe, NM 87504

© 1990 by RDR Syndicate
Cover ©1990 by John Muir Publications
All rights reserved. Published 1990
Printed in the United States of America

First edition. First printing

Library of Congress Cataloging-in-Publication Data

Rapoport, Roger.
    22 days around the world: the itinerary planner/Roger Rapoport,
    Burl Willes. — 1st ed.
        p.   cm.
    ISBN 0-945465-31-9
    1. Travel.   I. Willes, Burl, 1941-   . II. Title.   III. Title:
    Twenty-two days around the world.
    G153.4.R37   1990
    910'.2'02—dc20

                                                        89-42944
                                                        CIP

Distributed to the book trade by:
W. W. Norton & Company, Inc.
New York, New York

Cover Map and Inside Maps   Michael Taylor
Typography   Copygraphics, Inc.
Printer   McNaughton & Gunn, Inc.

Pages 156 to 159 excerpted with permission from *22 Days in France* by
Rick Steves and Steve Smith (Santa Fe, N.M.: John Muir Publications,
1989).

ACKNOWLEDGMENTS
We are indebted to many people who helped us map out this global
journey. Derk and Robin Richardson researched the Thailand and Bali
sections of the book. Earl Baldock assisted us in Lombok. Fred Stross,
Egyptologist extraordinaire, was a great help in Cairo. Tanya Gregory
shared her Venice secrets, and Linda Lancione Moyer did an excellent
job in Paris.
    At the *Oakland Tribune*, Bari Brenner, Wendy Miller, Ken Long,
Belinda Taylor, Eric Newton, Roy Grimm, Leroy F. Aarons, and Robert
and Nancy Maynard all deserve our thanks. The tourist offices of Hong
Kong, Thailand, Indonesia, Egypt, Greece, Turkey, France, and Italy also
assisted us. In particular, we'd like to thank Omar Zaher, Agostino Petti,
Catherine Remedios, Peachy Villanueva, and Rene Santiago. We'd also
like to acknowledge the assistance of Peter Beren, Rick Steves, and Peter
Tannenbaum. Finally, a special thanks to all of our friends at John Muir
Publications.

CONTENTS

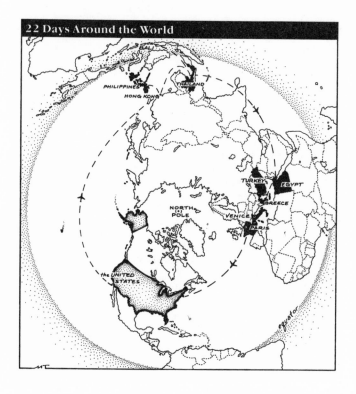

If you have at least three weeks and would like to see some of the world's most exotic destinations, we have good news. A dream trip to Hong Kong, Thailand, Egypt, Greece, and France is within your reach. Like Phineas Fogg, you can fly around the world, seeing these exotic places, and you can do it in 22—not 80—days. You may have a few predeparture questions before heading out. Perhaps you're curious about the logistics, cost, where to sleep, eat, and, of course, how to set sightseeing priorities. And that's where this book—the first self-guiding global itinerary planner—comes in.

Since the dawn of the jet age and special around-the-world airfares, savvy travelers have been taking the kind of trip that would have made Magellan or Jules Verne envious. And, of course, these passengers see a lot more than John Glenn, who circled the globe in less than two hours but bypassed every top tourist attraction in the process. Our book, based on firsthand experience, demystifies the process of planning an around-the-world trip, making it possible for you to easily realize this ultimate travel adventure.

Today, a three-week global trip is not only possible, it's far more rewarding than the standard round-trip journey to Frankfurt or Kenya. Why double back, when for a few extra dollars and a few more hours in the air, you can see one of the Seven Wonders of the World, sample the best cuisines of Europe and Asia, explore coral forests in azure seas, stay in a hotel room across the street from the Pyramids, and explore the finest island in the Aegean.

Because travel writers have no secrets, we are giving away all our favorite hideaways to ensure your trip is a great one. With around-the-world fares beginning at a little over $1,000, it's not surprising that more and more travelers are turning a three-week vacation into the trip of a lifetime. Full fare for our recommended itinerary is $1,899, and wholesalers can sell you the same trip at roughly 20 percent off. If you have more time, we've included additional information that makes it easy to add months to your trip. In fact, no matter how long you plan to spend on the global road, we can help. As you rough out your journey, you will find that these bargain tickets often have fewer strings attached than a Supersaver between Memphis and New York. You can create a flexible itinerary, fly on some of the world's finest airlines, and, best of all, choose among the most exotic destinations in the world.

These tickets ease your way to the world's great capitals, mankind's most celebrated antiquities, fabled beaches, and islands heretofore reserved for the rich and famous. On a single trip, you can sample second-century B.C. Egypt along the Nile, fifteenth-century Venice, eighteenth-century France, and twentieth-century Hong Kong. You will be pleased to discover our global itinerary offers prices comparable to single-destination resorts at home. And if you prefer a better class of service, an around-the-world business-class ticket can actually cost hundreds of dollars less than a round-trip business-class ticket between our country and Europe.

This book explains how to map out your trip, shop for the best airfare, and find the finest hotels and restaurants in all price categories. We cover the famous sights along with undiscovered gems missed by most tourists. We'll tell you where the best rooms are in the hotels we recommend, the best times to avoid crowds at popular attractions, and how to deal with visas, currency exchange, and jet lag.

Roger, travel writer at the *Oakland Tribune*, and Burl, a veteran travel agent, have written and collaborated on previous John Muir Publications guidebooks to Asia, the Caribbean, and California. We have joined forces to personally field-test this fascinating route, drawing on experts in each country and incorporating the suggestions of readers and clients who have tried out our day-by-day itineraries. You can plan this trip assured that we have slept in the hotels, eaten in the restaurants, visited the museums, and swum at the beaches recommended in this book. All our choices are based solely on merit. We traveled anonymously and accepted no gratuities or subsidies from any of the establishments mentioned in this book.

Because many travelers will want to augment the basic itinerary, which covers Hong Kong, Thailand, Egypt, Greece, and France, we have added options to the Philippines, Bali, Turkey, and Venice. If you are on a lengthy vacation, sabbatical, or open-ended trip, *22 Days Around the World* gives you the information you need to extend the basic itinerary into a much longer trip.

Whether you have three weeks, three months, or longer for your trip, rest assured that your ambition will be well rewarded. From your walk down Hong Kong's glorious Victoria Peak to your first night in Paris sailing past the illuminated monuments on the Seine, this is the sort of trip that will make you the envy of your friends. We're going to tell you about superb Thai restaurants, how to buy museum quality crafts in Egypt at bargain prices, Venetian islands where you can escape virtually all the tourists, and a wonderful Greek hotel that costs less than a night at Motel 6 back home. If you would enjoy staying in a comfortable Parisian apartment for about $70 a night or would like to step back a few centuries to a traditional village near Hong Kong, this is the trip for you. Along the way, count on meeting some of our favorite shopkeepers, restaurateurs, and hoteliers—people who will be just as memorable as many of the famous sites you'll see.

Keep in mind that one of the great advantages of this self-guiding itinerary is that you are free to adapt, augment, or change it at any time. Thanks to the great flexibility of around-the-world tickets, you will, for the most part, find it easy to alter your schedule once you leave home. Unlike an organized tour, you will not be required to pick up and leave just when things are getting interesting. Nor will our recommendations eat up your time with boring banquets that culminate in a pile of leftovers, mandatory visits to shops that provide kickbacks to tour guides, or hokey floor shows created primarily to lighten tourists' wallets.

By not trying to do too much, you'll be able to focus on the destinations that really matter. This is what the Greek poet Antipater had in mind when he created a list of travel priorities called the Seven Wonders of the World. The Greek dream was to visit all these best bets in a single lifetime. Today, only one of the Seven Wonders still stands (and is on our itinerary). But many other singular sights can be seen on a single trip. Selectivity and a workable itinerary are the keys to a successful trip.

This book concentrates on the highlights of five countries in a workable, proven itinerary designed to help you experience the sights and sounds of each culture without rushing about in a futile attempt to see everything. To make your trip more rewarding, we've divided this book into daily itinerary sections containing:

1. A general **overview** of each day.
2. **Suggested schedules** for travel, sightseeing, shopping and meals.
3. Summaries of major **sightseeing highlights** rated ▲▲▲ Don't miss; ▲▲ Try hard to see; ▲ Worthwhile if you can make it, with step-by-step walking tours and excursion directions to the most important sights.
4. **Food** and **lodgings** suggestions, from bargain and moderately priced favorites to deluxe splurges.
5. **Practical tips**—random tidbits that will help make your trip go smoothly.
6. **Itinerary options**—excursion suggestions for travelers who have more time.
7. **Maps** designed to point out walking routes, recommended restaurants, and sightseeing highlights.

Why Around the World?

Remarkably low airfares offered by nearly all major international carriers put global vacations within the reach of many travelers. Special discount deals, which we'll discuss later, make these trips even more affordable. In addition, many frequent fliers win around-the-world tickets.

If you have at least three weeks, you'll find it easy to arrange a worldwide trip. Hotel costs may actually run less than a standard three-week vacation at a major American resort. Food and incidentals will be about the same. Travelers who like to go first class will find that comfort is fairly priced along our route. For example, a night on the Nile at one of our favorite hotels in the world runs about half what you would expect to pay for similar accommodations in New York. A perfectly situated hotel on Hong Kong harbor can run as little as $40 a night. And if you want to save money, we have some great suggestions in Egypt, Thailand, and Venice for as little as $35.

Now let's consider a few of the rewards of your journey. To begin with, you are taking advantage of around-the-world airfares while they are at rock bottom. Second, you are seeing destinations, particularly in Thailand, Greece, and rural Hong Kong, that have escaped twentieth-century intrusion. Development threatens these remote places, and the sooner you see them, the better.

There's another reason to go around the world that you may not have thought about. Travel changes your life in big and little ways. Perhaps the best thing about a trip around the world is that it provides an excellent overview. If you've seen Europe but have never been to Asia, this is an ideal way to sample a new region. If you're curious about what's going on in the Middle East but have always put off the idea of going to Egypt, you now have the perfect excuse to go. A journey around the world is several trips in one. At a minimum, you'll sample at least three major regions. And, if you have extra time, you can even add lots of stopovers to see the relatives in our own country at no extra charge.

You'll begin in Hong Kong, a beautiful city where traditional Chinese life and a thriving Asian business center coexist peacefully. Blessed with wonderful restaurants, museums, and a delightful ferry system, this city is also handy to secluded islands that give you a look at rural Chinese villages.

Thailand, one of Asia's most popular destinations, is known for its golden temples, exotic restaurants, hill country tribes, and tropical islands with translucent bays. In this lush country—famous for its silk goods, orchids, elephants, and fascinating river life—you'll have a chance to see both modern and traditional ways of life.

Cairo, home of the Sphinx and the pyramids, will quickly transport you back to ancient times. Some of the world's greatest mosques and museums are found in this city, which is also home of a bazaar with an incredible 13,000 stalls!

Greece is a perennial favorite of Europeans, and after landing here, you'll understand why. Great weather, food, antiquities, beaches, inns, and food make this country a pleasure. From Athens to Santorini, you'll also enjoy some astonishing bargains.

Your last stop, Paris, is the perfect place to end an around-the-world journey. You'll enjoy some of the world's best-known museums and monuments and dine at a restaurant favored by chefs who vacation in Paris for the same reason you do. A relaxed walking tour leaves plenty of time to linger at sidewalk cafés, explore the city's fabulous parks, and, of course, browse in some of the world's most sophisticated neighborhoods.

How Much Will It Cost?

Perhaps you've read or heard about tours that will take you around the world on the Concorde for three weeks at a mere $30,800 per person. Don't be discouraged by this kind of extravagance. You don't have to take out a second mortgage on your house to afford a trip around the world. On a per-mile basis, a global trip is an excellent value. At a time when the carriers burden the typical traveler with endless red tape, around-the-world tickets remain relatively flexible. And bargain prices don't mean you have to sacrifice comfort or settle for rubber chicken. Depending on your routing, you can choose carriers like Singapore, Thai Airways and Cathay Pacific, all known for their excellent in-flight service. Other excellent choices, using wide-bodied, comfortable 747s, DC10s, and L1011s, include Canadian International, United, American, Northwest, TWA, Japan Airlines, China Airlines, Malaysian, and Garuda Indonesian.

Full-price, around-the-world tickets covering our itinerary on reliable carriers like TWA, Delta, or American in combination with Singapore (the latter was voted one of the three best airlines in the world by an experienced travelers' poll) run about $1,900. Your travel agent can easily obtain this ticket for you. If you don't have a travel agent, ask around for personal recommendations. If you're prepared to do a little extra work, you might be able to cut as much as 20 percent off this fare by dealing with a bonded wholesaler known in the trade as a consolidator. These companies, which advertise in such publications as the *New York Times*, the *Los Angeles Times*, and the *San Francisco Examiner-Chronicle*, put together discount deals on around-the-world tickets.

Some limited itineraries that do not include all the stops on

our 22-day plan start at a little over $1,000. These deals also
limit your choice of airlines. A consolidator might be able to
save you several hundred dollars off the full fare price quoted by
the airlines. The best way to buy these discounted tickets is to
find a bonded ASTA member travel agent who deals with consolidators. That way, you are protected against the possibility of
the discounter going bankrupt. To find an agent who works
with consolidators, ask friends who travel frequently for a
recommendation. Or simply call around to find the right kind
of agency. No matter who you work with, try to protect yourself
by paying for your ticket when you pick it up. If you decide to
deal direct with a wholesaler who lives in another town, be sure
to pin down the exact delivery date of your ticket with a written
contract. Another good idea when dealing with wholesalers is
to use your credit card. This approach gives you recourse
through the card company in case a seller fails to produce the
promised ticket.

If you can afford an extra $1,000, we encourage you to con-
sider paying extra for the added comfort, service, and good
food that come with business class. For $2,899, you can enjoy
our recommended itinerary in this higher class of service. If you
fly business class regularly, you may be surprised to learn that
this $2,899 global fare is several hundred dollars less than a
round-trip business-class ticket between cities like San Francisco and Rome.

Booking Your Flight

On the typical $1,899 ticket from carriers like TWA and Singa-
pore, reservations must be made at least 14 days before departure, and you must confirm your originating flight. All other
segments can be left open, and, space permitting, you can
change your flights. There is no minimum stay if you depart
from the United States, and tickets are generally valid for a maximum of six months to one year.

During the trip, you must remain on the carrier combination
that sold you the ticket. That means if the plane you want is full,
you may have to wait for the next flight out on your chosen carrier. The easiest way to avoid this difficulty is to make advance
bookings for each segment as soon as possible. We have chosen
a route with frequent service, which means that seat availability
should not be a problem. Reservations as far in advance as possible are a must for flight segments during holiday periods such
as Christmas, Chinese New Year (in Asia), and the height of the
summer season. It also makes sense to reserve a flight home at
the end of your journey.

On these tickets, you are required to continue in a westbound (or eastbound) direction around the globe. Backtracking is generally not permitted, and no foreign city may be visited more than once. It is possible to stop in some American cities more than once, depending on your carrier. In fact, it is possible to see a lot of our own country on a global ticket. For example, on the TWA/Singapore combination that covers our recommended itinerary, you can make as many as 12 extra stops within the United States at no extra charge. Children are typically allowed to fly at 67 percent of the adult fare. Infants under age 2 not occupying a seat pay 10 percent of the applicable adult fare. Because of the duration of this trip, however, and our belief that every passenger should, for safety's sake, be strapped in during takeoff and landing, we believe you are wiser to purchase a seat for every member of your family.

Many of these same rules apply for passengers flying on less expensive tickets purchased from consolidators. The big difference between the two fare plans is cancellation penalties and refunds. In general, full-fare around-the-world tickets will refund all your money if you cancel your trip two weeks or more before your departure. If you cancel less than 14 days before departure on tickets purchased in the United States, 75 percent of the fare will be refunded. And in most cases, you can get a full refund in the event of the death or serious illness of a traveling companion or member of the immediate family. In such cases, passengers are typically permitted to reroute their itinerary after departure without penalty. If you cancel your trip after departure, you get a refund of 75 percent of the fare paid minus the applicable fare for flights already taken.

If you are flying on a less expensive ticket purchased from a wholesaler, refunds are generally not available. No matter what kind of fare you're using, we believe no one should fly around the world without purchasing trip cancellation insurance. It typically costs about $5.50 per $100 of coverage. One of the best programs we know about is offered by Travel Guard at 800-826-1300 (in Wisconsin, 800-634-0644). In addition to refunds for standard reasons like illness, this company sells a policy that refunds up to half your cancellation penalty if you decide not to go for any reason.

While around-the-world tickets are flexible, perhaps the most important restriction to keep in mind is that you cannot switch destinations. That means if you are booked from Bangkok to Cairo, you may have a hard time adding a stopover in Bombay without an additional charge. For this reason, we urge you to plan your itinerary with care. Otherwise, you may end up spending extra money for add-on fares after leaving home. A complete discussion of cancellation insurance is available in the

January 1989 issue of *Consumer Reports Travel Letter*, available
for $5 from CRTL, 2506 Washington St., Mt. Vernon, NY 10553.
While you're at it, you might also want to order, for another $5,
their September 1988 listing of around-the-world airfare packages on 48 different airline combinations. This useful summary
shows which routes various carriers serve.

After deciding which cities, if any, you are adding which are
not covered by the major airlines, shop around for carriers.
You'll find they divide cities into three categories. An "on-loop"
destination can be reached eastbound or westbound. For example, Hong Kong is on-loop with Northwest and KLM, meaning
you can fly here in either direction. But Shannon is a "dead-
end," which means you can only fly here on an eastbound trip
that begins with a flight across the Atlantic. Lisbon is "off-loop,"
which means you can't get there on this airline combination.

Sometimes, the easiest way to include an optional city will be
to simply purchase an extra flight that supplements your global
ticket. This "off-loop" travel can be the least expensive way to
add extra stops. For example, a full-fare around-the-world ticket
that includes a stop in Nepal could run over $2,000. You may be
able to save money by supplementing a discount around-the-
world fare with an extra ticket between Bangkok and Nepal.

After doing your research, you may discover that it's not possible to buy an around-the-world ticket that takes you to all the
destinations you have in mind. For example, airline pairs that
take you to Bali may not get you to Venice. *Consumer Reports
Travel Letter* recommends "making your compromises in Western Europe where you can often use fast trains to fill the gaps."
That's one of the reasons we recommend going to Venice by rail
from Paris. (The other reason is that the train trip across the Alps
is a winner.)

Your choice of carrier combinations will be dictated by your
route. Generally, full-fare tickets are served by a pair of carriers.
If you plan to make a number of extra stops in the United States,
one of these carriers should be an American airline.

Be persistent when dealing with airlines. Keep asking questions when you talk to reservation agents. Some may not be
familiar with all the rules and routing possibilities on global
trips. If one carrier says you can't fly a certain route, call the
partner airline it works with to make sure this is true. If you're
dubious about the rules, ask to speak to a supervisor. When you
get the answer you want, be sure to take down the name of the
reservation agent helping you.

Safety

Reasonable precautions will ensure your safety on this trip. Take
your money in the form of a well-known brand of traveler's

checks. The exchange rate for them is usually more favorable than currency. You'll find currency exchange facilities at all major airports as well as at banks and hotels. Credit cards can be used at major hotels, restaurants, and some stores. Always carry your traveler's checks, credit cards, airline tickets, and passport in a money belt. Never carry valuables in a purse, bag, or pocket. Photocopy your airline ticket and the first page of your passport and pack them separately. We also recommend using hotel safe deposit boxes.

Money

We quote prices in this book in the local currency of each country, followed in parentheses by the approximate U.S. dollar values. These prices change constantly due to inflation and changes in international currency rates. You're likely to find that prices in some countries have remained roughly the same in local currency, while the U.S. dollar prices have changed; in other countries along your route, prices in local currency will have changed while U.S. dollars remain fairly accurate. Despite such changes, the prices we quote here will give you a good idea of relative values within each country. The approximate foreign currency exchange rates as of late 1989 are:

Hong Kong: 1 Hong Kong dollar (HK$1) = $.13; $1 = HK$7.8
Philippines: 1 peso = $.05; $1 = 20.8 pesos
Thailand: 1 baht = $.04; $1 = 25.2 baht
Bali (Indonesia): 1 rupiah = $.00056; $1 = 1,775 rupiah
Egypt: 1 pound = $.39; $1 = 2.55 pounds
Greece: 1 drachma = $.006; $1 = 167 drachmas
Turkey: 1 lira = $.0004; $1 = 2,295 liras
France: 1 franc = $.15; $1 = 6.5 francs
Italy: 1 lira = $.0007; $1 = 1,390 lire

Please keep in mind that all prices quoted in this book are subject to an inflation factor of 5 to 10 percent annually. If you're traveling during the holiday season, rates may be subject to a surcharge.

Lodging

In Hong Kong, the busy and well-located YMCA International Hotel faces the ferry terminal. Rates here start at $10 for a dorm room, $40 for a pleasant room in a modern high-rise, and $75 for the family suite with kitchen. Comfortable midrange hotels start around $75. Traveling deluxe ($150 and up), you will be pampered by huge staffs at some of the finest hotels in the world.

In both Thailand and Bali, the graciousness of the people is felt at $8-a-night beachfront cottages in Thailand or $5-a-night homestays on Bali. Western-style toilets and showers are the

rule in moderate ($15 to $50) and luxury ($50 to $200) categories but not so in budget accommodations, where floor toilets
and bucket showers are the rule.

In major Philippine cities like Manila and Cebu, an inexpensive room starts at around $30, with deluxe accommodations
running $75 to $100. On the resort island of Bohol, inexpensive
lodging runs as little as $10 a night, while first-class establish-
ments cost around $40.

In Egypt, expect to pay about $30 to $65 a night for a moderately priced hotel room. You can stay across the street from the
pyramids for as little as $60 a night. Luxury hotels charge $100
and up.

Some of our favorite midrange hotels in Greece run about
$35 a night, while luxury establishments are $75 and up.

We've mentioned a number of our favorite budget hotels in
excellent Paris locations. They run as little as $35. A moderate
Paris hotel room runs $50 to $100 with deluxe hotels charging
$150 and up. Comfortable apartments can be rented by the
week for $70 a night, complete with kitchen facilities.

In Venice, budget travelers who book ahead can find rooms
for as little as $35. Midrange hotels here run $60 to $100. The
sky is the limit on luxury establishments, which charge as much
as $400 per night.

If you are traveling during Christmas, Chinese New Year, or
the summer months of June, July, or August, hotel reservations
are essential in Hong Kong and Thailand. Confirmed hotel
space is always a good idea in Egypt, particularly during the
September to May season. Holiday and summer season reservations are also a good idea for other stops on our recommended
itinerary. Remember that the best rates in each category are
often booked months in advance.

Food

Hong Kong is a gourmet's paradise; food of every type and
description is available at small restaurants ($1 to $5) or in luxury restaurants with unique waterfront vistas.

Thai food is always fresh and generally spicy. Tropical fruits
abound and are very inexpensive. Moderately priced meals are
$3 to $6, and deluxe meals run $15 to $25.

On Bali, the food is less spicy and even less expensive. Fried
rice, noodles, and *gado gado* (hot vegetable salad with peanut
dressing) cost $1 to $3. Dinner at one of the finer restaurants in
our favorite Balinese town, Ubud, will run under $10. In the lux-
ury tourist resorts, allow $15 to $20 for a similar meal.

For health reasons, hotels and tour boats are our first choice
for dining in Egypt. You'll enjoy local specialties like *taamiya*

(falafel) and a spiced minced meat called *kofta*, as well as continental cuisine. Allow $5 to $10 for an inexpensive meal and $20 to $30 for a deluxe dinner. The round brown bread found at market bakeries is excellent.

In Greece, you'll find moussaka, lamb, pasta, and other specialties at moderate prices. For less than $10, you can dine well anywhere in the country. Expect to pay $20 and up in deluxe restaurants. Greek coffeehouses are the perfect way to start your day here.

France is famous for its cuisine but not for its prices. Follow our suggestions and you'll be able to choose between the best restaurants in all price categories. Mussels and other seafood dishes, steak and fries, and main dish salads can all be enjoyed at reasonable prices. We also have suggestions for café snacks like *croque-monsieur* (a grilled ham and cheese sandwich), crepes, pastries, and wonderful picnic food. Figure on spending $10 or less for a light meal, $15 to $20 for a moderately priced dinner. When it comes to haute cuisine (we have a great suggestion), you can easily spend over $100.

Venice can be pricey, with elegant dinners rivaling the prices you'd pay in Paris. But our favorite inexpensive *trattoria* offers elegant pasta dishes for about $10. You'll also enjoy fresh seafood, fish soups, and *risottos* at moderate establishments charging less than $20. The wine bars here, which serve sandwiches and snacks, are an excellent choice for a light meal.

Public Transportation

In Hong Kong, the ferry system is one of the world's best. Travel to offshore islands and nearby towns costs less than $2. Within the city, the subway is efficient, safe, easy to use and inexpensive. Cabs are very reasonable in Hong Kong as long as you avoid rush-hour traffic.

Bus travel in Thailand is efficient and inexpensive. For local trips within the cities, taxis are very reasonable.

On Bali, bemos (small public vans carrying five to eight passengers) are omnipresent and can take you wherever you want to go for minuscule sums. Private taxis can be hired by the hour or day at approximately $5 per hour.

In the Philippines, cabs are very reasonable. In Manila, you can rent them for $5 an hour. A car and driver leased from Avis for the entire day runs about $60. On resort islands like Bohol, a car and driver for the day runs $20 to $30. Small local taxis known as tricycles run under $1 for a short trip. Air transportation is excellent and inexpensive. For less than $60, you can fly from Manila to nearly any destination in the archipelago. Ferries are also very cheap.

Cairo taxis are a steal. A car with driver costs about $2 to $3 an hour. Most local flights within Egypt run under $60. Cruises on the Nile, including accommodations and all meals, cost $80 to $325 a day, depending on the class of service.

In Greece, taxis are inexpensive, as are domestic flights and ferries. Rental cars can be costly in Greece.

The moderately priced Paris Métro is one of the most efficient transportation systems in the world. The domestic train system is also a blessing for travelers, thanks to its frequent, fast service. Taxis are expensive.

In Venice, expensive gondolas serve as private taxis. A cheaper alternative are the public ferries, called vaporetti. Additional ferries known as traghetto connect St. Mark's with the Lido and other outlying islands.

Visas

Besides a valid passport, visas are required for Egypt. These visas are valid for three months from the date of issue. If you are on an extended itinerary, keep in mind that the clock starts running as soon as you pick up this document. Travelers who expect to complete their stay in Egypt or Nepal more than 90 days after leaving the United States will have to pick up their visas en route at embassies in Hong Kong or Bangkok.

No visa is required for stays in these countries up to the following limits. In the Western European countries and some other destinations, visas can be extended, provided you have sufficient funds and are not gainfully employed. Check with each country's consulate or embassy for details.

Hong Kong: 30 days
Thailand: 15 days
Indonesia (Bali): 2 months
Philippines: 21 days
Greece: 3 months
France: 3 months
Italy: 3 months

An easy way to obtain visas is to take advantage of a visa service. The very nominal extra charge is justified by the fast service and convenience. Two excellent companies we've used are Visas Unlimited (582 Market St., San Francisco, CA 94105; tel. 415-421-7351) and Visa Aides (870 Market Street, San Francisco, CA 95105; tel. 415-562-7137). Visa service companies are listed in most telephone yellow pages under Passport Photo and Visa Services. Your travel agent can also suggest reputable companies to assist you in obtaining visas. If you prefer to obtain visas directly, check with the appropriate consulates or national tourist information offices for details.

When to Go

The best months to start this itinerary are January to May and
September to November. Our climate chart (see below) provides
complete information on what climate to expect on your
journey.

	Hong Kong	Thailand	Philippines	Bali	Egypt	Greece Turkey	Paris
Jan	sunny, cool	sunny, hot	sunny, hot	sunny with rain	sunny, mild	cold, sun possible	cold, overcast, rain
Feb	sunny, cool	sunny, hot	sunny, hot	sunny with rain	sunny, mild	cold, sun possible	cold, overcast,
Mar	sunny, pleasant	sunny, hot	sunny, hot	sunny with rain	sunny, mild	sunny	cold
Apr	sunny, pleasant	sunny, hot	sunny, hot	sunny with rain	sunny, warm	sunny, pleasant	sunny, variable showers
May	sunny, warm	hot, some rain	hot, some rain	sunny, showers	very hot	sunny, pleasant	sunny, variable showers
Jun	sunny, hot	hot, some rain	hot, some rain	warm, light rain	very hot	sunny, pleasant	sunny, occasional rain
Jul	sunny, hot, humid	hot, some rain	hot, some, rain	warm, light rain	very hot	hot, dry	hot
Aug	hot, humid	hot, some rain	hot, some rain	warm, light rain	very hot	hot, dry	hot
Sep	stormy rainy, hot	rainy	rainy	warm, light rain	very hot	warm, occasional rain	sunny
Oct	warm	warm	warm	warm, pleasant	hot	warm, occasional rain	sunny, some rain
Nov	warm	warm	warm	hot and humid	sunny, pleasant	cold	crisp with rain
Dec	cool	warm	warm	rainy with sunny periods	sunny, pleasant	cold	cold with rain

Climate Chart

Health Precautions

We recommend that you heed your physician's advice on vaccinations, immunizations, and other precautions against malaria, hepatitis, venereal diseases, cholera, and typhoid fever. We are strong believers in preventive medicine on foreign trips. We always drink bottled water, beer, wine, or soft drinks rather than tap water. We avoid shellfish and raw food. In Asia, we carry our own chopsticks to use when eating any freshly cooked food from street stalls. Rather than use a vendor's dishes, which may have been washed with questionable tap water, we eat off paper utensils or simply take away items on wax paper provided by the stall.

Chances of getting malaria or dengue fever are minimal with protection against disease-carrying mosquitoes. We recommend an insect repellent that contains Deet. Be sure to protect your ankles, a prime mosquito target. At night, sleep under a mosquito net or fan if you are in an area where these insects are prevalent.

Jet Lag

Our itinerary goes westbound. There are practical reasons for this approach. First, your longest flight, from the United States to Asia, takes place when you are fresh. Second, a westbound trip means you will only have to sleep on the plane a maximum of one night on your trip, from Bangkok to Egypt. There are even daytime flights on this route for travelers who find them more convenient. If you flew eastbound, you would have to fly at least three nights on the plane when traveling from America to Europe, Cairo to Bangkok, and Asia to America. This fact alone tends to make an eastbound trip more tiring, because most people don't sleep as well on a plane as they do in a hotel room.

Another advantage to the westbound trip is that you lose time—16 to 19 hours—in one giant leap across the international date line on the first leg of your trip to Hong Kong. For the balance of the trip, you are gaining time while continuing westbound through Asia and Europe. This means that you arrive at new destinations like Thailand, Egypt, and Paris with extra time at your disposal. A good example is Egypt, where you pick up five hours on your trip from Bangkok. Using our itinerary, you'll be able to arrive early in the day and rest up before venturing out to see the city. Our itinerary generally calls for morning or early afternoon arrival at your destinations, making it easier for you to check into your hotels and get situated while local tourist offices, museums, banks, and other tourist facilities are open.

If you do plan a late arrival, try to let your hotel know when you'll be checking in. A deposit for your first night or a credit card guarantee will hold your room. Incidentally, if you have never been an early morning person, you will be one for at least four or five days as you begin your trip. This makes it easier to visit popular attractions first thing, before the crowds build up. By the way, due to time-zone changes, you shouldn't expect to take in much nightlife for the first few days of your trip. If you find yourself tiring during the early days of your trip, simply turn in early. Occasional naps can also be a good antidote for jet lag.

What to Pack
TRAVEL LIGHT! Ideally, take carryon baggage. You'll save time at your destination and often be one of the first through customs and immigration. Even more important, you'll eliminate the possibility of delayed or lost luggage. If you are checking luggage, try to limit it to one piece. Never, we repeat, never put anything valuable or irreplaceable in a checked bag. This includes glasses, credit cards, medicine, address book, money, and jewelry.

It's safer to check your luggage at the ticket counter than to use curbside check-in. Clearly label your suitcase inside and out. You might even attach a tag to the outside of the bag which indicates where the suitcase is headed that day and on what flight (e.g., United 801 to Hong Kong and the Victoria Hotel). For $15 a year, you can buy Bag Trak coverage from Travel Guard International (800-826-1300, or in Wisconsin, 800-634-0644). Special labels identify your luggage, and the company will use its resources to track down your missing suitcase.

Clothing
Wear your warm outfit on the plane—a sweater and a jacket if you are leaving in winter. A small portable umbrella can be useful in any month, especially when you are traveling with few changes of clothing. Lightweight rubber overshoes will keep your walking shoes dry during the rainy days. For the tropics, light cotton clothing is ideal. Women can buy a sarong to use as a skirt, but cotton shorts and pants are acceptable nearly everywhere. There's no need to take more than one pair of comfortable, all-purpose walking shoes, but do take a pair of rubber thongs or sandals for Thailand, Bali, the Philippines, and Egypt. Include a bathing suit, two light shirts, and shorts. Don't worry if you feel you haven't packed enough. In Thailand, Bali, and the Philippines, you'll find everything you need and more at very reasonable prices.

Even if you travel as lightly as you can, you'll still find certain items essential: an alarm clock, an eye mask, dark glasses, ear plugs, a pencil-size flashlight, and reading material. Bring antibacterial ointment, Band-Aids, prescription drugs, vitamins, sunscreen (#15 is recommended), and mosquito repellent.

Recommended Reading

This book is part of the 22 Days series, itinerary planners that cover the globe. The first title, *22 Days in Europe*, was written by Seattle author Rick Steves, who has gone on to write other 22 Days books covering Great Britain; France; Germany, Austria, and Switzerland; Spain and Portugal; and Scandinavia. Portions of this book on Hong Kong, Thailand, and Bali appear in different form in our book *22 Days in Asia*, which also covers Kyoto, Japan, and China. Many of the destinations in this book, such as Egypt, the Philippines, Lombok, Greece, and Turkey, make their first appearance here in a 22 Days volume. Our Paris itinerary (with the research and writing assistance of Linda Moyer) is supplemented with the introduction to this city written by Rick Steves and Steve Smith in their book, *22 Days in France*. Our thanks to all of them.

If you're planning to extend your itinerary, we believe *22 Days in Asia* and *22 Days in France* will be particularly helpful. Rick's other European titles and the 22 Days guides to Japan, China, and India may also fit into your travel plan. Each user-friendly title follows the same format, making it easy for you to add days and destinations. For a complete list of other 22 Days titles that will help you create a longer around-the-world itinerary, please see the back of this book. Use the series to design the trip that suits you best.

In addition to the 22 Days series, you'll want to do some background reading before leaving home. We've recommended armchair titles, as well as a few titles you might want to bring along or pick up when you're on the road. To lighten your luggage, copy the sections you need or simply send the surplus titles home after you finish up on each country.

Hong Kong: Jan Morris's book *Hong Kong* (New York: Random House) offers an up-to-date look at the crown colony. In Hong Kong, pick up a copy of *Hong Kong Walks* (Hong Kong: The Guidebook Company), a handy tour book full of fascinating information on both Chinese and British landmarks.

Thailand: *Chiang Mai and North Thailand* by John Hoskin (Hong Kong: Hong Kong Publishing Company) is worth reading if you plan to spend more time in the hill country. For general information, see the *Insight Guide Thailand* (Singapore: APA Productions).

Indonesia: *Island of Bali* by Miguel Covarrubias (New York: KPI), written in 1938 and recently republished, is a classic work that evokes the magic of Bali and is in no way outdated. If you read only one book on Bali before you leave, it should be this one. Copy relevant sections of *Bali and Lombok, A Travel Survival Kit* (Oakland: Lonely Planet) or Bill Dalton's *Indonesia Handbook* (Chico, Calif.: Moon Publications).

Philippines: Bring along a copy of *Philippines, A Travel Survival Kit* (Oakland: Lonely Planet). The security tips on pages 67-69 are excellent and useful for travel to any third world country. In Manila, pick up a copy of Jill Gale de Villa's *Philippine Vacations and Explorations* (Manila: Devcon). Also useful is the same author's *Manila: The Traveler's Companion* (Manila: Devcon). Must reading before you leave home is Stanley Karnow's superb history of the Philippines, *In Our Image* (New York: Random House).

Egypt: The touring information in *Frommer's Dollarwise Guide to Egypt* by Nancy McGrath (New York: Prentice Hall) is particularly useful. Bring it along on your trip or copy relevant sections.

Greece: You may want to carry the *Michelin Green Guide: Greece* (Paris: Michelin). *The Cadogan Guide: Greek Islands* by Dana Facaros (Chester, Conn.: Globe Pequot) provides excellent background. Every visitor to Greece will enjoy *The Greek Way* by Edith Hamilton and Henry Miller's *Kolosis of Marousi*. Another good pretrip bet is *Eleni* by Nicholas Gage.

Turkey: *Turkey, A Travel Survival Kit* by Tom Brosnahan (Oakland: Lonely Planet) is a useful general guide. You may want to copy relevant sections for your trip. The best-known popular history of the country is *The Ottoman Centuries* by Lord Kinross. For a background book on modern Turkey, try *The Turks* by David Hotham. Herbert J. Muller's *The Loom of History* is a good history from Hellenistic times to the present.

France: After arriving, you may want to pick up a *Michelin Green Guide on Paris* and the provinces or a red guide covering hotels and restaurants (Paris: Michelin). *French Country Inns and Chateau Hotels* by Karen Brown (New York: Travel Press/Warner Books) is excellent for finding comfortable lodging.

Italy: *The Companion Guide to Venice* by Hugh Honour (New York: Prentice Hall) is one of our favorites. Before leaving, read *Venice Observed* by Mary McCarthy.

For additional background on the countries covered in this book, contact the official government tourist organizations:

Hong Kong Tourist Association, 333 N. Michigan Ave., Suite 2323, Chicago, IL 60601-3966, (312) 782-3872.

Tourism Authority of Thailand, 3440 Wilshire Boulevard, Suite 1101, Los Angeles, CA 90010, (213) 382-2353.

Indonesia Tourist Promotion Office, 3457 Wilshire Boulevard, Los Angeles, CA 90010, (213) 387-2078.

Philippine Department of Tourism, 447 Sutter St., 6th Floor, San Francisco, CA 94108, (415) 456-4060.

Egyptian General Authority for the Promotion of Tourism, 630 Fifth Ave., New York, NY 10022, (212) 246-6960.

Greek National Tourist Organization, 611 W. Sixth Street, Suite 2198, Los Angeles CA 90017, (213) 626-6696.
French Government Tourist Office, 1 Hallidie Plaza, Suite 250, San Francisco CA 94102, (415) 986-4174.
Italian Government Travel Office, 360 Post St., Suite 801, San Francisco, CA 94108, (415) 392-6206.

Please Note

Always confirm plane reservations and transit schedules through your hotel desk. Special tour arrangements, drivers, and airport transportation should be arranged a day in advance. On arrival at each destination, we urge you to supplement this book with a local map. Museum and attraction hours and routings are, of course, subject to change. For this reason, it's always a good idea to inquire locally whenever possible. On this trip, we prefer to use local transit, take cabs, or hire drivers to get around. We never drive in Hong Kong, the Philippines, Thailand, Bali, or Egypt. You shouldn't either. Of course, there is no need for a car in Venice. Check the weather forecast before setting out for rural areas. Prices listed in this book are approximate, subject to change, currency fluctuations, and inflation. Because the least expensive rooms tend to be booked first, you may be quoted a higher rate. We welcome your comments and suggestions in care of the publisher.

Because of scheduling changes, all of the times and some of the carriers operating on this route may be different from the ones we mention. Use our flight times for a rough guideline and then confirm details with your travel agent.

DAY 1 Depart for Hong Kong, cross the international date line, arrive early the following day, and check into your hotel. Explore lesser-known Hong Kong Island. Take the tram to the top of Victoria Peak and walk down the mountain's backside to Pokfulam Reservoir. After lunch at Repulse Bay, shop for designer-label bargains in Stanley and then catch a cab to Shek-O to sample Chinese village life before riding back to bustling Hong Kong Central.

DAY 2 See the Hong Kong most visitors miss by ferrying to one of three fascinating outer islands: Cheung Chau, Lamma, or Lantau. Lunch at a monastery, swim at scenic beaches, cycle through farm and fishing villages, visit temples, or hike verdant peaks to enjoy the views. This is a delightful way to turn back the clock in the Hong Kong archipelago, and the ferry tab will only set you back a couple of dollars.

DAY 3 Get a preview of the colony's future by visiting the New Territories spread out along the Chinese border. You'll tour the Bamboo Forest Monastery, visit a traditional market, see farms tended by black-hatted Hakka women, and visit a local bird sanctuary. You can also enjoy a picturesque ferry ride through the fjordlike scenery of Tolo Harbour or, if you prefer, shop for bargains at some of the city's factory outlets.

DAY 4 After a day at leisure in Hong Kong sampling some of the city's finest museums, depart early in the evening for Bangkok, Asia's most exotic city.

EXTENSION #1: Philippines (6 Days) In Manila, you'll see the walled city of Intramuros, visit the City of the Dead, the Manila Hotel, and the incomparable Imelda Marcos shoe collection at the Malacanang Palace. From here, you continue to the nation's second largest city, Cebu, where another world traveler, Ferdinand Magellan, met his maker. Then it's on to the idyllic island of Bohol, home of the Chocolate Hills and beautiful beach resorts.

DAY 5 A jet boat whisks you to the Grand Palace and the Temple of the Emerald Buddha. Continue to Wat Pho, home of the Temple of the Reclining Buddha. Dine on inexpensive fresh seafood and fine curries before sampling Bangkok's legendary nightlife.

DAY 6 Your morning begins with a cruise to Wat Arun, the Temple of Dawn. After visiting this landmark, distinguished by its 282-foot-tall central spire, you'll continue to one of Bangkok's floating markets and then visit the handsome Royal Barges.

DAY 7 Fly to Chiang Mai, your base for a trip to the northern hill country. Explore the city and line up your trek or tour for the following day. Dinner at the Diamond Hotel's teak mansion.

DAY 8 Create your own personalized tour from a fascinating array of choices. You'll be able to visit traditional tribal villages and the ancient capital of Chiang Rai. Alternatively, you can go for a hill country elephant ride, cruise the Mekong River by longtail boat, or hike a jungle trail, where it's easy to cool off in the spray of a waterfall.

DAY 9 Explore Chiang Mai's finest temples, such as Wat Chiang Man, Wat Phra Singh, and Wat Phrathat. Tour handicraft workshops and shop for lacquerware, wood carvings, silverware, jewelry, parasols, and celadon pottery. After dinner, enjoy the carnival atmosphere of the night bazaar, where you can continue to shop, sample delicacies from the food stalls, listen to music, and kibitz.

DAY 10 Return to Bangkok and catch your evening flight to Cairo.

EXTENSION #2: Bali/Lombok (8 Days) The cultural hub of Indonesia, Bali offers a chance to see the legendary legong dancers of Ubud, explore the little-known ruins of Yeh Pulu and the idyllic beach at Candi Dasa. On neighboring Lombok, you'll spend a night in the off-the-beaten-track village of Tetebatu at the foot of one of the nation's largest volcanoes. Then visit the Gili Islands, a snorkeling paradise.

DAY 11 You'll arrive in Cairo early in the morning, head for your hotel, and relax. In the afternoon, visit two of Islam's greatest mosques, the Citadel and a grand home from the British Colonial era.

DAY 12 Visit the fascinating Egyptian Museum, home of a 250,000-piece collection that spans 5,000 years of national history. Among the highlights is the famous Tutankhamen collection. Then continue to the famous City of the Dead necropolis. Later in the day, you'll visit Khan el-Khalili, a bazaar with more than 13,000 shops. In the evening, enjoy the Pyramids Sound and Light Show.

DAY 13 A trip to the Giza Plateau gives you a chance to visit the Great Pyramids and see the Sphinx and the Solar Boat Museum. Explore the Cheops Pyramid tomb chamber via a long passageway. In the afternoon, visit one of the nation's finest craft centers in Harrania.

DAY 14 On your last day in Egypt, you'll see museums and synagogues that tell the story of the region's leading religions. The Islamic Museum, Coptic Museum, and Synagogue of Ben Ezra are the ideal way to round out your visit. Most of the afternoon is at leisure, giving you a chance to relax, revisit your favorites, or shop. If you have extra time to spend in Egypt, on a five-day cruise, you can see life on the Nile as it was centuries ago. You'll fly to Luxor, where you board the boat that serves as your hotel. Highlights of your voyage include the statues of Ramses II, King Tut, the Valley of the Kings, and the Colossi of Memnon. A short drive from Luxor takes you to the superb temples of Abydos and Dendra. Your cruise ends in Aswan, where you'll catch a flight back to Cairo.

DAY 15 Fly to Athens. Walk through the old medieval section, the Plaka. Then visit the National Archaeological Museum, home of the archipelago's most important treasures. Continue to the Acropolis and Parthenon, two of Western Civilization's most famous landmarks. In the evening, join the promenade and have a leisurely dinner.

DAY 16 Fly to Santorini, the most spectacular island in Greece. Visit Ia, one of the most beautiful villages in the Aegean, famous for its caves, ancient churches, and winding streets. Swim in a quiet cove. Your afternoon is at leisure, and you'll take your dinner at an outdoor café on the rim of the mountaintop.

DAY 17 Watch the sunrise at the site of ancient Thera. After a visit to the local museum, take a boat trip in the volcanic crater lake. You'll enjoy lunch at a beachfront taverna on neighboring Thirassia Island and return to your hotel to relax before dinner and an evening stroll.

EXTENSION #3: Samos, Greece/Ephesus and Kusadasi, Turkey (2 Days) Fly from Athens to Samos. Explore Samos town, the picturesque island capital, or head east to see the

Monastery of Zoodohos Pigi. Then continue by ferry to
Kusadasi, Turkey, a charming port with exotic minarets and
open-air markets. In the afternoon head out to Ephesus, home
of the best-preserved archaeological ruins in Turkey.

DAY 18 Fly to Paris in the morning and check into your hotel.
After dinner, board a bateau mouche for a romantic evening
cruise down the Seine. Along the way, you'll see some of the
city's illuminated landmarks.

DAY 19 A walking tour takes in Notre-Dame and Sainte-
Chapelle and breaks for lunch at the Printemps rooftop restau-
rant. After visiting the Grands Magasins (department stores),
resume strolling the right bank and relax at a sidewalk café.
After dinner, visit the Place de la Concorde/Champs-
Elysées/Arc de Triomphe.

DAY 20 Walk though the beautifully restored Marais quarter
and the Halles district, once home of Paris' best-known food
market. Two of the city's most popular museums—the Picasso
and the Centre Pompidou—are also on the itinerary. After dinner in the Les Halles area, stroll past the city's handsomely lit
buildings and monuments.

DAY 21 The Musée d'Orsay, a train station that has been converted into a museum of nineteenth-century art, is your first
stop. After leaving the museum, explore some of the nearby
streets depicted by the Impressionists. The Musée Cluny and
Tour Eiffel are also on today's schedule.

DAY 22 After a morning visit to the Louvre, the world's most
famous museum, you can choose an excursion to the glorious
Gothic cathedral at Chartres or Louis XIV's lasting monument,
Versailles. Celebrate the last night of your around-the-world
journey at the ultimate Paris restaurant, Le Grand Vefour.

EXTENSION #4: Venice (3 Days) An overnight train ride from
Paris takes you to Venice and the Piazza San Marco, where you
visit the Doge's Palace and then visit Palladio's church of San
Giorgio. You'll go by vaporetto and foot to see the Accademia
Museum, the Scuola degli Schiavoni, and the Peggy Guggenheim Museum. There's also time for trips to less crowded outer
islands such as Murano, Torcello, and Burano.
    Fly back to the United States the next day.

HONG KONG CONTRASTS

Today you depart for one of the world's great destinations,
Hong Kong. You're arriving in time to see the twilight of British
rule, set to end in 1997. This itinerary, which covers both urban
and rural Hong Kong, offers you a chance to see some of the
colony's greatest sights. Although some people visualize Hong
Kong as a jam-packed Asian metropolis, it is actually an
archipelago of great physical beauty where modern commerce
and rural villages coexist peacefully. The contrasts are especially
rewarding to tourists, who can sample old and new China
tinged with a bit of Merry Old England—a wonderful place to
shop for bargains, sample new cuisines, or explore remote backcountry villages.

Suggested Schedule

9:00 a.m.	Explore central Hong Kong.
11:00 a.m.	Tram ride to Victoria Peak and walk down the mountain to Pokfulam Reservoir.
1:00 p.m.	Lunch at the Verandah Restaurant at Repulse Bay.
2:30 p.m.	Shopping in Stanley.
3:30 p.m.	Cab to Shek-O.
4:00 p.m.	Explore Shek-O area.
5:30 p.m.	Bus and subway back to central Hong Kong. Evening at leisure.

Hong Kong

Few cities offer greater contrasts and more diverse opportunities for tourists than Hong Kong, a metropolis of 5.7 million
people. The population is 98 percent Chinese, but there are also
healthy smatterings of Vietnamese, Thai, Filipinos, Indonesians,
Koreans, Japanese, Pakistanis, and Europeans. Most of them live
in the business center, Hong Kong Island, and the dense urban
factory centers of the Kowloon Peninsula. North toward the
Chinese border are the modern new towns of the New Territories. But most of this region and the colony's 235 outlying
islands remain a rural outpost where you can glimpse traditional
Chinese life and visit ancient walled villages.

Although Hong Kong's contemporary image is relentlessly
urban, with residents crammed into towering apartment blocks,
the colony was a backwater when the British took it over in
1841 during the Opium Wars. Only 3,650 Chinese lived in the

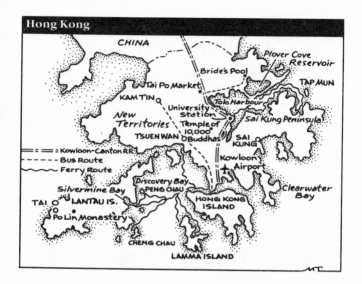

Hong Kong

CHINA

Plover Cove
Reservoir

Bride's Pool

TAP MUN

Tai Po Market

KAM TIN

University
Station

*New
Territories*

Tolo Harbour

Sai Kung Peninsula

TSUEN WAN

Temple of
10,000
Buddhas

SAI
KUNG

=== : Kowloon-Canton RR.

----- Bus Route

— Ferry Route

Kowloon
Airport

Silvermine Bay

Discovery Bay
PENG CHAU

Clearwater
Bay

TAI O

LANTAU IS.

Po Lin Monastery

HONG KONG
ISLAND

CHENG CHAU

LAMMA ISLAND

little fishing villages dotting the harbor. Under British domin-
ion, this small outpost gradually expanded its boundaries and
became China's commercial link with the world. Ultimately,
Hong Kong replaced Shanghai as Southeast Asia's key business
center. Although the colony remains overwhelmingly Chinese
today, English is also widely spoken.

In 1997, when Hong Kong reverts to the Chinese, more than
the politics of this city is likely to change. In a sense, Hong Kong
is what much of China would like to become, a moderately
prosperous Asian land with a dependable industrial base. The
colony also has much of the infrastructure that Chinese cities
covet—the roads, the subways, and the tourist facilities that
meet the standards of demanding foreign visitors. Hong Kong
also has an international flavor that brings together the best of
East and West and makes it a bit of a novelty among major Asian
centers. The city is famous for offering quality goods at very fair
prices. As you shop alongside Japanese visitors, who find that
cameras made in their own country sell for less in Hong Kong,
you will get a sense of this colony's business acumen.

Although the business centers have been Westernized, you
need only turn the corner into a residential neighborhood to be
quickly reminded that this is, at heart, a Chinese land where the
teachings of Taoism, Confucianism, and Buddhism are the religious order of the day. Of course, the Protestant work ethic

holds sway in the small shops that are commonly open twelve
hours a day, seven days a week. A seemingly nonstop port town,
Hong Kong is also an extremely efficient community. While you
are visiting this modern city, keep in mind that you are seeing
the last of the good old Western-style days. When the Union
Jack is lowered in 1997, Hong Kong is destined to become the
same—only different.

Arrival
Depending on the airlines you choose for your around-the-
world trip, you can count on today's trip to run between 14 and
18 hours. From San Francisco, a major Pacific gateway, the Singapore nonstop departs about 1:00 a.m. and puts you into Hong
Kong on the morning of the following day. The sun never sets
on this 14-hour trip across the international date line. Your
specific flight arrangements may be different, of course,
depending on your point of departure.

Perhaps the most centrally located major airport in the world,
Kai Tak is in the middle of Kowloon, one of Hong Kong's two
major population centers. On one approach pattern, the blast
from your jet will help dry the laundry hanging from teeming
apartment buildings. After clearing customs, stop by the Hong
Kong Tourist Association booth to pick up free maps and
guides. Then change a small amount of money (you'll probably
get a better rate at the banks downtown). The Hong Kong dollar
(HK$) is pegged to the U.S. dollar, presently HK$7.8 to $1. For a
quick mental conversion from Hong Kong to U.S. dollars, multiply the Hong Kong value by 13 and move the decimal point two
places to the left. For example, HK$100 equals approximately
US$13. Although cab fares into town are reasonable, there may
be a line when you arrive. It may be quicker to take the Airbus
(HK$6-$8, or about US$0.77-$1.02) to your hotel. The only
catch is that you won't get any help putting your luggage on
board.

Lodging
Hong Kong has an outstanding variety of accommodations in all
price ranges. From well-situated YMCAs and mountaintop
monasteries to five-star hotels, this city accommodates every
taste. Keep in mind that because you are flying west and crossing the international date line, you'll want to reserve your first
night's room for the day after your departure date. For example,
if you take off from the United States on June 18, you'll need to
have your first night's reservation for the 19th. Inexpensive
hotels run under HK$400 (about $50), moderate hotels cost

HK$400 to HK$800 ($52-$104), and expensive hotels start around HK$1,000 ($130).

The **YMCA** operates three hotels in the Hong Kong area. Oldest and best known is the branch on Salisbury Road, Kowloon. It's next door to the expensive Peninsula Hotel and across the street from the harbor. Rooms here are inexpensive (tel. 3692211). Because this hotel is often full, you may want to try the **YMCA International House** at 23 Waterloo Road, Kowloon. This modern hotel offers rooms in the inexpensive and moderate categories (tel. 7719111).

On the Hong Kong side, consider the moderately priced **Harbour View International House** at 4 Harbour Road, Wanchai (tel. 5-201111). Close by, in roughly the same price range, is the **Harbour** at 116 Gloucester Road (tel. 5748211).

Naturally, Hong Kong has many fine upscale hotels. One of the best is the **Hotel Victoria**, just steps from the Macau Ferry Terminal and not far from the Outer Islands Ferry Terminal. It is expensive, but the harbor location at 200 Connaught Road is tops (tel. 5407228). If you prefer a more remote location, consider the moderate **Surf Hotel** on Sha Ha Beach at Sai Kung, about half an hour by bus from Kowloon. Far removed from the clamor of Hong Kong, Sai Kung is a charming village. The hotel on Tai Mong Tsai Road offers swimming, tennis, canoeing, windsurfing, and a good seafood restaurant. Rooms start around HK$440 ($59) a day (tel. 7924411).

On a tight budget? Contact the **Hong Kong Youth Hostels Association** at 1408A Watson's Estate, North Point, Hong Kong (tel. 5706222, or after hours, 8175715). This organization operates hostels on Hong Kong Island and more remote locations, such as the Sai Kung Peninsula and the outer islands. Guest membership and accommodation charges are inexpensive. Some of the outer island hostels have camping facilities. A detailed listing of accommodations is available from the Hong Kong Tourist Association, Shop 8, Basement, Jardine House, 1 Connaught Place C., Hong Kong (tel. 8017177).

Food

Westerners tend to divide Chinese food into such familiar categories as Cantonese, Szechuan, and Peking. In fact, there are numerous other categories, such as Shanghai, Chiuchow, and Hakka. All are found in Hong Kong, one of the best and most reasonably priced restaurant towns in the world. While here, you'll certainly want to sample Chiuchow cuisine, famed for its shellfish dishes, such as steamed lobster and crabmeat balls. A good place to experiment is the moderately priced **Chiuchow Garden Restaurant**, at Hennessy Centre, 500 Hennessy Road,

Causeway Bay (tel. 5773391). For dim sum, the **North Sea Fishing Village** in Tsimshatsui East's Auto Plaza is a good bet (tel. 7236843). Be sure to try the shrimp dumplings. Thai food is also a very good bet in Hong Kong, and some of the best is served at the **Chili Club**, a moderately expensive establishment at 68-70 Lockhart Road, Wanchai. Try the spicy chicken or deep-fried fish and chili cakes (tel. 5272872). For ambience, you'll have a hard time beating **Spices**, an eclectic Asian restaurant at 109 Repulse Bay Road, Repulse Bay (tel. 8122711). It's on our itinerary for Day 13 .

Getting Oriented

After settling into your hotel, you may want to relax and turn in early. But if you rested well on the plane, perhaps you'll feel like taking a good walk and seeing a little of the most accessible city in Asia. The local subway (MTR) is an efficient way to get around town. Cabs are moderately priced (just ask the hotel desk to write out instructions for the driver in Chinese), and there's a good bus and ferry system. And as you'll discover dur-

ing the next few days, the Kowloon-Canton Railway provides efficient service to the New Territories.

On the Hong Kong side, it's fun to ride one of the old trams from the central district out through Wanchai to the Causeway Bay shopping area on the western end of Hong Kong Island. One of the few areas on this side of the island that hasn't been overwhelmed by high-rises, it features old shops selling Chinese herbs, salted fish, and dried seafood. On your way back to central Hong Kong, stop at Causeway Bay's Food Street, off Gloucester Road, where you'll find many varieties of Chinese food as well as restaurants specializing in Japanese, Taiwanese, Vietnamese, Spanish, and American cuisine. Vast shopping malls and some of the city's best boutiques are also found in this neighborhood. Many are open until 9:00 p.m. or later. If you want to sample both sides of the harbor, take the Star Ferry, a short ride connecting Kowloon with Hong Kong. It will give you a feel for some of the longer trips you can enjoy in this archipelago aboard the Hong Kong Ferry Company fleet.

Travel Route
Your day begins in the Hong Kong Visitors Information Center, where you can obtain maps and brochures that will orient you to the region (tel. 7225555). After walking through the central district, head over to the Victoria Peak Tram Station, one block above the Hilton Hotel on Garden Road. From the top, descend on the Hong Kong Trail to Pokfulam Reservoir, then catch the #73 bus or a cab to Repulse Bay Hotel for lunch or continue via bus #73 to Stanley Village for lunch. Afterward, take a cab to Shek-O. Later, take bus #9 to the Shau Kei Wan MTR Station, where the subway will return you to central Hong Kong.

Sightseeing Highlights
Central Hong Kong is a fascinating blend of Asia's new and old. This morning, you'll have a chance to explore the central business district and see famous markets, craft and herb shops, and the memorable work of artisans next door to tourist kitsch.
▲**Central Market**—Start your day, as many residents do, at the Central Market, Queen Victoria Street and Des Veoux Road Central. The largest of the city's 65 public markets, it has over 300 stalls selling everything from fresh shark to medicinal herbs. Continue on Des Veoux Road across Jubilee Street and you'll be surrounded by tempting street-food stalls selling fried dough sticks, bowls of shrimp dumplings, and noodle dishes.
▲ **Cloth Alley**—Continue on Des Veoux Road and turn left at Wing On Street. This small street is an excellent place to bargain for shirt fabrics, wool, linen, and velvet.

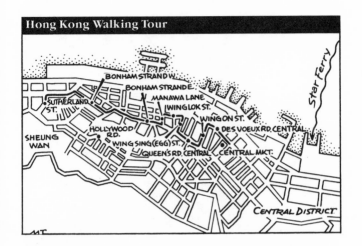

Hong Kong Walking Tour

▲ **Egg Street**—After turning right on Queen's Road Central and passing the Jet Kee Record and Cassette stall, you'll reach Wing Sing Street, also known as Egg Street. The city's primary egg distribution center, this is where dealers grade and repackage pale green duck eggs, goose eggs, delicate pigeon eggs, and speckled quail eggs, along with mundane chicken eggs. Each egg is inspected for freshness by holding it up to a bare light bulb. If the yolk appears to move easily, it's a winner.

You may be surprised to learn that preserved eggs are just as popular as fresh eggs here. To see what you've been missing back home, try one of the city's great delicacies, the 100-year-old egg. The name is something of a misnomer. Actually, these duck eggs are soaked in batches for a month with lime, wood ash, and tea leaves. They are then preserved for up to six months in mud, ash, and rolled rice husks. This delicacy is usually found to be an acquired taste.

▲▲ **Bonham Strand East**—Turn left on Wing Lok Street and then left again on Man Wa Lane. After passing the chop or seal carving shops (you can buy your own seal as a souvenir), turn right on Bonham Strand East. From October to February, the snake shops here are booming. In season, there are always plenty of tasty pythons and cobras to choose from. You'll find restaurants in this area serving snake soup; or, if you prefer, go for a snake banquet, where you can have a shot of snake gall wine, made from the gall bladder. This drink is considered to be just the thing for rheumatism. Or order a glass of snake wine (don't bother ordering the red or white; this liquor made from bile only comes in green). If you miss the snake season, have a

Hong Kong Island

Star Ferry · VICTORIA HARBOUR · NORTH POINT · WAN CHAI · CENTRAL DIST. · CAUSEWAY BAY · Victoria Peak · Victoria Peak Tram · SHAU KEI WAN · HIKING TRAIL · Pok Fulam Reservoir · ABERDEEN · OCEAN PARK · REPULSE BAY · HIKING TRAIL · SHEK-O · TAI TAM BAY · STANLEY

look at some of the fascinating medicine shops, which have just the herbs you'll need to balance your yin and yang. There's nearly always an herbalist on duty.

▲▲▲ **Victoria Peak Tram Tour**—This tram is an easy way to begin your look at the backside of Hong Kong Island. Take a taxi to the tram terminal or retrace your path on Bonham Strand East until it turns into Queen's Road Central. At the Hilton, turn right on Garden Road to the tram. When she's in town, famed travel writer Jan Morris takes her constitutional on this peak. When you reach the top, you'll quickly see why this spot is such a favorite of Hong Kong visitors. A 45-minute walk in either direction takes you around the peak via Harlech and Lugard roads. This is an ideal way to gain perspective on the Hong Kong region. It's also a lot of fun. After enjoying views of the harbor, begin the Hong Kong Trail, which descends 1.2 miles down the mountain spine through lush countryside to the Pokfulam Reservoir. If you have a couple of days to spare, you could continue on this 30-mile walking route through all five of the island's county parks; but today's walk ends at the reservoir. Hail a cab on Peak Road or take the #7 bus and connect to the

#73, disembarking at the old Repulse Bay Hotel site, 109 Repulse Bay Road, for lunch.

▲ **Repulse Bay Hotel**—In earlier decades, this white hotel was famous for its whitewashed veranda, where you could sit and enjoy a drink while looking out over one of the island's most popular beaches. To the horror of preservationists, this colonial landmark was demolished in 1982. Fortunately, this establishment has become the Lazarus of the Hong Kong hotel world. Rebuilt on the original oceanfront site, it no longer offers lodging, but you can still enjoy the ambience of this Hong Kong classic at the Veranda restaurant or Spices, an expensive eatery serving everything from Indonesian nasi goreng (rice, chicken, eggs, chilies, and prawns) to a Thai-style chicken curry. Or, if you prefer, just have a look around this historic place and take the #73 bus on to Stanley village for lunch.

▲ **Stanley**—Popular with bargain hunters, the shops and stalls of Stanley are a good place to look for brand-name garments at considerable savings. Rattanware and Chinese furniture are also sold at factory prices. The village beach is less crowded than the one at Repulse Bay. Take a break at a little British pub called Stanley's, 86 Stanley Main Street (tel. 8138873). While enjoying lunch in the second-floor dining room, you'll have a fine harbor view. You may overhear passionate shoppers at adjacent tables conducting postmortems on their day's outing.

▲▲ **Shek-O**—Many Hong Kong natives have never been to the southwestern tip of their own island. Few tourists have even heard of this area. A ten-minute cab ride from Stanley will take you to this little headland village. The beaches here and at nearby Big Wave Bay are two of the finest in the archipelago. On a clear day, you'll enjoy a panoramic view of the Sai Kung Peninsula. A short walk north takes you to an old Chinese settlement. If you have extra time, hike up the Dragon's Back in adjacent Shek-O County Park. This moderately strenuous hike offers fine marine and mountain views. For more information, inquire at the Hong Kong Tourist Association Office. If you don't have time to make it to one of the outer islands, by all means see Shek-O. It will give you a good feel for the colony's village life.

HONG KONG'S OUTER ISLANDS

Most of Hong Kong's 5.7 million residents live either in Kowloon or on Hong Kong Island. Surrounding these two hubs are 235 other islands that comprise the Hong Kong archipelago. From Cheung Chau (population 20,000) to uninhabited islands stretching out into the South China Sea, these retreats are an ideal way to go back in time. Today you'll do just that, compliments of the Hong Kong Ferry Company. It only costs about HK$12 ($1.50) for the ride out to your choice of outer islands. The only hard part is choosing among the islands, where you can explore mountaintop monasteries and Buddhist temples, stroll deserted beaches, cycle past rice paddies, dine at fresh seafood restaurants, and shop for Chinese crafts. Of course, if you fall in love with one of these islands, it's usually possible to spend the night.

Suggested Schedule

8:15-8:45 a.m.	Arrive at Outlying Districts Ferry Terminal, Hong Kong. Board a vessel for Cheung Chau, Lamma, or Lantau.
10:00 a.m.	Arrive on the island of your choice.
4:00-5:00 p.m.	Return to Hong Kong. Evening at leisure.

Transportation
The Outlying Districts Ferry Pier is located on Pier Road off Connaught Road Central. Star Ferry passengers arriving from Kowloon should turn right when they disembark in Hong Kong and walk down to the Outlying Pier. If you're traveling on a weekend or holiday, purchase your ticket in advance. Hotel reservations are also recommended on weekends or holidays. It's a good idea to arrive 15 to 20 minutes before sailing time on weekends, when the vessels are extremely crowded. Call the ferry company at 5423081 for schedule information (also available from the Hong Kong Tourist Association, tel. 8017177). Purchase a round-trip ticket. Be sure to carry change for exact-fare ferries. Round-trip fares range from HK$10 to HK$30 ($1-$3.84). Don't forget to double-check the return ferry times after arriving at your destination.

Sightseeing Highlights: The Outer Islands

▲▲ **Cheung Chau** (suggested departure: 8:45 a.m. from Hong Hong Outlying Districts Ferry Pier)—One of the best outings from Hong Kong, this trip is made in the company of locals enjoying a daylong holiday. A highlight is cruising through Hong Kong Harbour, where junks, sampans, freighters, and cruise liners coexist peacefully. After an hour of threading through the Hong Kong archipelago, the ferry slows for the floating neighborhood that bobs about in Cheung Chau Harbour.

About 10 percent of the 20,000 residents on this dumbbell-shaped island just 7.5 miles west of Hong Kong live on junks. Inhabited for over 2,500 years, Cheung Chau emerged as a major port for cities along the south China coast in the sixteenth century. It was also a haven for pirates, including the infamous Cheung Po Tsai, who hid in a cave on the southwestern side of the island. Today, the island remains a shipbuilding center. Near the pier, you can watch shirtless shipbuilders create these handsome junks without the aid of blueprints. You may also find uniformed schoolchildren tossing balls, old men reading newspapers while sipping tea, and vendors selling barbecued fish on skewers. On the pier, you'll find vendors selling fruit, vegetables, and fresh seafood.

One thing you won't find in this village is cars. They are banned on the island, which has preserved many preindustrial traditions and is dominated by clans and trade guilds. A short walk north takes you to Pak Tai Temple, notable for its two excellent stone dragon carvings and a sword forged during the Song dynasty (A.D. 960-1279). Return to Cheung Chau's Pak She Street and you'll find incense shops, groceries, craftsmen polishing jade, and Gee Jat Po, a paper-bundling shop selling items for funerals. Most of these goods will become part of cremations, helping loved ones prosper in the next world. The rest will be set out on the anniversaries of their deaths.

Just ten minutes east of Cheung Chau Pier is Tung Wan Beach, where windsurfers and swimmers entertain themselves near a large rock adorned with Bronze Age carvings. After pausing for tea at the Warwick Hotel, take Hak Pa Road to Kwun Yum Wan Beach and Kwun Yum Temple, dedicated to its namesake, the Goddess of Mercy. Then return to Fa Peng Road and central Cheung Chau. Following lunch, take a local ferry to Sai Wan, another pleasant waterfront village. Walk up to the temple of Tin Hau, Queen of Heaven and Goddess of the Sea. It's adjacent to the pirate cave of Cheung Po Tsai. Return to Cheung Chau Pier by foot or motorized sampan in time to catch the 4:30 p.m. ferry back to Hong Kong.

Of course, it's also possible to spend the night on the island. Rooms at the comfortable waterfront Cheung Chau Warwick on East Bay are moderate in price (tel. 9810081). More modest accommodations are available at the Cheung Chau Star House, 149 Tai Sun Back Street (tel. 9812462). Rooms are inexpensive on weekdays and moderate on weekends. Advance reservations are always a good idea, particularly on holidays and weekends.

▲▲ **Lantau** (suggested departure: 8:15 a.m. ferry from Hong Kong Outlying Districts Ferry Pier to Silvermine Bay)—Twice the size of Hong Kong Island, Lantau has less than 16,000 residents. With verdant mountain peaks, ruins of an old fort, traditional Chinese villages, temples, monasteries, and more than 40 miles of trails leading through two country parks, this is an ideal day trip. Inhabited since Neolithic times, Lantau's economy centered around fishing, salt-making, and lime-burning for many centuries. Today, tourists eager to see this rugged place make an important contribution to local commerce. One of the island's most popular beaches is located just five minutes from the ferry dock at Silvermine Bay. You can also explore the area on foot or on a bike rented at the stand in front of the Silvermine Beach Hotel. Head up Mui Wo Rural Committee Road through lush fields and you'll come to Man Mo Temple, which pays homage to both the civil god and the martial god. Adjacent to this landmark is a fabulous mansion with a pagoda-style roof and squadrons of gardeners grooming the estate's topiary garden. The island's old silver mine is a short walk uphill from the mansion.

After returning to the wharf and exploring the Silvermine Bay area, turn in your bike (if you rented one) and catch a bus or taxi to visit the island's leading attraction, the Po Lin Monastery. A pair of two-story temples here feature bronze Buddha statues that are bathed in holy water every May during a Lord Buddha birthday celebration. On an adjacent plateau, you'll see the tallest Buddha statue in Southeast Asia, built at a cost of more than $8 million. Be sure to enjoy the vegetarian lunch served at Po Lin. If you've ever wanted to spend the night at a monastery, this is your chance. Naturally, the boards are harder than what you're used to sleeping on. Inexpensive rooms at Po Lin include three vegetarian meals per day; there are communal bathrooms. Telephone 9855426 or write to the Po Lin Monastery, Ngong Ping, Lantau. Accommodations are also available at the Trappist Haven Monastery northeast of Silvermine Bay. In addition, there are numerous campsites to serve hikers on Lantau as well as a variety of hotels. For a complete list, contact the Hong Kong Tourist Association.

There are many other attractions on Lantau, including Hong Kong's only tea gardens, the nineteenth-century Tung Chung

Fort, shipbuilders creating junks and modern yachts on Penny's Bay, and the old salt-panning village of Tai-O. If your image of Asia is homes built on stilts, temples, Buddhist markets, coffin shops, herbal medicine stores, and fishermen unloading their catch onto the town dock, you've come to the right place. Some of the best seafood in the archipelago is found here. Two-mile-long Cheung Sha Beach is another popular Lantau spot. It's 20 minutes by bus from Silvermine Bay.

▲ **Lamma** (suggested departure from Hong Kong Outlying Districts Ferry Pier is 8:35 a.m. to Yung Shue Wan)—Just 40 minutes from Hong Kong, this outer island is prized for its beaches and its ban on cars. Your first stop will be Yung Shue Wan (Banyan Tree Bay), where shops and stalls sell everything from dried fish to candles. There are no big monasteries, but as you walk south across the island, you will come to Tin Hau Temple, guarded by a matched pair of granite lions. A strenuous trail beginning at the temple leads up to the peak of 1,100-foot-high Mt. Stenhouse, where there is a fine view of Hong Kong and neighboring islands. Continuing through the fields from Tin Hau Temple, you'll come to one of the island's best beaches, Hung Shing Ye. After relaxing at this popular spot, continue up the road into the hills and you'll be rewarded with a fine view of Lamma, Hong Kong, and several other islands.

Sok Kwu Wan is an excellent place for a seafood lunch or dinner before catching the ferry back to Hong Kong. You might want to try the Cantonese Peach Garden Seafood Restaurant at #11 Sok Kwu Wan First Street or Man Fung Seafood Restaurant, First St. #5 in Yung Shue Wan. If you want to see more of the island, take the 30-minute walk east along the beach to Mo Tat Wan. It's adjacent to the 300-year-old village of Mo Tat. From here, you can return to Sok Kwu Wan and catch the ferry back to Hong Kong. Or, if you prefer, take the local boat across to Aberdeen on Hong Kong Island and then catch a #7 bus back into central Hong Kong.

Other Outer Islands—While Cheung Chau, Lantau, and Lamma are the most visited outer islands, you may also want to stop off en route. Peng Chau, which also endures happily without the benefit of automobiles, can be reached as a stopover on the Lantau route. In addition, you can reach Po Toi on the way to Lamma's Sok Kwu Wan. Since the population here is only 200, you'll find plenty of elbow room and great views of Hong Kong.

HONG KONG: THE LAND BETWEEN

One of Asia's most important political transformations will occur in 1997, when Britain will retreat from Hong Kong after 150 years of colonial rule. This, of course, raises the political question of the decade in Asia: will the crown colony become a shadow of its former self, like Shanghai? Or will capitalism continue to flourish under Chinese Communist rule? A good place to look for answers is Hong Kong's New Territories, where old walled villages and farms tended by Hakka women are found just a few miles from China's booming new manufacturing plants on the border. After a tour of this fast-developing region, you'll enjoy lunch on a terrace overlooking Tolo Harbour and then cruise out into this waterway, which resembles a Norwegian fjord.

Suggested Schedule

8:30 a.m.	Join Land Between tour.
9:30 a.m.	Bamboo Forest Monastery, Kowloon.
10:30 a.m.	Hong Kong's highest mountain, Tai Mo Shan, traditional market at Leun Wo, Hong Kong-China border area, Kam Tin walled village.
12:00 noon	Visit Plover Cove County Park.
1:00 p.m.	Lunch at Yucca de Lac.
3:00 p.m.	Return to Hong Kong or cruise Tolo Harbour.
Rest of day	Shopping, exploring Kowloon or central Hong Kong.

Sightseeing Highlights
▲▲ **Land Between Tour**—At HK$220 ($28), this tour of the New Territories is a fine way to get out beyond urban Hong Kong and see the terraced fields, parks, duck ponds, and rural villages on the Chinese border. Named for the area that bridges the gap between old and new Hong Kong, this tour offers an excellent introduction to traditional Chinese village life. The tour can be booked through the Hong Kong Tourist Association Office in Jardine House (tel. 8017177), the information center at the Kowloon Star Ferry Concourse in Tsimshatsui, or the Royal Garden Hotel in Tsimshatsui East. The pick-up for the tour is Queen's Pier Central at 8:30 a.m., the Holiday Inn Golden Mile

Hotel at 9:00 a.m., or the Holiday Inn Harbour View Hotel at 9:10 a.m. Be sure to confirm these departure times the day before. The tour price includes lunch.

Your trip begins with a stop at Chuk Lam Sim Yuen, the Bamboo Forest Monastery, best known for its three Precious Buddha statues. Also here are the Laughing Buddha, the Four Heavenly Kings, the Lord of the Western Paradise, and the 18 Lohans (disciples) of Buddha. On both sides of the main hall is the home for the aged, run by the temple nuns. After contributing $3,000 to $4,000, the elderly can live here for the rest of their lives.

From here, the tour proceeds north to Tai Mo Shan, where you'll get a fine view of Hong Kong before heading down through fish-breeding ponds and chicken farms to Luen Wo Market, where stalls offer dried fish, herbs, vegetables, fruit, flowers, meat, and poultry. After passing through a bird sanctuary that's home to Chinese pond herons, you'll continue to a Hong Kong-China border overlook. In the distance, you'll see China's special incentive zone at Shenzhen, where foreign investment has created vast industrial development. The tour continues through farmland worked by the Hakka women, who tend the fields while their husbands handle domestic chores. You'll ride through mountainous Plover Cove County Park before returning to the market town of Tai Po and your luncheon banquet at the hillside Yucca de Lac restaurant. If you're as impressed by the view of Tolo Harbour as we were, consider leaving the tour at this point and taking a four-hour trip out into this mountain-rimmed bay that resembles the fjords of Norway.

The Land Between tour ends back in Hong Kong about 3:00 p.m.; but if you want to depart from the group after lunch at the Yucca de Lac restaurant, here are options to consider for the balance of the day.

Tolo Harbour Tour—Just a short distance from the Yucca de Lac by cab is Ma Liu Shui, port for the Tolo Harbour Ferry. This ferry leaves every afternoon at 3:15 p.m., returning to Ma Liu Shui at 7:10 p.m. If you're looking for a long, relaxing ride to historic Chinese villages, consider this trip. It's possible to get off at Tap Mun (Grass Island) at 4:50 p.m. and then catch the same ferry back to Ma Liu Shui at 5:50 p.m. If you choose this stopover, be sure to be back at the Tap Mun Pier in plenty of time to catch the 5:50 p.m. boat. It's the last one of the day. Since departure times are subject to change, you'll want to confirm the entire ferry schedule in the "Places of Interest by Public Transport" brochure available from the Hong Kong Tourist Association Office. When you reach Ma Liu Shui, a ten-minute walk will take you across a bridge to University Station, where you can catch the train back into Kowloon. Incidentally, you don't have to take the Land Between tour to see Tolo Harbour.

Just catch the Kowloon-Canton line at Kowloon Railway Station. Get off at University Station and walk over to the ferry dock at Ma Liu Shui. In addition to the 3:15 p.m. trip, a morning Tolo Harbour run departs Ma Liu Shui at 7:25 a.m. and returns at 11:05 a.m.

▲ **Bride's Pool**—Located in Plover Cove County Park, this landmark is easily reached by cab from the Tai Po Station on the Kowloon-Canton Railway line (about HK$50, or $6.40). A pleasant mile-long trail will take you past this series of romantic waterfalls. When you're finished, catch the #75K bus from Tai Mei Tuk back to Taipo Market Station and pick up the Kowloon-Canton Railway back into Kowloon.

▲ **Kam Tin**—A popular New Territories stop, this is the best known of Hong Kong's five walled villages. You can reach Kam Tin by taking a taxi direct from the Yucca de Lac restaurant. A less expensive but more time-consuming route is to take a taxi from Yucca de Lac to University Station, where you can take the Kowloon-Canton Railway train back to the MTR and connect to Tsuen Wan Station. Then pick up the #51 bus from the stop above the station on Tai Ho North Road for the 40-minute ride out to Kam Tin.

According to Hong Kong author Barry Girling, this is the crown colony's largest precolonial historical monument and military fortification. Today, it is home to 400 descendants of the Tang dynasty, during which it was founded more than 300 years ago. Communities such as Kam Tin were designed to protect the Chinese from pirates, brigands, and other invaders. They were also an occasional refuge for former aristocrats, such as the last members of the Song dynasty, who took shelter here. The village is entered through an old gate that was seized by the British in 1898 and ceremoniously restored as a token of goodwill 27 years later. Hakka women wearing their black hats and smoking long pipes will gladly pose for about a dollar. Exploring the back streets here, you'll have a chance to visit ancestral halls, a shady market, and small shops. Some of the streets in this tiny town are barely wide enough for a bicyclist. In the evening, you might want to check out a walled village hot spot called the Sweet Garden Night Club.

▲ **Temple of Ten Thousand Buddhas Monastery**—If you're feeling energetic, get off the Kowloon-Canton Railway at Shatin and take the half-hour walk to this landmark, where you'll find 12,800 statues of Buddha. A strenuous walk to the top of the pagoda will give you a memorable view of the New Territories.

▲ **Factory Outlets**—People come from all over the world to shop at Hong Kong's factory outlets. Dozens of reputable firms

manufacturing designer apparel, leather goods, jewelry, silk
goods, and beaded track suits are listed in the Hong Kong Tourist Association's brochure on this subject. The crown colony
also has some of the world's best bargains on computer soft-
ware. They're found at the Golden Shopping Arcade. Take the
MTR to Sham Shui Po, where the station agent can direct you to
this computer mall.

▲ **Tea at the Peninsula**—The Peninsula, one of Asia's most
elegant hotels, is located near the Kowloon waterfront, just a
short walk from the Star Ferry Terminal. The lobby of this Hong
Kong landmark is an ideal place to rest after a hard day of sightseeing.

Macau

If you have extra time, an easy way to get a taste of Portugal in
Asia is to take the one-hour hydrofoil ride from Hong Kong to
Macau. In 1999, after more than four centuries of Portuguese
rule, this island, like Hong Kong, reverts to the Chinese. While
many visitors come to gamble at the city's casinos, this colonial
city is also a good place to search for antiques, visit museums
and temples, take a pedicab ride along the tree-shaded Praia
Grande, and enjoy *feijoada* (a Brazilian stew), dim sum, or a
prego steak in a crisp roll.

Founded by Portuguese traders and missionaries, Macau is an
island of pastel-colored palaces, baroque churches, and for-
tresses that are now elegant hotels. A six-square-mile peninsula
on the southeast coast of China, Macau is also the gateway to
China's Guangdong Province. After arriving, you can arrange a
city tour or head off on your own to visit highlights like the
ruins of St. Paul's Church on Rua de São Paulo. All that remains
of this seventeenth-century landmark is a facade rising in five
colonnaded tiers covered with carvings and statues. A few
blocks away on Praça Luis de Camões is the Camões Grotto, a
garden with beautiful fern and flower beds and giant banyan
trees honoring Portugal's national poet, Luis de Camões. While
here, you'll also want to visit one of the city's Buddhist temples.
Kun I Am Tong on Avenida do Coronel Mesquita, built in 1627,
has open courtyards leading to the Three Precious Buddhas.
Behind the temple are terraced gardens with small fountains,
bamboo groves, and shrines.

While most of the colony's history focuses around China and
Europe, Macau also has some important links to our own country. Here, in 1773, British ships took on the tea that was dumped
in Boston Harbor during the famed tax protest. Although most
visitors come for the day, there are excellent accommodations
available such as the Pousada de São Tiago. For $67 to $80, you

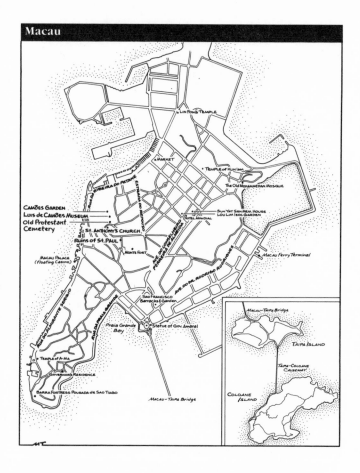

Macau

can take one of this hotel's 23 rooms built inside the walls of a seventeenth-century fort. Refurbished with period furniture and hand-painted tiles, the hotel has a memorable oak-shaded veranda with a panoramic view of the South China Sea. (From Hong Kong, call 8910366 for reservations.) Like Hong Kong, Macau also has its outer islands. On Taipa and Coloane, you'll find small Chinese villages, rice fields, and sandy beaches. Both islands are easily reached via a causeway road.

For more information on visiting Macau, call the island's Hong Kong office at 3677747.

HONG KONG TO BANGKOK

Today you'll spend the morning and early afternoon at leisure, enjoy more of Hong Kong's highlights, and depart in the early evening for Thailand.

Suggested Schedule

Morning/early afternoon	At leisure.
Evening	Depart for Bangkok.

Museum Tour
Why not visit some of Hong Kong's leading museum exhibits? They range from the Han dynasty to the space age. Here are a few of the best:

Hong Kong Museum of Art—This collection of 2,800 pieces of Chinese antiquities includes rubbings, ceramics, bronzes, lacquerware, jade cloisonné, paper cuts, and embroidery. The historical picture collections have more than 1,100 paintings, prints, drawings, lithographs, and engravings that provide a pictorial record of Sino-British contacts in the eighteenth and nineteenth centuries. The museum (tel. 5-224127) is located on the 10th and 11th floors of the City Hall on High Bloc, two minutes walk east of the Star Ferry Pier. Open 10:00 a.m. to 6:00 p.m. daily, 1:00 to 6:00 p.m. on Sundays and public holidays, closed Thursdays.

Fung Ping Shan Museum—Located at Hong Kong University, this museum has an excellent collection of bronzes as well as good collections of paintings and ceramics from the Han, Tang, Song, Ming, and Qing dynasties as well as stone, jade, lacquer, and bamboo carvings. The museum is at 94 Bonham Road (tel. 8592114). Open Monday-Saturday, 9:30 a.m. to 6:00 p.m. closed Sundays.

Museum of Chinese Historical Relics—Artifacts from thousands of years of Chinese culture are frequently discovered in China. Some of the best are displayed here. Copies of some of the artifacts are available in the souvenir shop. The museum (tel. 8320411) is located on the 1st floor, Causeway Centre, 28 Harbour Road, Wanchai, Hong Hong near the Wanchai Ferry Pier. Enter from the China Resources Building. Open daily 10:00 a.m. to 6:00 p.m.

Hong Kong Museum of History—This collection offers an excellent introduction to the city's past. Photographs and ethnographic collections document Hong Kong traditions in arts and crafts, customs and beliefs, agriculture, and the rapidly disappearing rural style of life. Antiquities, coinage, and currencies are also on display. Located at Kowloon Park, Haiphong Road, Tsimshatsui, Kowloon, a two-minute walk from the Haiphong Road exit of MTR Tsimshatshui Station or a 10-minute walk from Kowloon Star Ferry Pier 2. Open daily except Fridays from 10:00 a.m. to 6:00 p.m. Tel. 671124.

Hong Kong Space Museum—One of the world's largest planetariums is found at this museum's space theater. For a fresh view of the sun, look through the solar telescope in the hall of solar sciences. Located on Salisbury Road east of the Star Ferry in Kowloon. Open Monday, Wednesday, Thursday, and Friday 2:00 to 9:30 p.m., Saturdays and holidays 10:30 a.m. to 9:30 p.m. Phone 7212361 for space theater schedule.

Since museum schedules change, you'll want to phone the Hong Kong Tourist Information Services offices at 8017177 for the latest information. Most are closed on public holidays. This office also provides a detailed "Museums & Arts & Crafts" brochure that tells where you can watch artisans at work. Many of these locations can easily be incorporated in the main Hong Kong itinerary. You may even want to substitute them for some of our other suggestions.

Hong Kong Departure

Following our primary 22-day itinerary, you'll fly from here to Bangkok this evening. Singapore Airlines connects to the Thai capital via its Singapore hub.

If you have more time for your around-the-world adventure, you can spend an extra week in the Philippines, where many Hong Kong residents take their vacations. Both Cathay Pacific and Philippine Air provide convenient nonstop flights. The 1-hour-and-45-minute morning flights will put you in Manila by midday.

If you are using Cathay, you'll have to return to Hong Kong to pick up a flight to Bangkok and rejoin the main itinerary on Day 5. Another possibility is to fly Philippine Airlines or Thai Air nonstop on the Manila-Bangkok leg.

Due to rush-hour traffic considerations, it's a good idea to leave your hotel at least two hours before flight time. Ask the hotel desk for advice on your departure time before arranging for a cab or inexpensive airport bus. Don't forget to reconfirm your departure. If possible, it's always a good idea to settle your room bill the night before checkout to avoid the morning line.

PHILIPPINES

With 7,000 islands, more than 100 tribes, and numerous dialects, this Asian land offers one-of-a-kind opportunities for travelers on an around-the-world itinerary. Only 90 minutes by air from Hong Kong, the Philippines make an easy side trip for travelers searching for an exotic locale, beautiful architecture, unique museums, and some of the best beaches in Asia. Nothing here suffers in the translation, thanks to the fact that English is a national language equal to, and in some places surpassing, Tagalog. In all the popular tourist areas, you can count on communicating with ease and never needing to refer to a dictionary. And Manila has more English newspapers than any city in America.

The Philippines is also an incredible travel bargain. Blessed with an excellent air transport system, offering some of the lowest-priced domestic flights in the world, it's a breeze to see the nation's beach resorts, Spanish colonial treasures, volcanoes, rain forests, rice terraces, and beautiful fiestas.

Anyone who has visited here can tell you about the landmark hotels, the superb snorkeling and diving, the exotic cuisine, and the endless array of vacation possibilities. But what makes this nation special—perhaps even unique—is that once you get past the urban centers, you find yourself in Old Asia, a place you thought only existed on library shelves and in film archives.

Although this is a third world country, where the average annual income is less than $1,500 a year, the Philippines is rich in natural and scenic resources. Torn by civil and religious wars that continue to smolder in certain provinces, the Philippines is also a place where you need to respect limits placed by the government on tourist traffic. Certain regions remain military hot spots plagued by guerrilla warfare and some of the last pirates to ride the high sea. They are definitely off-limits to tourists.

Most of the major areas of tourist interest—the urban centers of Manila and Cebu, the mountain town of Baguio, and resorts such as Puerto Azul and Boracay—are considered generally safe. With its Spanish colonial past, you'll discover the Philippines exists as a kind of Eurasian hybrid, with beautiful old Catholic churches and festivals that bring together the best of West and East. For our week-long extension, we recommend seeing Manila, the popular southern resort hub of Cebu, and a superb getaway island called Bohol. If you have more time, you can, of course, add other destinations.

The Philippines is a complex country, an anomaly of sorts in the East Asian community of nations. Although this is a well-

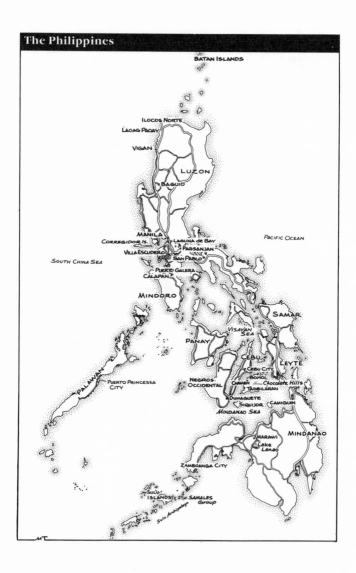

educated nation by third world standards, Spanish and American colonialism, the devastation of World War II, and most recently the rapacious Marcos oligarchy help explain why the Philippines has failed to match the economic miracles of Japan, Singapore, and nearby Taiwan. While the country is richly endowed with minerals, timber, fisheries, and other resources, there's a growing realization that it can no longer abdicate to developers who would just as soon strip the nation's treasured rain forests into pastureland. Similarly, there is a sense that the Philippines' unspoiled fishing villages, tribal homelands, and jungle highlands offer welcome relief from the contemporary urban model. Today, the government believes tourism can help rebuild the nation's economy on a kind of Small Is Beautiful model. Many communities feel they have the scenic, cultural, and artistic assets to attract paying guests from all over the world. We agree. For the discerning visitor, the Philippines is one of Asia's most important destinations.

Manila, with its incomparable Malacanang Palace, the original Spanish walled city of Intramuros, Jeepney factories, and Chinese Cemetery (where homes serve as incredible mausoleums), is the natural starting point for a visit.

Helpful Hint

Before leaving the United States, you need to check with the U.S. State Department in Washington or your local U.S. passport office for information on areas that are not considered safe for tourism. Your travel agent may be able to retrieve these travel advisories via their computerized reservation service, and additional assistance is available from the Philippine Department of Tourism and the U.S. Embassy in Manila or consulate in Cebu. To be on the safe side, travel to established tourist areas in the Philippines. It is a mistake for tourists to travel alone in rural areas, especially at night. We do not recommend massage parlors or Filipino bars outside tourist hotels. There's no need to drive in this country, which offers inexpensive cabs and moderately priced hire cars.

FIRST DAY: HONG KONG TO MANILA

Your visit begins with a trip to one of the city's most historical districts. You'll also have a chance to leisurely explore some of its grand parks, shop for incredible bargains, and sample the country's famed cuisine and nightlife.

Manila

A sprawling city of 10 million, Manila is your port of entry to the Philippine archipelago. Rebuilt after devastating Japanese raids that killed more than 100,000 residents during World War II (after Warsaw, the highest civilian casualty figure in the war), contemporary Manila is a crowded Asian capital that provides an excellent introduction to Filipino life. It is also a convenient gateway to some of the country's most fascinating resorts, volcanoes, jungles, and military monuments. Excellent hotels and restaurants, shopping, and one-of-a-kind attractions like the Malacanang Palace are all compelling reasons to visit.

Arrival

After landing at Ninoy Aquino International Airport (named for President Aquino's husband, who was assassinated while deplaning here in 1983), you'll claim your luggage and then head to the bank to pick up some pesos. (For a quick mental conversion from peso prices to dollar equivalents, simply multiply pesos by 5 and move the decimal left two places. For example, 400 pesos equals about $20.) If you don't have reservations, head over to the hotel desk. All the major hotels have representatives, and you may be able to bargain for a commercial rate or other discount. Car services are available, but you'll probably find it's less expensive to take a taxi to your hotel.

Domestic Air Ticketing

Before leaving the airport, you should take care of all travel arrangements for domestic air travel. Philippine Airlines, the carrier that flies to your next destinations, Cebu and Bohol, will only confirm domestic flights for foreign passengers if they fly to Manila on one of their international routes. Unless you came over on Philippine Airlines or have a friend in Manila who can make domestic reservations, you will need to get your tickets as soon as you land in Manila. Our plan calls for you to take the 8:30 a.m. flight from Manila to Cebu on the fourth day of your itinerary extension and the 4:00 p.m. flight from Cebu to Tagbilaran, Bohol. On the seventh day, you will catch the 1:20 p.m. flight from Tagbilaran to Cebu and connect to the 3:40 p.m. flight to Manila. Here you'll pick up a flight to Bangkok and

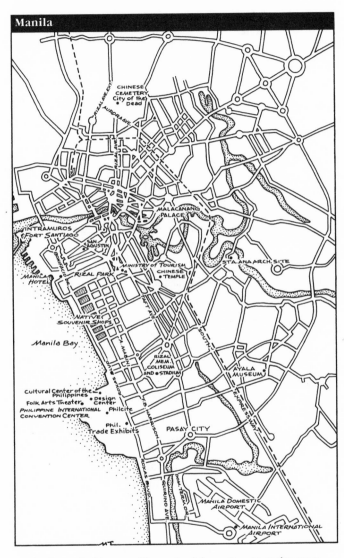

rejoin the main itinerary. If you don't have time to make your Philippine Air bookings at the airport, take care of them in Manila. By the way, don't panic if you can't get a flight to Bohol, as there is convenient daily ferry service between Cebu and Tagbilaran.

Lodging

Advance reservations are essential during Christmas, Easter, and the Chinese New Year season. During the remainder of the year, many hotels offer special weekend packages and commercial discounts. If you can afford it, the **Manila Hotel**, General Douglas MacArthur's home base in the days leading up to World War II, is an excellent choice. Rooms start around 2,000 pesos ($100) a night. It's located on Rizal Park (tel. 470011). A less expensive alternative—around 1,200 to 1,400 pesos ($60 to $70) a night—is the **Holiday Inn** at 3001 Roxas Boulevard (tel. 597961). For budget accommodations, try the **Bayview Hotel** at 1118 Roxas Boulevard (tel. 503061) for about 500 pesos ($25).

Food

Kamayan at 47 Arnaiz Road is the place to eat Filipino food with your hands (tel. 883604). A broad menu features seafood, lumpia, suckling pig, and dozens of other specialties. For a light lunch or coffee, try **Cafe Adriatico** at 1790 Adriatico, Remedios Circle, Malate (tel. 584059). At the **Manila Hotel** (tel. 470011), patio dining on the harbor is an excellent way to end the day. The same hotel offers the Manila dinner show, complete with native dancing. After the show, Imelda Marcos—the most famous size 8 in Filipino history—loved to dance to the disco beat. **Seafood Market** on J. Bocobo (tel. 505761) lets you choose your dinner and have it cooked to order.

Getting Around

Taxis are so inexpensive in the Philippines that you'll want to use them everywhere. With the assistance of your hotel door-man, you can easily arrange to hire a taxi for around $5 an hour. Alternatively, you can rent a car and driver from a company like Avis for up to 18 hours at around $60. Hired cars tend to be more comfortable, and the drivers often can do limited guiding.

Sightseeing Highlights

▲▲▲ **Intramuros/Fort Santiago**—The walled city of Intramuros, built by the Spanish in 1571, is a historic and cultural center that will introduce you to Manila's colonial heritage. Living separately from the Filipinos inside the walls of this city, the Spanish ruled their island colony for three centuries. While earthquakes and wars have leveled many of the residences, Intramuros has been partially restored. In and around this walled city are craft shops, museums, the San Agustín Church, and Casa Manila, the reconstructed home of a wealthy Filipino family. Also here is Fort Santiago, which has been occupied by British, American, and Japanese troops. National hero Dr. José

Rizal was imprisoned here prior to his execution in December 1896. In the museum are Rizal memorabilia as well as translations of his best known poem, "Mi Último Adiós." Continue up to Plaza Moriones and Bastion San Francisco, where Admiral Dewey's victorious troops first raised the Stars and Stripes in 1898. Don't miss the display of Filipino presidents' antique autos on the lower level.

SECOND DAY: MANILA

Today you'll see the spoils of the Marcos regime at the Malacanang Palace, get an overview of Filipino history at the Ayala Museum, tour the City of the Dead, and visit the legendary Manila Hotel.

Suggested Schedule	
9:00 a.m.	Malacanang Palace.
11:00 a.m.	Chinese Cemetery.
1:00 p.m.	Lunch at Manila Hotel.
3:00 p.m.	Ayala Museum.
5:00 p.m.	Cultural Center of the Philippines.

Sightseeing Highlights
▲▲▲ **Malacanang Palace**—Your day begins with a cab ride to the Malacanang Palace, one of the best reasons we can think of for adding the Philippines to your itinerary. Among President Aquino's most important decisions upon taking office in 1986 was to not move into Malacanang, the Philippine White House. While she does hold cabinet meetings and receptions in the 200-year-old palace, Aquino has done a great public service by opening the Marcoses' private quarters to public tours, daily except Wednesday and Sunday from 9:00 to 11:00 a.m. and 1:00 to 3:00 p.m. Visitors are guided by docents who liberated the palace during the 1986 People's Power revolution.

On your tour, you'll see the mansion just the way Imelda and Ferdinand left it. With their own barber and beauty shops, hospital, private chapel, chandeliered bedrooms, and $7,900 toy cars for the grandchildren, the Marcoses clearly got by just fine on a civil servant's salary. Although the Marcoses made off with about 75 percent of their clothing during their hasty exit from the country in 1986, the basement wardrobe area does showcase 57 racks of First Lady dresses, including one gown made from silver threads. In this tropical climate, the First Lady also had plenty of fur around to ward off the chill of the air-conditioning. For example, she could wear a different mink coat every day for two weeks. Another tour highlight is the bullet-proof vest section. Among the imaginative designs here is a bulletproof London Fog raincoat. "When it fell off the hanger," says the guide, "it was so heavy the guard taking care of this section couldn't pick it up."

Clearly the highlight of this portion of the tour is Imelda's collection of more than 3,000 pairs of shoes, including her disco footwear with blinking lights in the translucent heels. Although Ferdinand bought most of his shoes in his homeland, the docents point out that only about 18 percent of Imelda's size 8 footwear was domestic. While some exhibits such as the Pampers boxes the first couple used to take cash out of the country are lost to history, there is no shortage of curatorial opportunities in this collection. A new Malacanang hall of fine and decorative arts is showcasing the best of Philippine fashion and design. Recent curated exhibits have featured the shawls of Imelda, the fans of Imelda, and the religious art of Imelda. The possibilities are endless.

It would be easy to dismiss the Marcos collection as the demented spoils of a 21-year regime. But this denies the possibility that Imelda and Ferdinand had a higher purpose in mind: to demonstrate the important role shopping plays in the political process. On Imelda's nightstand is a mirror with a digital time display across the bottom. When the alarm sounds, the mirror suddenly illuminates with a color photograph of the Marcoses. It's that image—fleeting though it may be—that offers hope to those who have hit the limit on their Visa card. Have faith, they seem to be saying, and perhaps one day you too will become the highest size 8 in the land.

Other Sightseeing Highlights
▲▲▲ **Chinese Cemetery**—This 135-acre City of the Dead was built in the mid-nineteenth century as the last resting place for Chinese who were banned from Spanish cemeteries. As your taxi or driver enters the south gate off Aurora Avenue, you'll find the streets lined with handsome mausoleums, including some with fully equipped kitchens, wet bars, and party rooms to accommodate relatives who come to honor their dead. More than 387,000 Filipinos have been buried or cremated in this cemetery. With the help of a guide (agree on a fee in advance), you can tour some of the more opulent homes and townhouses that cost as much as $1,000 a month to maintain. Along the way, you may find relatives watching color TV or entertaining their children in playrooms built next to some of the beautiful

mausoleums that are bigger than most Manila homes. Perhaps the most opulent cemetery in Asia, this graveyard functions like a village complete with restaurants and drink and souvenir stands.

▲▲ **Manila Hotel**—When General Douglas MacArthur's troops stormed Manila in 1945, one unit's mission was to liberate the Manila Hotel from the Japanese. "We were told that the Boss (MacArthur) wanted his old room back, intact," one of his soldiers explained years later. From 1935 until the Japanese took Manila in 1941, MacArthur, military adviser to the Philippine Commonwealth Government, lived here in the penthouse with his family. Like the general, who said he wouldn't accept the Manila posting unless he was given this suite, many guests consider this establishment a mandatory stop on a tour of the archipelago. Designed by architect Daniel Burnham, the California mission-style hotel (now complemented by a modern tower) is a landmark building featuring Doric columns finished with adobe, graceful arches, and ornate Spanish lanterns. The ceiling of the vast, wood-paneled lobby is highlighted by three chandeliers made of brass, crystal prisms, and seashells. The small museum here covers the hotel's many links to Filipino history. In the summer of 1986, leaders loyal to deposed President Marcos seized control of the hotel during a four-day coup attempt against the Aquino administration. The dissidents gave up when the kitchen ran out of food. Of course, you'll be able to choose from an impressive menu when you lunch on the patio overlooking Manila Bay.

▲ **Ayala Museum**—Located on Makati Avenue in the Greenbelt complex, this small museum features historical dioramas that provide an overview of Philippine history. You'll learn about early hunters, Chinese traders, the spread of Islam, Magellan's tragic death in Cebu, the Spanish colonial period, and the execution of Rizal. From the American conquest of Manila in 1898 through the Battle of Bataan in 1941 and Douglas MacArthur's dramatic return with the American forces at Leyte in 1944, this is a carefully authenticated look at the evolution of the archipelago. All the wooden figurines in the dioramas were carved by skilled craftsmen. Also here are galleries covering the nation's maritime, archaeological, and religious heritage. Open 9:00 a.m. to 6:00 p.m. Tuesday through Sunday.

▲ **Cultural Center of the Philippines**—The center is located on Roxas Boulevard, Pasay City. On the 4th floor, you'll find excellent displays of excavated artifacts, Stone Age tools, Iron Age pottery and metalware, ancient jewelry, and an extensive collection of ceramic tradeware from China, Thailand, and Cambodia. In the same complex, the Contemporary Art

Museum of the Philippines exhibits contemporary painting, sculpture, mixed media, printmaking, and performance and video art. Together, these two venues provide an excellent introduction to Filipino arts and crafts. Also worthy of your attention is the Coconut Palace, a grand home built almost entirely of coconut wood for the visit of Pope John Paul II in 1981. While the pontiff declined to stay here, many friends of the Marcos family, such as Cristina Ford and George Hamilton, did check in.

Also located in this complex is the Manila Film Center. Seven workers perished in a construction accident while completing this building. To avoid postponing the film center's grand opening, orders were issued to leave the dead men in the quick-drying cement, where they remain entombed to this day. Not long after this tragedy, the administrator who gave the order to not recover these victims died in a car accident. This tragedy took place after she saw ghosts of the victims on a roadway and ordered her driver to swerve. He did and hit a tree. The driver was unhurt. The Cultural Center is open daily 9:00 a.m. to 6:00 p.m. and the Contemporary Art Museum is open daily 9:00 a.m. to 8:00 p.m. The Coconut Palace is open Tuesday through Sunday.

THIRD DAY: MANILA

Today you can choose between three popular day trips from Manila: a look at the region's military history, a delightful estate, or an exciting jungle river cruise. Corregidor was MacArthur's base of operations at the beginning of World War II and a major battleground. Villa Escudero gives you a panoramic look at the opulent colonial life-style. For an adventure travel experience, Pagsanjan is ideal. Just be sure to bring a change of clothes.

Suggested Schedule	
8:00 a.m.	Leave your hotel for Corregidor, Villa Escudero, or Pagsanjan Falls.
6:00 p.m.	Return to your hotel. Evening at leisure.

Corregidor—Reached by ferry, this island 24 miles from Manila was the command post of General MacArthur and Philippine President Manuel Quezon from December 1941 to March 1942, when more than 12,000 American and Filipino troops surrendered to the Japanese. Thousands of these prisoners died in the Bataan Death March, the infamous 100-mile Japanese evacuation of prisoners to a POW camp. The island was taken back from the Japanese in a 1945 attack that began with an assault that took the lives of more than 1,000 Japanese defenders. Their situation hopeless, the Japanese refused to surrender. Instead, they detonated an underground arsenal in a mass suicide that killed more than 2,000 of their own soldiers as well as a number of Americans. Daylong tours, which leave Manila at 7:30 a.m., include a two-hour bus tour of the island's monument, a visit to the Pacific War Memorial and museum, and a buffet lunch. Boats return at 4:00 p.m. The tour costs about 8,000 pesos ($40) and can be booked through your hotel.

Pagsanjan Falls—This daylong excursion to Laguna Province begins with a *banca* (canoe) ride down the Pagsanjan River. Add to your adventure by switching to a raft for the ride beneath Magdapio Falls and a chance to ride the rapids. The rapids are at their best in the late summer. You'll also enjoy swimming in the river near the bottom of the falls. You can make this tour an overnight trip by checking into the Pagsanjan Rapids Hotel. Due to heavy crowds, weekend trips are best avoided. Used as a location for a portion of Francis Ford Coppola's *Apocalypse Now,* Pagsanjan is easily reached by tours from major hotels. Be sure to bring along a change of clothing and a plastic bag to protect your camera.

Villa Escudero—About an hour and a half south of Manila, Villa Escudero is a charming coconut planation that now doubles as a resort. You'll be serenaded by musicians as horse-drawn carts take you around this Spanish-style hacienda. Villa Escudero guests are welcome to see coconut processing exhibits and visit a museum dedicated to treasures of the colonial area. We recommend the plantation's waterfront restaurant, and there are handsome cottages for those who want to extend their stay. A few minutes away is San Pablo, a city surrounded by seven lakes. Continuing south toward Sariya, you'll see a number of other imposing mansions built by Filipino coconut barons in colonial days. The easiest way to reach Villa Escudero is to take a hired car or taxi. Don't even consider driving your own car in this country.

FOURTH DAY: CEBU/BOHOL

Fly south to Cebu, the second-largest city in the Philippines and a resort region popular with tourists from all over Asia. After exploring some of the highlights of Cebu, you'll continue by plane or ferry to Bohol, home of the legendary Chocolate Hills, outstanding beaches, and coral reefs perfect for diving and snorkeling.

Suggested Schedule	
8:30 a.m.	Fly to Cebu on Philippine Airlines.
9:40 a.m.	Arrive in Cebu, take taxi into town.
10:30 a.m.	Visit Fort San Pedro.
11:30 a.m.	See Magellan's Cross and Basilica Minore del Santo Niño.
12:30 p.m.	Lunch.
1:30 p.m.	Taoist Temple.
4:00 p.m.	Fly to Tagbilaran, Bohol, on Philippine Airlines.
4:30 p.m.	Arrive in Tagbilaran, Bohol.
5:00 p.m.	Check into your hotel.

Cebu

At the Manila Airport, check your bags through to Bohol and then catch a flight to Cebu, the oldest city in the Philippines. Home of the first church, school, and commercial street in the Philippines, Cebu became the cradle of Christianity in the Far East when Magellan planted his cross here in 1521. The city was colonized four decades after these explorers arrived. Today this city of 500,000 is an important port and commercial center and the gateway to many popular beach resorts in the Visayan region. Your flight lands at the airport on Mactan Island, where you'll want to catch a taxi for the half-hour ride into town. Bargaining with drivers at the curb will probably get you a cheaper fare than using one of the transportation desks inside the baggage claim area.

Now is the time to reconfirm your onward flight to Tagbilaran, Bohol, this afternoon. If you can't get a flight from Cebu to Bohol, simply take one of the ferries to Tagbilaran. The Sweet Heart and Sweet Time make the four-hour trip over from Cebu every day at noon and Mondays and Fridays at 10:00 p.m. Call Sweet Lines at 97415. You can confirm these and other ferry schedules to Bohol by checking with the Cebu tourist office at Fort San Pedro.

Cebu Sightseeing Highlights

▲ **Fort San Pedro**—The oldest fort in the nation, this stone and mortar landmark was built in 1565. Over the centuries, it has defended the island from Muslim raiding parties and served as a headquarters for Filipino revolutionaries, an American military base, and a Japanese prisoner-of-war camp. Walk along the walls and you'll enjoy a fine view of Cebu Harbor. Be sure to visit the Department of Tourism Office inside the fort to get maps and information on touring the region.

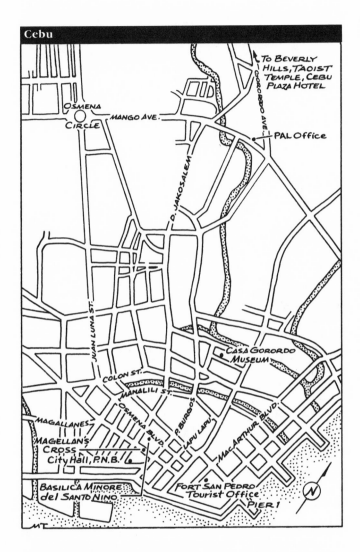

Cebu

▲ **Magellan's Cross and Basilica Minore del Santo Niño**—
After he arrived in 1521, Magellan gave thanks for his safe journey by planting a cross here. Today, the monument is a short
walk from Fort San Pedro. Cross the Plaza Independencia and
walk four blocks up Magallanes Street (the tourist office at the
fort can assist you) to see Magellan's cross sheltered in a little
pavilion. The king and queen were baptized along with several

hundred of their people, an event re-created in the ceiling mural you can see over the cross.

It was in Zebu, as the village was then known, that Magellan gave the queen an image of the Holy Child (Santo Niño). Forty years after Magellan's death, the Santo Niño was found amidst the ruins of the village, which had been largely destroyed in fighting between villages and the Spanish. To this day, the survival of the Santo Niño is celebrated as a miracle. It is now located in the Basilica Minore del Santo Niño, across the street from the cross. The schedule of liturgical services is listed on signs that also advertise Coca-Cola.

▲▲ **Casa Gorordo**—Walk out of the church to Burgos Street and turn left. Continue six blocks to a triangle where the road forks. Stay to the right and you'll come to this restored Spanish home, now a museum of eighteenth-century antique furniture as well as a gallery for Filipino art. Restored by a wealthy family, the wood-paneled home was the residence of the first Cebuano bishop. Built around a beautiful garden, this Cebu highlight is open Monday through Saturday 9:00 a.m. to 12:00 noon and 2:00 to 5:00 p.m.

▲ **Taoist Temple**—Taxi up into Cebu's affluent Beverly Hills neighborhood to see this aerie dedicated to the teachings of Chinese philosopher Lao Tze. Both believers and nonbelievers hike up the 99 temple steps to have their fortunes read daily. With its pagoda roofs and fearsome dragon sculptures, the temple makes a great setting for picture-taking. After enjoying the panoramic view, ride over to the Cebu Plaza on Nivel Hill (tel. 92431) or the Golden Cowrie on Salinas Drive (tel. 91633) for lunch. Less expensive fare is available at Alavar's Seafood House on Archbishop Reyes Avenue (tel. 96120).

On your way back to the airport (leave town at least 90 minute before flight time), ask the cab driver to take you down Colon, the oldest street in the Philippines. If you have extra time, you may want to ask the driver to stop off at the Magellan monument near the airport. It was here that Magellan, who had been warned not to go ashore by locals and Spanish royalty, was killed by Chief Datu Lapu-Lapu two weeks after reaching Cebu.

Helpful Hint
Cebu is a major resort hub. If you would like to remain in the area, simply check with the tourist information office at the airport or Fort San Pedro for suggestions on the many waterfront resorts in and near the area.

Bohol
An emerging Filipino resort, home of the mysterious Chocolate Hills, Bohol is an ideal tropical retreat that offers a chance to see

unreconstructed village life. This island is blessed with exceptional beaches and diving opportunities that draw the scuba certified from all over the world. After seeing two of the country's major cities, you'll find on this island the kind of deserted beaches, jungle scenery, remote rivers, and verdant landscapes that make the Philippines an excellent vacation choice.

Most of the island's 800,000 residents live in rural villages, where the economy is focused on fishing, coconut plantations, rice paddies, and cornfields. The fruits of all this labor find their way into many of the wonderful dishes served at local restaurants. An emerging craft center, Bohol is an excellent place to shop for inexpensive seashell necklaces and woven products such as Panama hats, basketry, and straw mats.

An important Asian trading center as far back as the fifth century, Bohol, like Cebu, was colonized by the Spanish in the sixteenth century. Here the Jesuits built what is today the nation's oldest church at Baclayon. Over the next century, other sanctuaries skillfully blended Moorish, European, and Mexican design. Bohol is also the site of the first known and recorded international treaty of peace, the blood compact signed in March 1565 between Spain's Miguel Lopez de Legazpi and Bohol's Chief Datu Sikatuna. To seal their friendship, both men drank a few drops of their blood mixed together in a cup. In this spirit of peace and harmony, the Boholians continue to welcome foreign visitors to their shores. If you're the kind of person who likes to discover a dream retreat ahead of the masses, look no further.

After checking into your hotel, you may want to take a swim before dinner. In the evening, you can shop for crafts downtown. For short trips, it's easy to get around using the inexpensive little three-wheeler cabs called "tricycles." These ubiquitous vehicles are the city's principal form of transportation. Before turning in, ask your hotel desk clerk to line up a taxi driver for the next day's tour. Expect to pay about $25 to $35 for the day.

Lodging

Catch a taxi at the airport or ferry dock to your hotel. Most tourists head out across the causeway to one of the beach resorts on Panglao Island. The most expensive at 800 pesos (about $40) a night is the **Bohol Beach Club** (tel. 522-2301 in Manila for reservations). For about 600 pesos ($30) a night, or 1,000 pesos ($50) for a cottage, you can stay at the nearby **Alonaville Beach Resort** (tel. 32-86). The **Momo Beach Resort** in the same area charges 600 pesos ($30) a day including meals (tel. 3182). All these resorts are ideal for beachcombing and diving. But because they are 20 to 30 minutes from

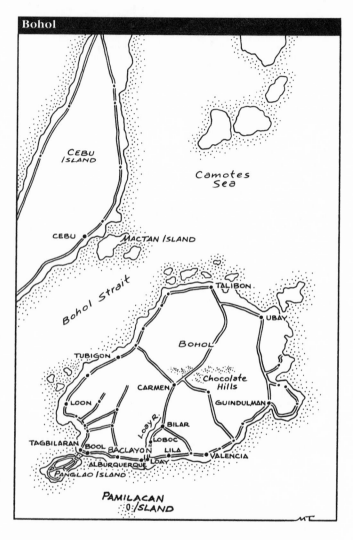

Tagbilaran—your hub for most tourist activities in Bohol—you will find yourself doing a fair amount of commuting back into town to follow our suggested itinerary.

An alternative worth considering is **Island Leisure** on Bohol, about five minutes from Tagbilaran. While the beach here is not as perfect as those at the aforementioned Panglao resorts, air-conditioned rooms are available for about 350 pesos ($17.50) a night (tel. 2482). There's also a lovely terrace restaurant and full facilities for snorkeling and diving. The advantage to this location is that you will be closer to popular spots like the Chocolate Hills and the Loay River Cruise. You'll still be able to head out to perfect beaches whenever you want to kick back. If you enjoy strolling around town, checking out museums, shops, and new restaurants (instead of always ending up at the resort for meals), you'll appreciate this location convenient to Tagbilaran.

Food
Most of the major tourist restaurants are found in the resort hotels—**Island Leisure**, the **Bohol Beach Club, Momo Beach Club**, and **Alonaville Beach Resort**. Inexpensive Chinese and Filipino food is available at the **Gie Garden Hotel** in downtown Tagbilaran on Garcia Ave. (tel. 3182). A modest terrace café at the **Chocolate Hills Complex** is a good choice in this area.

FIFTH DAY: BOHOL

Today you'll travel up-island, visiting Bohol's historic churches en route to the Chocolate Hills. After touring these geologic landmarks, which fascinate scientists and metaphysicians alike, you'll return to Loboc and take the Loay River trip to see Busay Falls. Your driver will pick you up at the end of this cruise and take you back to the hotel, where you can relax or swim before dinner.

Suggested Schedule	
8:00 a.m.	Breakfast at your hotel.
9:00 a.m.	Visit Bohol Museum in Tagbilaran.
9:30 a.m.	Drive up-island to see Bohol's churches at Baclayon, Aburquerque, Loay, and Loboc.
11:00 a.m.	Arrive at Chocolate Hills.
12:00 p.m.	Lunch at Chocolate Hills.
2:00 p.m.	Loay River cruise.
5:00 p.m.	Return to your hotel.
	Evening at leisure.

Sightseeing Highlights
▲ **Bohol Museum**—Your driver will take you to this little Tag-bilaran museum located near the plaza. Here you'll get an over-view of the island's past which will add to your enjoyment of today's tour. Artifacts, archives, and exhibits tell the story of Bohol's tribal customs, religious revolts, political evolution, and role in World War II. On display are weaponry, basketry, altar-pieces, wood carvings, and beautiful colored shells. Open 9:00 a.m. to 4:00 p.m. weekdays.

▲▲ **Baclayon Church**—Heading north out of town, you can pause briefly at the monument commemorating the site of the famous Blood Compact between Spain's Miguel Lopez de Legazpi and Bohol Chief Datu Sikatuna. A few minutes up the road is the landmark Baclayon Church, built in 1595 by natives under the direction of two Jesuits. The coral blocks are mor-tared together by lime mixed with egg whites. Inside, you'll find a museum featuring religious art, ecclesiastical vestments, and Latin librettos printed on animal skin. Also here is a dungeon used to punish natives who violated Christian law. Children playing in the churchyard create great photo opportunities. The church is four miles from Tagbilaran. Continuing east up the island, you can also stop to visit the church in Aburquerque. Wednesday market days transform this spot into a community center. Inside, you'll want to see the handsome painted ceilings. You'll find more ceiling paintings worth seeing at the church in Loay.

▲▲▲ **Chocolate Hills**—Bohol's best-known destination, these 1,200 hills, shaped like giant Hershey kisses, are located near the town of Carmen. Rising an average of 100 feet above the surrounding rice paddies and coconut plantations, the mys-terious hills have inspired many legends. One popular local the-ory maintains that the hills sprang from teardrops left behind by a local giant who lost the love of his life. The late Erik Van Daniken had another explanation (that's right, UFOs). Of course, geologists would tell you how limestone uplifted from the sea to create this phenomenon. You can develop your own theories as you hike through the neighborhood; then retire to the hostel restaurant, which serves excellent corn soup and fresh lemonade (the waitress on the terrace picks the lemons from a tree). A modest hostel provides lodging for those who want to spend the night.

▲▲▲ **Loay River Cruise**—Returning back toward the coast, your driver will take you to Loboc, where you'll board a motor-ized outrigger canoe for a trip up the tropical Loboc River. This popular tour can be arranged through the desk at your hotel, but your driver can often make individual arrangements on short notice. Just be sure to have your hotel tell him to put the cruise on your day's itinerary. The cruise begins in Loboc (you may want to visit the historic church here) with a ride up to Busay Falls, a good place to swim before heading down the palm-shaded stream to Loay. On this river trip, you'll be able to see the stilt houses, small farms, and villages of rural Bohol. Friendly kids race along the banks as you descend the Loay. The river trip takes roughly an hour and a half and will cost about 400 pesos ($20). Be sure to make arrangements to have your driver pick you up at the dock in Loay for the ride back to your hotel.

SIXTH DAY: BOHOL

Today is devoted to exploring some of Bohol's coral reef highlights. You can choose between an organized trip to one of the popular scuba sites or making your own way out to an undiscovered island that the Boholians consider one of their secret treasures.

Suggested Schedule

9:00 a.m.	Catch a boat or outrigger canoe to Balicasag or Pamilacan Island.
10:00 a.m.	Snorkel, dive, or beachcomb.
12:00 noon	Lunch.
1:00 p.m.	Return to the beach.
4:00 p.m.	Ride back to your hotel.
	Evening at leisure.

On the Bohol Waterfront

Bohol is a big hit with the diving and snorkeling crowd. Some of the best reef life is found in the vicinity of two small nearby islands, Pamilacan and Balicasag. You can join an organized trip from Bohol with the Island Leisure, the Bohol Beach Club, or other major hotels for about 1,000 pesos ($50). Or, if you prefer, have your driver arrange for a motorized outrigger canoe to take you from the dock at Baclayon to Pamilacan Island. It's easy to make the latter trip on Wednesday, when the people of Pamilacan come into Bohol for market day. You may also find plenty of navigators after church at Baclayon on Sunday. But with the help of your driver, you should be able to arrange a trip to

Pamilacan any day. Whenever you go, expect to pay about 400 pesos ($20) for the round-trip ride.

Sightseeing Highlights

▲▲▲ **Balicasag**—You can take an organized trip to this popular diving spot and rent diving or snorkeling gear from the tour operator. You'll be in the hands of an experienced dive master from one of the major resorts such as Island Leisure or the Bohol Beach Club. Because of the support provided by these operators, this is the trip divers should take first. Snorkelers who prefer the security of a group will also want to take these 1,000-peso ($50) organized tours.

▲▲▲ **Pamilacan Island**—An excellent choice for snorkelers. After beaching at the little village here, walk to the left a few hundred yards (ask the canoe skipper to show you the way), where you'll find fine beaches and a luminous reef with brown, black, and red corals that attract manta rays, swordfish, and scores of other species. On Pamilacan, you'll get a look at village life, complete with corn growing in the front yard, pigs sleeping underneath homes, and a little store that only sells canned food and soda. The truly adventurous can spend the night in little dirt-floored huts for $1. This is not the Hyatt, and it would be a good idea to bring your own food if you plan to stay over. Use the buddy system when swimming off Pamilacan Island. This trip is only for strong swimmers with snorkeling or diving experience.

If you don't feel like heading out to Balicasag or Pamilacan, why not swim at one of the popular beaches on Panglao Island, near Tagbilaran? Among the popular spots are Alona Beach and Bikini Beach. Check at any of the resort hotels for additional suggestions.

Departure

Many visitors to Bohol find this island so relaxing that they choose to extend their stay for a day or two. After you complete your extension on this romantic island, you'll want to rejoin the main itinerary on Day 5 in Thailand. Catch a 1:20 p.m. flight back to Cebu and connect to the 3:40 p.m. flight arriving in Manila at 4:50 p.m. In the capital city you can take a nonstop evening flight to Bangkok, leaving at 8:25 p.m. and arriving at 10:35 p.m. Or you can return to Hong Kong and pick up a Bangkok flight there.

BANGKOK: THE GILDED CITY

From the hills and jungles of the Golden Triangle, through the teeming urban metropolis of Bangkok, to the white sand beaches and turquoise waters of its southern peninsula, Thailand is one of the most diverse and complex countries in Asia. Known to many Westerners only through *The King and I* stereotypes, Thailand is a many-faceted society held together in an intricate web of history, culture, religion, and political independence. Home of some of Asia's most beautiful palaces, Bangkok is a gilded city of canals, temples, and reclining Buddhas. From colorful silk to fiery seafood, Bangkok's pleasures belong on any Asian itinerary. Today you will get an overview of this society shaped by Siamese kings and Buddhist priests. Like Kyoto and the Forbidden City, this royal capital is the kind of place you'd expect to find at the end of a yellow brick road.

Suggested Schedule

1:00 a.m.	Check into your Bangkok Hotel.
12:00 noon	Lunch.
1:00 p.m.	Temple and Grand Palace tour.
7:00 p.m.	Dinner.

Thailand

Occupying the central and western part of the Indochina Peninsula, with Burma to the west, Laos to the north, Kampuchea to the east, and Malaysia to the south, Thailand is about the size of France or Texas. Its mountainous north, geologically linked to the great Himalayan range, slopes down into a semiarid northeastern plateau and a fertile central plain. The country is squeezed into a narrow isthmus in the south, bordered by the Gulf of Thailand and the Andaman Sea. Thailand's tropical climate supports a tremendous variety of vegetation (including over 1,000 varieties of orchids) and animals—elephants, tigers, snakes, birds, and monkeys. While the country's economy is being rapidly modernized (exporting tin, rubber, and textiles), three-quarters of the population works in agriculture, mostly related to rice production. Bangkok is a major hub of Asian travel, with all the amenities and symptoms of a modern city; yet much village life remains insulated from twentieth-century civilization.

The history of Thailand, known as Siam until 1939, is the story of independent Asian civilizations—ancient cultures of the Chao Phraya River Basin, the southern peninsula, and the northern mountains—gradually merging into a unified society. Starting in 1239 during the century-long reign of the Sukhothai Kingdom (the "dawn of happiness"), Thais were first united under a single monarch, King Ramkamhaeng, and a single religion, Theravada Buddhism. There followed a succession of kingdoms, including the great Ayutthaya era in the seventeenth century, and encounters with foreigners, notably aggressive Burmese rulers and influential French traders. In 1782, General Chakri, crowned Rama I, moved the Siamese capital to Bangkok and founded the royal dynasty that endures to the present.

Foreign trade flourished in the mid-1800s, but, unlike all of its neighbors, Siam was never governed by an imperial power, and political independence and cultural integrity were important factors in preserving Thailand's unique character. In 1932, a bloodless coup, the first of many throughout the twentieth century, led to the establishment of a constitutional monarchy governed by a prime minister but strongly shaped by the military.

Thailand's ethnically mixed population of 52.8 million descends mostly from Mon, Khmer, and Thai peoples but has absorbed waves of migration from China as well. Ninety-five percent of the people are Buddhist, and men typically spend at least three months in the monkhood as they become adults. This abiding spirituality influences the Thai people's universally kind and friendly demeanor. Everywhere you will meet people who go out of their way to make you feel welcome. In return, you can observe a few simple customs. It is impolite to touch people, including children, on their heads, or to sit with the soles of your feet pointing at another person. Buddhist monks are not allowed to touch women and will sometimes refrain from social contact with them altogether. The royal family is the object of great affection in Thailand, and respectful behavior is expected of foreigners. Losing one's temper is virtually taboo. The Thai people seem to live by the wisdom of mai pen rai, which can be translated as "it doesn't matter," but which actually implies a much deeper acceptance of the moment.

The tonal Thai language is extremely difficult to master. Pronunciation is so complex and crucial that phrase books tend to be of little help. But because tourism has become the country's major industry, giving rise to an efficient infrastructure of plane, train, bus, and taxi transportation, most people involved with travelers speak some English and make great efforts to help visitors enjoy their country.

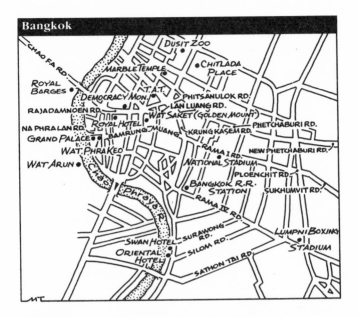

Bangkok

The greater metropolitan area of Thailand's largest city covers 580 square miles and is home to over 5 million people, almost one-tenth of the country's population. Bangkok's contradictory potpourri of ancient temples and high-rise hotels, quiet canals and frenetic expressways, tranquil saffron-robed monks and hustling drivers of *tuk-tuks* (motorized versions of the old three-wheeled pedicabs) is enough to warrant Thailand's reputation as the most exotic city in Asia. Since King Rama I made it the country's capital in the late eighteenth century, Bangkok has grown into a city that is at once magnificent and mad. The old "Venice of the East," a maze of *klongs* (canals) supporting fishermen and floating markets, is now traversed by bustling avenues carrying 90 percent of Thailand's automobile traffic. Look up from the congested streets to the sharply curving spires of an ancient temple and understand why the Thais call their capital city "Krung Thep," the "City of Angels." In a noisy sidewalk café, dip into a spicy seafood soup or a hot chicken curry and be transported into a paradise of exotic aromas and flavors.

Bangkok proper is bordered by the curving Chao Phraya River on the west. The old royal city was built next to the water. The Dusit area, with the new royal palace, government buildings, and zoo (developed under King Rama V), is just to the

northeast of the Old Royal City, across the Klong Phadung.
"Modern" Bangkok, where you'll find many of the new hotels,
towering office buildings, and exclusive shops, extends to the
south and east along New Petchburi, Sukhumvit, and Silom
roads. The combination of Western influences and Asian traditions and the imposition of helter-skelter modern development
on an ancient culture that in many ways is still thriving make
Bangkok wild, foreboding, exciting, and endlessly intriguing.

Getting Around
When you arrive at the Bangkok airport, many of the anxieties
about disembarking in a foreign country with a difficult language are quickly dispelled. Once you clear immigration and
customs, young English-speaking women from the Thai Tourist
Authority approach travelers and cheerfully assist in arranging
ground transportation. They will also try to sell you package
sightseeing tours, but you can just have them secure a taxi to
your hotel. You can also change money at one of the currency
exchange bank windows in the airport lobby. For a quick mental conversion from baht to dollars, multiply the baht amount
by 4 and then move the decimal point two places to the left. For
example, 100 baht equals about $4. Taxi fares to downtown
Bangkok are about 300 baht ($12) and the drivers race along the
expressway at breathtaking speeds.

    One of the first things you notice about Bangkok is the traffic,
a mad swirl of speeding cars, trucks, buses, motorbikes, bicycles, and tuk-tuks. Only the bravest of short-term visitors
would rent a vehicle and venture out into the apparent chaos.
Fortunately, Bangkok has a well-developed bus system and a
seemingly inexhaustible supply of taxis and tuk-tuks. Buses
cost two baht (about $.08) for short local trips, 5 to 20 baht
($.20-$.80) for longer crosstown routes. Taxi fares are
negotiable—bargain before you get in. Tuk-tuks provide both
the cheapest transport and the most down-to-earth views
of the city. They, too, are negotiable, starting at 10 baht ($.40) for
the shortest (two- or three-block) rides. Boats can be hired
along the riverbank for about 300 baht ($12) per hour, regard-
less of the number of passengers.

Travel Route
From the Royal Hotel, turn left (south) down Rachini Road (on
the far side of the canal). At Bamrung Muang Road, turn right
(west), and at the end of the block, you will see the tall, white
walls of the Grand Palace. The entrance is around to the right on
Naphralan Road. From either the Oriental or Swan Hotel, take a
bus, taxi, or tuk-tuk to the Grand Palace. Or take a jetboat up

the Chao Phraya River to the dock near Naphralan Road and walk straight ahead to the Grand Palace.

On leaving the Grand Palace, turn left (west) and walk along Naphralan Road, turning left (south) again on Maharaj Road. Walk along the west wall of the Grand Palace grounds until you reach Charoen Krung Road. Turn left (east). The entrance to Wat Pho is in the middle of the block. Return to your hotel by tuk-tuk; there are always several waiting outside the temples.

Sightseeing Highlights

▲▲▲ **Grand Palace**—Here is the one sight that best captures the checkered history, royal splendor, and religious symbolism of premodern Bangkok. Construction on the sprawling grounds was initiated by King Rama I when he moved the country's capital to Bangkok in 1782. The compound includes the palace buildings, a model of the magnificent Khmer temple at Angkor Wat, and the spectacular Temple of the Emerald Buddha.

Among the royal buildings is the Chakri Maha Prasat, the British-designed royal residence built for Rama V to commemorate the 100th anniversary of the Chakri dynasty. It features an Italianate facade and a three-tiered Thai roof. Visitors are allowed into the reception rooms, featuring paintings, busts, and artworks that reveal the close ties Rama V developed with European royalty.

To the right of the Chakri Maha Prasat is a pinnacle of classic Thai architecture, the Dusit Maha Prasat, or audience hall, built under Rama I in 1789. Next door is the elegant Aphon Phimok Pavilion, or king's disrobing pavilion. Guides at the entrance offer their services for about 450 baht ($18), but you can easily tour the grounds yourself with the pamphlet provided at the gate.

Other sites include the Forbidden Quarters, used in the past to house the king's wives; the Borompiman Hall, residence of the crown prince who became Rama VI; and the Amarin Vinichai Hall, a gorgeously painted audience hall originally built by Rama I and still used for special ceremonies. The Grand Palace is open daily 8:30 to 11:30 a.m. and 1:00 to 3:00 p.m. Admission is 100 baht ($4).

▲▲▲ **Wat Phra Keo**—Located in the Grand Palace complex, the Temple of the Emerald Buddha is deservedly one of Bangkok's two most famous temples—out of more than 400. Its pavilions and spires create one of the most absorbing visual spectacles in Thailand. Rama I built this remarkable chapel to enshrine the legendary Emerald Buddha image brought down from northern Siam. The image, actually carved from jasper, was discovered in Chiang Rai in 1434 when lightning cracked open an old *chedi* (spire pagoda), but its exact origin remains unknown. It stands less than two-and-a-half feet high and is enthroned in a towering altar. From the gilded entranceway, it glows on high in the distant darkness of the chapel. A nine-tiered umbrella sits above the Emerald Buddha, flanked by crystal balls representing the sun and moon. With the turning of each of Thailand's three seasons, the king ascends the altar and changes the statue's costume—a golden diamond-encrusted tunic in the hot season, a gilded robe in the rainy season, and a head-to-toe robe of solid gold for the cool season. Though nearly overshadowed by the gloriously detailed chapel, which features reflecting glass chips, blue tile, and great interior murals of the *Ramakien* (the Thai version of India's Ramayana story), it remains the most sacred of the country's Buddha images.

▲▲▲ **Wat Pho**—The oldest temple-monastery complex in Bangkok, Wat Pho (also known as Wat Phra Chetupon) is most famous for its immense Reclining Buddha. The grounds are a maze of chapels, pavilions, Buddha images, chedis, and marble reliefs. In keeping with the role of the early temple as an institution of education as well as worship, many of the objects and paintings were originally installed at Wat Pho for the edification of the public, without any explicit connection to religion. Hence the temple has been known informally as Thailand's first university. Buildings and chedis were constructed here over the course of four centuries. The complex is fascinating but does not adequately prepare you for what you see when you enter the sixteenth-century Temple of the Reclining Buddha. Occupying nearly the entire structure, the figure of Buddha lying on his side is 145 feet long and 50 feet high; it is built of plaster-covered brick and plated with gold leaf. The soles of its feet are inlaid with 108 mother-of-pearl images of the auspicious signs of Buddha. The walls surrounding the immense figure are painted with elaborate murals, which, although deteriorating, are in the finest traditional Thai styles. The temple was enlarged and remodeled in 1789 by Rama I and has undergone constant reconstruction and repair in recent years. Around the grounds are many souvenir stands and stalls, where visitors can make offerings to help support the renovations. Wat Pho is open daily 8:00 a.m. to 5:00 p.m. Admission is 10 baht ($.40).

Lodging
As the travel hub of Southeast Asia, Bangkok offers a mind-boggling variety of accommodations, from the most minimal dormitory-style rooms to the splendor of grand hotels. The legendary jewel in the crown is the **Oriental Hotel** at 48 Oriental Avenue, New Road, Bangkok, 10500 (tel. 236-0400). Its over

400 rooms are beautifully appointed, and the lavishly adorned hotel overlooks the Chao Phrang River. The rates—3,100 to 4,000 baht ($124-$160)—reflect the Oriental's luxury and legendary status. Far more reasonably priced and more convenient to old Bangkok and the Grand Palace is the **Royal Hotel** at 2 Rajadamnern Avenue (tel. 222-9111). Its 300 rooms are clean and comfortable, the staff is helpful, and the large, bustling lobby has a heady international atmosphere. Rates are 508 to 823 baht ($20-$33). The **Swan Hotel**, at 31 Custom House Lane, Charoen Krung Road (tel. 234-8594), directly behind the Oriental, is a good economy accommodation with funky decor and low rates (290 to 360 baht, or about $12-$14). The **Boston Inn**, 4 Soi Si Bamphen, Rama IV Road, is popular with budget travelers for its cheap, clean rooms and friendly feeling. Dorm beds go for 60 baht ($2.40), while rooms with private bath are 120 to 190 baht (about $5-$7.50). Low-priced guest houses can be found in the Baglamphu District along Khao San Road just north of the Democracy Monument. The **PB Guest House**, 74 Khao San Road, for instance, charges only 60 baht (about $2.50) for a double room with fan and shared bath.

Food

Dining will undoubtedly be one of your most memorable activities in Thailand. Becoming the culinary rage the world over, Thai cuisine takes relatively simple ingredients—white rice (steamed or "sticky"), pork, beef, poultry, seafood, herbs, and spices—and creates soups and main course dishes that are amazingly complex. The sumptuous red and green curries sometimes literally bring you to tears, especially when the fiery native chilis are used in abundance along with garlic and ginger. Lemon grass, coriander, mint leaves, shrimp paste, fish sauce, and tamarind sauce add to the astonishing mix of flavors. Although Bangkok caters to every national taste, it would be a crime to ignore the superb native cooking available in all price ranges, from the thousands of street vendors to resplendent restaurants. A cornucopia of sweets is concocted from eggs, beans, rice flour, roots, seeds, palm sugar, and coconut. The selection of Thai fruits includes bananas, pineapples, oranges, mango, papaya, sapodilla, mangosteen, rambutan, jack fruit, pomelo, and rose, custard, and crab apples.

Such luxury hotels as the **Oriental**, the **Imperial**, and the **Shangri-la** offer fabulous spreads, but we've had splendid meals in the moderately priced restaurants. **Silom Village**, 286 Silom Road between Pramual and Pun roads, is part of a tourist-oriented trade center; yet the patio restaurants offer fresh seafood and mouth-watering curries at reasonable prices. For less than 250 baht ($10), two people can gorge on dry beef curry, chicken-coconut milk soup, green and red curry dishes, and other tempting delicacies. **Djit Pochana II** serves Thai dishes in a beautiful riverside setting directly across the water from the Oriental Hotel. Take the ferry from the dock next to the hotel. **Vijit**, at the corner of Rajadamnern Klang Avenue and Prachathiptai near the Democracy Monument, is popular and noisy (a musical combo plays loud pop music). But the chili oil prawns and garlic, chicken curry, and other dishes are well worth the clamor. **Lemon Grass**, at 5/1 Sukhumvit 24 (Soi 24), eschews the court-based Thai cuisine presented in most of Bangkok's tourist-oriented fancy restaurants, in favor of homestyle recipes. Special care is given to the presentation, which is akin to nouvelle or California cuisine in its elegance and balance. The **Whole Earth Restaurant**, at 93/3 Soi Lang-suan, Ploenchit Road, serves vegetarian dishes starting at 55 baht ($2.20) for lunch as well as a wide range of beautifully pre-pared nonvegetarian soups and curries. One afternoon, looking for a fast lunch, we slipped into the **Sky-High Restaurant**, around the corner from the Royal Hotel. It may have looked like an ordinary coffee shop, but we were served an extraordinary charcoal-fired pot of hot and sour prawn soup for 100 baht ($4), indicative of the delicious, individually prepared dishes avail-able all over the city. If you have a cast-iron stomach and a sense of adventure, try eating from streetcorner carts, where you can point to the ingredients that are most enticing, but first seek advice from a local resident on how to order.

Nightlife

Bangkok is notorious as a wide-open city when it comes to nightlife, a reputation enhanced by the presence of more than a quarter of a million hostesses, escorts, bar girls, and masseuses. Some say that the sex industry is the largest single component of Thailand's tourist business. The most intense concentration of nightclubs, go-go bars, gay clubs, and massage parlors is in the Patpong District, along Patpong I, II, and III, between Silom and Suriwongse roads, and along Soi Cowboy, between Soi 21 and 23 off Sukhumvit Road. Barkers on the street, as well as tuk-tuk and taxi drivers, often hand out small cards listing the types of attractions, including sex acts, available in different clubs. If this is your type of scene, however, remember that tourists are sometimes viewed as easy marks for hustlers and con artists. And the specter of AIDS (Acquired Immune Deficiency Syn-drome) among prostitutes has become a growing concern for Thai officials in the past two years.

Bangkok also offers a wide variety of more conventional and less risky entertainment for foreign travelers. Cultural shows, featuring traditional costumes and classical dances, are presented at most of the big hotels, at the **Silom Village Trade Center**, and at such restaurants as **Baan Thai** (7 Sukhumvit Soi 32), **Ala Norasing** (Sukhumvit Soi 4), and **Tump-Nak-Thai** (131 Ratchadaphisek Road). Thai and Western pop music is often played by live bands in the scores of open-air restaurants in the city, notably along Lard Prao Road.

Thai boxing, the acrobatic form of fighting in which everything goes but head-butting, is a popular attraction. Since the fights take place with the accompaniment of traditional music, they are like a cross between martial arts and modern dance. They are held at the **Lumpini Stadium** on Rama IV Road on Tuesday, Friday, and Saturday evenings at 6:00 p.m., with a Saturday matinee at 1:30 p.m. Seats are from 30 to 150 baht ($1.20-$6). At **Rajadamnoen Stadium**, on Rajadamnoen Nok Avenue, matches are held on Mondays, Wednesdays, and Thursdays at 6:00 p.m. and Sundays at 5:00 and 8:00 p.m.; admission is 25 to 125 baht ($1-$5).

Helpful Hint
The Tourist Authority of Thailand, or T.A.T., has its head office on Rajadamnoen Nok Avenue (tel. 282-1143-7) and can provide pamphlets, brochures, and reams of helpful information about Bangkok and the rest of Thailand.

BANGKOK WATERFRONT

Next to the tranquillity offered by the courtyards and chapels of Bangkok's temples, the most peaceful respite from the city's wild disorder is on its many waterways. Before the building booms of the twentieth century, the canals (*klongs*) were such an important part of Bangkok's transportation system that the city was known as the Venice of the East. Today, you will enjoy life on the waterfront, Thai-style.

Suggested Schedule

6:00 a.m.	Rise for early breakfast
7:00 a.m.	River cruise to visit the Thonburi Floating Market, Wat Arun, and the Royal Barges.
12:00 noon	Lunch.
1:00 p.m.	Waterway boat tour of Bangkok's klongs.
5:00 p.m.	Relax at your hotel.
7:00 p.m.	Dinner and Thai classical dancing.

Getting Around
Nearly every tourist hotel in Bangkok has a tour information desk or a tour program of its own which includes trips to the Floating Market, Wat Arun, and the Royal Barges. Regular tours leave the Oriental Hotel pier daily at 7:00 a.m. and return around 11:00 a.m. The Supatra Company, Ltd., at 254 Arun Amarin Road, Thonburi, arranges single- and double-deck riverboat cruises with set destinations or custom itineraries. In addition to water taxis that cruise the klongs on a regular basis, smaller, speedy longtail boats (*hang yao*) can be chartered for about 200 to 300 baht ($12) per hour. Boats can be hired at the Oriental Hotel pier, at the landing near Silapkorn University in the Grand Palace section of the city, at the Ekamai Bridge on Soi 63, Sukhumvit Road, and at Prakanong Klong Tan Bridge on Soi 71, Sukhumvit.

Sightseeing Highlights
▲▲▲ **Wat Arun**—Located across the Chao Phraya River from Bangkok, in the sister city of Thonburi, the Temple of Dawn is one of the most memorable sights in this metropolis of dazzling physical wonders. It is just southwest of Wat Pho and the Grand Palace. In the early nineteenth century, King Rama II decided to expand an earlier temple, Wat Chaeng, established by King Tak-

sin on the site. Wat Arun, with a 282-foot-tall central spire (prang) derived from Khmer religious architecture, is the result of his vision. Raised on a series of terraces above the soft ground of the riverbank, the spire is embedded with colored Chinese porcelain and shards of crockery. The grounds include four small corner prangs, four pavilions housing Buddha images, and many statues. Staircases up the tower lead to a commanding view of the river and the surrounding area. In the misty early morning hours, the beautiful silhouette of the spire earns the temple its name.

▲▲▲ **Floating Market**—Although it couldn't help but smack of commercialism, given the heavy tourist traffic that has built up over the past two decades, the Floating Market at Thonburi, on Klong Dao Kanong, is still one of Bangkok's most colorful attractions. Women sell all kinds of produce and goods from their long wooden boats, starting at the crack of dawn and finishing up well before the morning gives way to noon.

▲▲▲ **The Royal Barges**—Housed in a shed on Klong Bangkok Noi, upriver north of Wat Arun, the Royal Barges are elaborately carved boats that were used in state ceremonies until 1967. At the end of the rainy season, the king would bring gifts across the river from the palace to the Buddhist monks at Wat Arun. The oldest and most ornate of the barges is *Sri Supannahong*, a fantastic vessel with tiered umbrellas and a marvelous golden pavilion. A crew of 60 was needed to sail it. The last time the barges were put into action was during the centennial of the Chakri dynasty in 1982.

CHIANG MAI: ANOTHER WORLD

Today, you slip away from twentieth-century civilization and the clamor of Bangkok to another world altogether. In the northern hill country, where odd-shaped, forested mountains rise from the sloping plains and rivers and waterfalls course through the jungle, tribal villages cling to traditional customs. Visiting Thailand's second-largest city, you will meet people whose culture is much closer to nineteenth-century ways of life.

Suggested Schedule

8:00 a.m.	Breakfast at hotel and checkout.
9:00 a.m.	Taxi to Bangkok Airport for late morning flight.
12:45 p.m	Arrive in Chiang Mai.
1:30 p.m.	Check into hotel or guest house. Lunch.
2:30 p.m.	Explore Chiang Mai and investigate trek and tour options.
7:00 p.m.	Lanna Khantoke dinner at Diamond Hotel.

Chiang Mai

In 1296, when King Mengrai was looking for a new capital for his kingdom, he came upon an auspicious location where two white barking deer and five white mice were seen together. Located 450 miles north of Bangkok on the banks of the Ping River, Chiang Mai ("New Town") was the great city of the north, the civilization center of Lanna Thai, the "land of the rice fields." From the late sixteenth through the late eighteenth century, its power declined, but it began a rebirth in 1796 under the increasing influence of Siam. The old part of the city is still surrounded by a 200-year-old moat and fortified gates, while development has expanded the city in every direction. Still an important center of trekking activity (which has shifted somewhat to Chiang Rai) and increasingly popular with tourists, Chiang Mai remains a unique and charming city, still reflecting the Burmese and, to a lesser extent, Laotian influences that shaped much of its history, art, and architecture. From October through January, it is the focus of many religious and cultural festivals.

Although it is Thailand's second-largest city, Chiang Mai is only one-fortieth the size of Bangkok's metropolitan area, and it

Chiang Mai

retains many attractive small-town features. Most of the temples, shops, hotels, and restaurants are within an area of less than four square miles. Along the roads leading out of the city (Highways 107 and 108, Roads 101, 1009, and 1096), scores of handicrafts villages and factories attract eager shoppers. The cottage industries and larger-scale operations include umbrella-making, lacquerware, earthenware, celadon, woodcarving, silversmiths, and world-renowned Thai silkweaving in the village of San Kamphaeng. Beyond the city, the landscape takes on the unique characteristics of northern Thailand, marked by steep hills and mountains, hardwood forests, verdant valleys, jungle rivers, and beautiful waterfalls. Orchid farms, hot springs, caves, and elephant training centers are among the attractions in the countryside.

Getting Around
Your Thai Airways flight from Bangkok to Chiang Mai takes one hour. We suggest catching the 11:45 a.m. departure. At the airport, catch a taxi to your hotel. If you choose a hotel or guest house along the Ping River or on nearby Chaing Khlan Road, most of Chiang Mai is readily accessible on foot. Tuk-tuks can be hired, starting at 10 baht ($.40), to take you to specific sites or on tours of your own choice. There are also minibuses and taxis

for hire all over the city at negotiable rates, from 5 or 10 baht ($.20-$.40) for a short trip to 500 baht ($20) for an all-day tour. At the taxi stand on the corner of Tha Phal and Chang Khlan roads, drivers pick up passengers headed for the same destinations. Four main bus routes crisscross the city and extend into the countryside. The inner-city buses are yellow, and the fare is only 2 baht. Bicycle and motorbike rentals are available around most hotels and guest houses. For day tours to the north, simply contact one of the many tour companies around each hotel and guest house. Bamboo Tour (tel. 236-501), S.T. Tours & Travel (tel. 212-829), Meo Tour Services (tel. 235-116), Chiang Mai Honey Tour (tel. 234-345), and Lamthong Tour (tel. 235-440) are just a few of scores of trek and tour services available.

Lodging
Consistent with its burgeoning tourist trade, Chiang Mai offers a full range of accommodations, from high-rise hotels to humble guest houses. The **Dusit Inn**, 112 Chang Khlan Road (tel. 214-372), has 200 rooms, a swimming pool, restaurants, and a nightclub. It is located on the street where the night bazaar is held. Rates are 940 to 4,000 baht (about $38-$160). The **Chiang Mai Orchid**, at 100-102 Huay Kaew Road (tel. 221-625), is one of several high-rise luxury hotels on the outskirts of town. In addition to 267 rooms, it has a pool, restaurants, disco, convention facilities, and a shopping arcade. Rates are 1,210 to 9,680 baht ($48-$387). The **Chiang Mai President**, 226 Wichayanon Road, is conveniently located on the northeast corner of town and has a pool and bar. Its 150 rooms go for 350 to 1,150 baht ($14-$46). One of the newer additions to Chiang Mai's guest houses is the **River View Lodge** at 25 Charoenprathet Road, Soi 2. Clean, beautifully appointed rooms with fans or air-conditioning overlook tidy gardens and the Ping River. It has an attractive patio restaurant near the river. Rates are 500 to 700 baht ($20-$28). The **Chiang Mai Guest House**, 91 Charoenprathet Road (tel. 235-402), accommodates travelers on more modest budgets with 28 rooms, from dorm style to air-conditioned doubles, at 80 to 400 baht ($3-$12).

Food
The cuisine of northern Thailand, influenced by Burma, has subtle differences in spices from that of southern regions. The **River View Lodge** serves special Chiang Rai dinners upon request. The **Whole Earth** serves impeccably prepared vegetarian and nonvegetarian dishes, curries, soups, and seafood in a pleasant Thai-style elevated restaurant on Sri Dornchai Road. No visit would be complete without a Lanna Khantoke

dinner, in which dishes such as pork curry, sweet-and-sour sauce, fried chicken, fried noodles, pork rinds, and cucumbers are served with plain rice and sticky rice. One of the best is served in the teak mansion at the **Diamond Hotel**, 33/10 Charoenprathet Road, followed by demonstrations of classical Thai dancing and traditional music. Although the entire presentation of food and floor show is designed for Western tourists, the experience is pleasant, and the unlimited portions of food are delicious. Chiang Mai is full of small restaurants and cafés, as well as tantalizing food stalls such as those on Loi Kroa Road between Charoenprathet Road and Chang Khlan Road. You can find fresh coconut ice cream, fried coconut milk, fish cakes, and several exotic delicacies for the adventurous palate, such as fried frog skins or grasshoppers. Western food is available at many restaurants, and there is even a German beer garden across the street from the Diamond Hotel.

NORTHERN THAILAND

Explore the northern hill country, meeting residents of tribal villages and discovering artifacts of ancient kingdoms. From the current trekking capital of Chiang Rai to the famous Golden Triangle, where the Thai, Burmese, and Laotian borders meet on the Mekong River, the north is a rich, largely unspoiled region. Opium poppies used to be the primary cash crop among the tribes here; although the government outlawed and cracked down on cultivation about 20 years ago, opium-smoking rituals are still part of the guarded indigenous culture.

Suggested Schedule

6:00 a.m.	Rise for early breakfast.
7:00 a.m.	Leave on driving tour of northern Thailand.
5:30 p.m.	Return to Chiang Mai.
7:00 p.m.	Dinner.

Getting Around
Although you can rent a car in Chiang Mai and attempt to negotiate the roads and traffic yourself, you are better off hiring a driver for a predetermined or personalized tour. For 900 baht ($36) per person, most touring companies will take you on a daylong round-trip to Chiang Rai, Mae Sai, the Golden Triangle, and a hill tribe village. Many options, including elephant riding, waterfall visits, and one-day treks, are available.

Sightseeing Highlights
▲▲▲ **Chiang Rai**—Founded by King Mengrai in 1262, this provincial capital, as yet relatively undisturbed by tourist development, is now a favorite starting point for trekkers. Supposedly founded when Mengrai followed his runaway favorite elephant to the banks of the Kok River, Chiang Rai has two interesting temples: Wat Prasingh, which once housed a significant Theravadan image, and Wat Phra Keo, the original location of the Emerald Buddha. The bones of King Mengrai are assumed to be housed in a wat atop Ngam Muang Hill to the west of Wat Phra Keo. In town, at 935 Phahonyothin Road, a modest restaurant called the T. Hut offers dishes that stand up to the finest cuisine in the rest of the country. Miss Siripan Boonyarasai serves up a mouth-watering *kaeng ped ped yang* (roasted duck curry) and an incomparable sun-dried beef with oyster chili sauce.

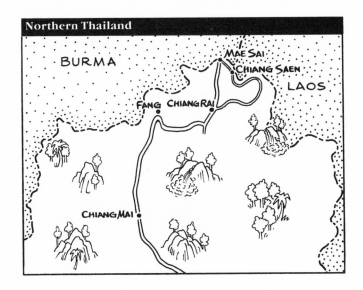

Northern Thailand

BURMA

MAE SAI
CHIANG SAEN

LAOS

FANG CHIANG RAI

CHIANG MAI

▲▲▲ **Hill Tribes**—Between 250,000 and 500,000 villagers from various Southeast Asian ethnic minorities still live in tribal settings tucked into the folding foothills of the Himalayas. There are seven major tribes, each with distinctive dress, rituals, and customs. The largest is the Karen, of Tibetan-Burmese stock, many of whom practice an adapted form of Christianity. The Meo, also known as the Hmong, migrated from southern China and were among the most prolific opium poppy growers. The Akha, who came from southern China via Burma, form one of the smallest and poorest tribes, but the women's costuming is among the most intricately sewn and beaded. The Lahu are believed to derive from Tibetan ancestry and still tend toward nomadic ways. The Lawa may be the survivors of original Mon and Khmer peoples. The Lisu are twentieth-century immigrants from southern China, cultivators of opium, and practitioners of animist religions. The Yao migrated from central China, through Laos and Burma, in the early twentieth century. In recent years, development and assistance agencies, such as the government-sponsored Hill Tribe Foundation, have attempted to bring education and health services to the tribes, change cultivation from opium to legal crops, and develop markets for the many tribal handicrafts. Assimilation and ''civilization'' may be inevitable, but, at present, tribal practices still survive.

▲ **Golden Triangle**—Although there is little more here than a garish sign indicating the location, several handicraft and sou-

venir stands, and a restaurant, the Golden Triangle is a popular
stop on northern tours. The Mekong River reaches out to Burmese and Laotian shores, and longtail boats will take you for
fast, exciting rides up and down the smooth-surfaced water.
Good, fresh, spicy fish dishes are available at the small restaurant that overlooks the river.

▲▲ **Chiang Saen**—Downriver from the Golden Triangle, 37
miles northeast of Chiang Rai, this ancient capital, founded in
the thirteenth century, was the center of power for King Mengrai's consolidation of the north. It came under Burmese control in the sixteenth century, was regained by the Chakri
dyanasty, and later was destroyed by Rama I, who sought to
fend off another Burmese invasion. Rama V initiated the city's
resurrection, and in 1957, it became a district seat. Among the
intriguing historical sights are Wat Pa Sak, a restored chedi from
1295, Wat Phra That Chom Kitti, a tenth-century hilltop chedi,
and Wat Chedi Luang, a thirteenth-century chedi rising 186 feet
from an octagonal base. You won't want to miss the displays of
tribal artifacts—including various Buddha images and temple
relics, plus a wide variety of hunting gear and antique opium-
smoking paraphernalia—at the small museum next door to Wat
Chedi Luang.

Itinerary Option: Trekking

Most trek operators offer three- to seven-day treks through the
hills around Chiang Mai, Chiang Rai, and the increasingly popular Mae Hong Son region. These tours often include bus or car
transportation to a starting point, hiking through the jungle
with local guides, traveling by elephant, and eating meals and
staying overnight with one or more of the hill tribes. To accommodate travelers on tight schedules, some operators have developed one-day "treks" that reveal less of the authentic backcountry way of life but offer a chance to visit a hill tribe, ride an
elephant, or take a raft trip. In Chiang Mai, such companies as
S.T. Tours & Travel (tel. 222-174 or 212-829) and Bamboo Tour
(tel. 236-501) arrange tours and treks of varying length and com-
plexity.

One typical three-day trek might start with a bus ride from
Chiang Mai to Thaton, followed by a three-hour boat trip on the
Mae Kok River to a Karen tribal village, where you take dinner
and spend the night. On the next day, you ride an elephant for
several hours to a Yao village for lunch and then walk for two
hours to an Akha village to eat dinner and sleep. After breakfast
with the Akha, walk to a Shan village and then ride by truck to
Chiang Rai and by bus back to Chiang Mai. Other itineraries can
take you to Meo and Karen tribal villages in the lush region of

Mae Hong Son. A trip to this latter area of misty hills and river valleys should include a stop at the Doi Inthanon National Park, named for Thailand's highest mountain and featuring a spectacular series of waterfalls. Before committing yourself to one trekking company, debrief other travelers in guest houses, hotels, and restaurants about their experiences and see who they recommend. Shop around among the tour operators to find the kind of excursion that fits your taste for comfort and/or adventure.

CHIANG MAI: UP CLOSE

This is the day for your closest inspection of Chiang Mai, taking in its historic temples and many handicraft workshops. Don't miss the panoramic view of the city from the fantastic mountaintop temple on Doi Suthep. In the evening, stroll through the exciting night bazaar, one of Thailand's best.

Suggested Schedule

9:00 a.m.	Explore temples and shops.
12:30 p.m.	Take handicrafts tour.
3:30 p.m.	Visit Doi Suthep.
6:00 p.m.	Dinner.
7:00 p.m.	Stroll through the night bazaar.

Sightseeing Highlights
▲▲▲ **Wat Chiang Man**—Chiang Mai's oldest temple, on Rjaphakinar Road, built in typical Lanna style with Laotian influences, was the residence of King Mengrai while he oversaw the construction of his capital city. It houses the revered Crystal Buddha (Phra Setang Khamani) and a bas-relief stone Buddha (Phra Sila) believed to have come from India after the eighth century.

▲▲▲ **Wat Phra Singh**—This large compound at the corner of Singharat and Rajadamoen roads dates from the reign of King Pha Yu in 1345 and contains a variety of buildings in different styles. The most important is the small, old chapel in which the Phar Singh Buddha image is enshrined. According to legend, the statue originated in Sri Lanka more than 1,500 years ago and was brought to Chiang Mai during the Sukhothai period.

▲▲ **Wat Chedi Luang**—A violent earthquake that shook Chiang Mai in 1545 brought down much of the giant, 283-foot-high pagoda here, and the chedi was never repaired. But its enormous base and partial spire, originally constructed in 1401, are still the most significant structures in this Phra Pokklao Road temple area. The Emerald Buddha was enshrined here at one time. Legend says King Mengrai died close by when struck by lightning. The "spirit of the city" is allegedly safeguarded by the towering gum tree near the wat's entrance.

▲▲ **Handicrafts**—Thanks to the tourist influx, Chiang Mai has northern Thailand's largest concentration of cottage industries. All along the roads to Bor Sang (the "umbrella village") and San

Kamphaeng (the center of silk and cotton weaving) are miles and miles of indigenous crafts. Any tuk-tuk or minibus driver will be delighted to take you to buy and witness the making of lacquerware, wood carvings, silverware, jewelry, celadon pottery, umbrellas, and silk. Silverwork ranges from the intricately hammered bowls of the city's artisans to the rougher jewelry of the hill tribes. Dyed and hand-painted paper umbrellas create rainbows of color in Bor Sang. On the road to Cham Thong, the lacquerware factories provide an intimate view of this difficult craft, in which layer after layer of lacquer is applied to a carefully shaped bamboo framework. In Sam Kamphaeng, the young women of the region—legendary for their beauty—labor over silk looms, each producing up to six meters of finished fabric a day. Just to the east, celadon craftsmen maintain the pottery tradition founded three centuries ago by Chinese artisans. Drivers should charge no more than 120 baht (about $5) per person for a full tour of the handicrafts areas.

▲▲▲ **Wat Phrathat**—About ten miles northwest of town, past Chiang Mai University and a strip of luxury hotels, the land begins a steep rise culminating in a peak over 3,000 feet high. Here sits the dazzling Wat Phrathat, an intricately detailed mountainside temple rife with gilded Buddha images, parasols, and gold-tiled chedis. Two long, colorful dragons snake down as railings alongside the 290 steps leading to the temple. This vantage point offers a grand view of Chiang Mai and the surrounding hills and plains.

▲▲ **Phuping Palace**—Farther up the mountain from Wat Phrathat is the summer palace of King Bhumibol, evidence of royalty's good judgment in choosing a retreat from Bangkok's sweltering heat and pollution. Audience halls, official buildings, guest houses, kitchens, and dining rooms make up the complex, but only the grounds—bursting with bright tropical flowers—are open to the public.

▲▲▲ **Night Bazaar**—Chiang Mai has plenty of markets, such as Warorot for produce (at the corner of Chiang Mai and Wichayan), Suan Buak Hat for flowers (next to the Suan Prung Gate), and Somphet for fruit (at the northeast corner of the moat). But the night bazaar along Chang Khlan Road is the most exciting. Before dusk, hundreds of vendors begin opening their stalls or setting up on the sidewalks. Hill tribe people come into the city to sell their crafts, including jewelry and clothing. There are fascinating collections of meticulously preserved butterflies, spiders, and insects next to tables of tennis shoes. General merchandise stores entice customers with piles of goods and garish displays. The latest Western rock and roll clashes with Southeast Asian pop blaring from various music tape stores. The entire street is a peaceful riot of buyers and sellers, natives and tourists, music, food, crafts, and trinkets. It's a combination crafts fair and international block party that will be one of the memorable highlights of you visit to Chiang Mai. It gets under way around 6:00 p.m.

Koh Samui

If you can add a few days to your global itinerary, you'll find that southern Thailand offers an ideal interlude on your around-the-world tour. Thousands of tourists are finding their way to such burgeoning resort areas as Pattaya, known as the "Thai Riviera," and Phuket, the large west coast island in the Andaman Sea. Koh Samui, the largest island off the east coast in the Gulf of Thailand, is rapidly become popular as an alternative to those busy tourist spots. Although they attract growing numbers of sunseekers from around the world, the relaxing beaches of Koh Samui remain a perfect place to ditch the harried schedules, traffic congestion, and high prices of civilization. And you don't have to rough it.

Admittedly, very little of the southern Thailand coastline is truly undiscovered anymore. On the western side of the peninsula, Phuket is dotted with large hotels, and even the immensely attractive Koh Phi Phi—a scantly populated island "paradise" of perfect white beaches, four hours by boat from Phuket—is garnering international attention. Krabi, a quiet mainland village across the bay from Phuket, is still relatively secluded and undeveloped but probably destined for tourist growth in the near future.

Koh Samui is certainly developing but still offers the right balance of convenience and peaceful privacy for the traveler seeking a few days of hassle-free respite. It is made more attractive by the fact that even during the wettest part of the rainy season (in September, when the west side of the peninsula is often drenched under monsoons), the showers on Koh Samui are usually intermittent, and the sun shines throughout much of the day.

Of the 80 islands in this part of the gulf, only four are inhabited, and Koh Samui is the largest. Its population of 32,000 was originally sustained by fishing and coconut farming, but as with the entire southern region of Thailand, it is increasingly oriented toward tourism, catering to visitors from Japan, Malaysia, and the West. A well-paved road runs approximately 34 miles around the circumference of the island. Tourist bungalows are chockablock on many beaches, but it is easy to find your own empty expanse of sand. The island interior is covered with dense jungle and crisscrossed by rivers that cascade down the

Koh Samui

hills into two major waterfalls. Coral reefs off the southern and western coasts provide fine opportunities for snorkeling and scuba diving.

A regular Thai Airways flight leaves Bangkok at 11:00 a.m. and arrives an hour later in Surat Thani. You can make reservations ahead of time at most Bangkok hotels and travel agencies for bus transportation from the Surat Thani airport to the ferry dock and for the Songserm Express Boat that leaves for Koh Samui at 12:30 p.m. (An earlier boat departs at 7:30 a.m.) By midday, you are cruising along the typically calm seas off the southeast Thai peninsula, between limestone formations that rise from the water in haunting shapes. The boat ride, which you will likely share with dozens of fellow international travelers, takes two hours. By late afternoon, you will be stretching out on great beaches and wading in warm, gentle waters.

The Songserm Express Boat docks in Nathon, near the north-west corner of Koh Samui. Small pickup trucks, converted into taxis with padded benches and covered beds, congregate on the street corner about 100 yards to the left (north) of the pier. Drivers charge set rates to each of the beach areas, from 10 to 20 baht ($.40-$.80). Motorbikes (150 baht, or $6 for 24 hours) and jeeps (500 baht, or $20) can be rented in Nathon and at many hotels and bungalows.

On the Express Boat from Surat Thani to Koh Samui, you will be approached by young men and women recruiting guests for various bungalows. Do not feel obligated to accept any offer. With the abundance of accommodations available, you do not have to rely on these young agents. Everything from the most minimal bungalows with outside plumbing to luxury resorts with doting service and lavish buffets is available. You might want to ask whether the place you are considering shows videos: it has become popular to show American movies on videotape, and the action can get noisy.

The most beautiful beach on Koh Samui, Chaweng, naturally has the most hotels and bungalows. The **Imperial Samui**, with more than 70 rooms, lush grounds, and a swimming pool, is one of the island's grand hotels. It charges 1,400 to 2,600 baht ($56-$104) per night for the privilege of a visit. The **PanSea** is close competition in the Club Med mold, offering half-pension and deluxe bungalows for 1,980 to 2,940 baht ($80-$118). The **White House** and the **Village** are much smaller (10 to 20 bungalows) but give the same attention to comfort and more opportunity for privacy at 700 to 1,200 baht ($28-$48). Prices go down as you move to other beaches. On Lamai Beach, the **Pavilion** (350 to 450 baht, $14-$18) and the **Sand Sea** (500 baht, or $20) are attractive, clean, and comfortable. Bo Phut Beach is not as pretty as Chaweng or Lamai (the sand is not as white and the waves are not as dramatic), but, like nearby Mae Nam, it is less crowded and quieter. Here, the **World** bungalows are pleasantly arranged along a garden walk to the beach, and three young women, Tik, Jead, and Yai, offer cheerful service with a wonderful sense of humor. Choen Mon Beach, tucked into a bay on the northeast tip of the island, offers a restful, private getaway at the **P.S. Villa** (40 to 200 baht, or $1.60-$8) and **Su's Place** (400 to 800 baht, or $16-$32), operated by the same management as the White House and the Village. If you are staying for more than one or two nights, take your time checking out accommodations at various beaches and find the combination of seclusion and amenities that suits you best.

Dining can be as much a pleasure on Koh Samui as anywhere else in this country. Every set of bungalows has its own restaurant, and given the high quality of local cooking, it is virtually impossible to go wrong. Two people can eat well on fresh fruit, seafood, a variety of soups, curries, rice dishes, and desserts for less than 200 baht ($8) per day at the medium-priced accommodations. Eating where you stay also offers the chance to get to know fellow travelers and meet the locals.

The main reason to come to Koh Samui is to stretch out on the sand, beachcomb, and enjoy the transparent ocean waters. But it is also rewarding to explore the man-made sites and natural wonders of the island—at a leisurely pace, of course. From your hotel or bungalow, rent a motorbike or catch a taxi and ride toward Bo Phut, turning east at the junction that leads to Big Buddha. As you approach Plai Laem Bay, situated at the northeastern tip of Koh Samui, you can see a large figure looming up from Farn Isle, as if rising from the seas. This is Big Buddha, a gigantic seated image at Hin Ngu Temple. The massive figure dwarfs everything around it, including the other carved figures of the temple grounds and the nearby row of souvenir stands.

From Big Buddha, if you return to the main road, turn left (south), and drive past Chaweng to the southern tip of Lamai Beach, you will see a sign directing you left to Hin Ta. Here are the Grandmother and Grandfather rocks captured on many of Koh Samui's most popular postcards. Some of the rocky promontories poking out of Thailand's southern waters assume bizarre and mysterious shapes, and none is more arresting than the famed Grandmother and Grandfather rocks at Hin Ta. These formations are reached by walking down the short path from the paved road turnoff.

From Hin Ta, the main road continues southwest. Turn right (west) at Baan Hua Thonan, where the road heads inland. At about one-and-a-half miles, at Baan Thurian, turn right on the dirt road leading to Namuang Waterfall. If you turn right from Baan Thurian and continue northward about five-and-a-half miles, you will reach Baan Lip Yai where you can turn right to the Hinlaad Waterfall. Most people never leave the beaches on Koh Samui, which leaves these inland jungle areas virtually untouched. Both of these beautiful waterfalls were important to early Buddhist inhabitants and are marked by old stone carvings. You can either continue your loop around the island or return along the same route.

If you want even more isolation than you find on Koh Samui, the islands of Koh Phangan and Koh Tao are only just beginning to foster tourism. Koh Phangan is about 5 miles due north of Koh Samui, and Koh Tao is another 30 miles northwest. Both are for people who really want to get away from it all and are visited predominantly by backpackers. On Koh Phangan, most of the bungalows are primitive, bare wooden structures built on platforms at the beach, many without electricity or private toilets. If you take the 45-minute boat ride from Nathon to Thong Sala, young men and women will recruit you to their bungalows, typically renting for 30 baht ($1.20) per night. Many of these accommodations are simple in the extreme, consisting of tiny thatched huts right on the beach, with nothing more than a raised platform and thin mattress for a bed. They attract a largely young, friendly clientele of backpacking adventurers, and the conversations around the dinner tables in the small patio restaurants are rife with colorful stories. Haad Rin, the southern peninsula with the most beautiful beaches (some people rank them with the best in the world), is more developed, with less of the Robinson Crusoe atmosphere of the more remote sites. More fully equipped bungalows rent here for up to 200 baht ($8). A day trip or overnight excursion to Koh Phangan is possible if you take the 40-minute boat ride from Bo Phut Beach (just past the Oasis) on Koh Samui to Haad Rin. It leaves at 9:30 a.m. and 3:30 p.m. and makes the return trip at 9:00 a.m. and 2:30 p.m. The fare is 50 baht ($2).

Koh Tao is a tiny island with clear, sheltered waters that are perfect for swimming and snorkeling. Some bold adventurers swim with sharks in the peaceful bay at Haad Nang Yuan. Bungalows are available on the western and southern beaches. Boats leave from Koh Samui at Bo Phut twice a week from January through April (for 120 baht, or $4.80) and from Koh Phangan five times weekly from January through March and twice weekly from April through December (80 baht, or $3.20). If you really feel the need to escape, this is one of Thailand's most remote and idyllic island getaways.

After your blood pressure has plummeted and you have grown accustomed to spending most of the day sifting sand with your bare toes, you might want to give some thought to returning to the main around-the-world itinerary. Simply make arrangements to be at Nathon on Koh Samui in time for the 7:30 a.m. Express Boat to Surat Thani. The bus connection will get you to the airport for a 12:30 p.m. flight to Bangkok. You'll arrive about 1:30 p.m. and can enjoy the afternoon and early evening in town before returning to the airport and catching your flight to Cairo, where you'll pick up Day 11 of our trip plan.

THAILAND TO EGYPT

Today you'll fly back to Bangkok and catch an evening flight to Cairo. Or, if you're extending your trip to Bali, you'll connect to Indonesia. The day plan is flexible, allowing you a choice between more time in the hill country or Bangkok.

Suggested Schedule	
Morning	At leisure in Chiang Mai.
After noon	Depart for Bangkok.
Midafternoon	Arrive Bangkok.
6:00 p.m.	Dinner in Bangkok. Then depart for Cairo.

Because Day 10 has an open itinerary, you're free to spend the morning and early afternoon in Chiang Mai. Or if you'd like, catch an early morning flight to Bangkok and enjoy another day there before flying on to Egypt.

Singapore Airlines connects to Cairo via Singapore. Depart in the evening and you'll be in Cairo on the morning of Day 11 at 5:35 a.m.

If you're planning to extend your trip to Bali, we suggest spending the night of Day 10 in Bangkok. Tomorrow morning, catch the 9:00 a.m. Garuda Indonesia flight to Denpasar, Bali, arriving at 6:00 p.m. After visiting Bali and Lombok, you can catch the 3:55 p.m. Garuda flight from Denpasar, arriving in Jakarta at 4:40 p.m. From there, you can fly back to Singapore and pick up a flight to Egypt.

BALI AND LOMBOK

The stunning physical beauty and cultural harmony of Bali are two of the many good reasons to visit this island, located five hours by air from Bangkok. A 2,000-square-mile volcanic island lying eight degrees south of the equator in the Indonesian archipelago, Bali is just a few miles east of Java but a world apart. Most of its 2.5 million inhabitants are Hindu, whereas most of Indonesia is Moslem; their religion, oriented toward the mountains that sweep up from the sea, is a uniquely balanced and taboo-free form of Hinduism. Spiritual concerns are inextricably interwoven with the routines of daily life. Worship—of ancestors and spirits manifested in nature but unified in a single god—is a constant state of mind underlying and shaping material existence. Offerings of woven straw, rice, and flowers are made throughout the days in homes, fields, workshops, and temples. Balinese arts reflect and extend this harmonious world view.

Mexican artist Miguel Covarrubias visited Bali in the 1930s and recorded his detailed impressions in *Island of Bali*, still in print and available through Pacific Basin Books. He wrote about the unity of Balinese life and its environment. "Like a continual undersea ballet, the pulse of life in Bali moves with a measured rhythm reminiscent of the sway of marine plants and the flowing motions of octopus and jellyfish under the sweep of a submarine current. There is a similar correlation of the elegant and decorative people with the clear-cut, extravagant vegetation; of their simple and sensitive temperament with the fertile land."

Today, Bali is struggling with the overlay of civilization that was spurred on by Dutch colonialism in the late nineteenth and early twentieth centuries. Over 200,000 people visit Bali annually in a tourist tide that started in the 1930s. Hordes invade the beach resorts of Kuta, Legian, Nusa Dua, and Sanur, attracted to the surfing, the hotels, the nightlife, the shopping, and the beaches. Far fewer stay inland, where the heart and soul of Balinese culture are still vibrantly intact.

The capital city, Denpasar, is the center of commerce, with a bustling population of more than 100,000. By far Bali's biggest city, overshadowing Gianyar, Klungkung, and Singaraja, it is crowded and energetic. But out in the villages, which are organized under eight governmental districts corresponding to ancient rajadoms, most people still work in the rice fields or at their crafts. Their social lives revolve around work, temples, and communal economic and fraternal groups. During the Dutch

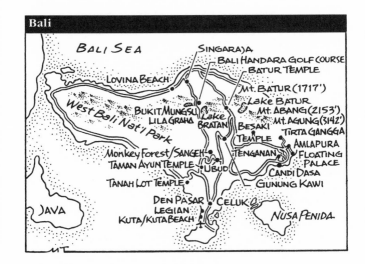

colonization, which formally ended in 1949, the Balinese
strongly resisted foreign influence, and as one of 26 provinces
of the Republic of Indonesia, founded by Sukarno in 1956, the
island still has an independent character.

Living under the watchful spirits of the Batur, Abang, and
Batuku volcanoes, the Balinese go about their daily lives in
deep, calm rhythms that have not been thrown off by the significant new invasion of travelers. They welcome visitors not
only as consumers of arts, crafts, food, and lodging but also as
honored guests in their homes. Although many villagers speak
only native Balinese, most islanders speak Bahasa Indonesian, a
relatively easy language to learn. A good phrase book, such as
Lonely Planet's *Indonesia Phrasebook*, can provide enough
words and grammar for the conscientious visitor to communi-
cate. The Balinese are extraordinarily accommodating.

FIRST DAY: UBUD, BALI

Melt into the easy pace of Balinese life as you explore the fascinating village of Ubud and its surroundings, where every
other person seems to be an artist. Start with a sunrise walk that
will steep you in tranquil rural rhythms. Step back ten centuries
and explore a largely unvisited ruin etched with religious meaning. Learn about the history of the Indonesian people, their fine
arts, and intricate crafts. Sample Balinese cuisine and enjoy the
island's world-famous dance performances.

Suggested Schedule	
6:00 a.m.	Take a prebreakfast walk along Campuhan Ridge.
8:00 a.m.	Breakfast at hotel.
9:00 a.m.	See Ubud's historical sites and arts and crafts.
12:00 noon	Lunch in Ubud.
1:00 p.m.	Bemo to Yeh Pulu and the woodcarving village of Mas.
5:00 p.m.	Return to your hotel. Make driving arrangements for the next day.
6:00 p.m.	Dinner in Ubud. Make arrangements for tomorrow's banana chicken or smoked duck dinner at Satri's.
7:30 p.m.	Attend dance performance.

Arrival

On arrival at the Denpasar Airport, after clearing immigration and customs, exchange money at one of the bank offices located just outside and to the right of the building exit. The exchange rate, about 1,700 rupiah to the dollar, varies by only a few rupiah from one official money changer to the next. For a quick mental conversion from rupiah prices to approximate dollar equivalents, multiply by six and move the decimal left four places. For example, 10,000 rupiah equals about $6.

The most reliable transportation from the airport to Ubud can be arranged at the taxi desk, which is situated just outside the airport doors and toward the left end of the building. The prices are fixed, and the 45-minute to one-hour ride to Ubud should cost about 26,000 rupiah ($21.60). Some independent drivers, waiting outside the airport, will negotiate slightly, but not dramatically, lower rates. Don't rent a car or hire a driver on a long-term basis. Wait until you are in Ubud, where prices are lower.

Ubud

The capital of Balinese culture, Ubud is a fascinating blend of ancient traditions and gradual modernization. Although it has become a busy, prosperous village catering to tourists on day trips from Bali's beach resorts, Ubud moves to a calm basic pulse. You will meet "visitors" who have settled in for weeks, months, or years.

Driving into Ubud from the airport can be disconcerting at first if you are expecting a quaint tropical town of dirt roads and straw huts. There is one main thoroughfare, a straight, paved road extending about a mile from Peliatan on the east end to

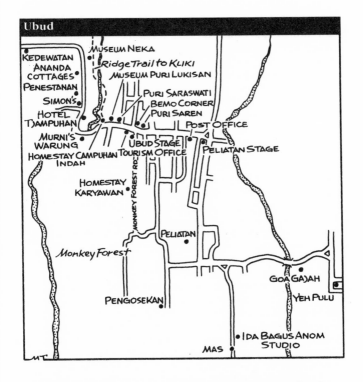

Campuhan on the west. A second important road, Monkey Forest Road, forms an intersection at the center of town and extends about half a mile south into a real monkey forest. Both roads are lined with shops, studios, and restaurants. On market days—every third day—Ubud gets congested with trucks and bemos. But soon you spy the many temples between the storefronts and see villagers setting out offerings of incense, rice, and flowers. Behind the shops, on the narrow side streets of cloistered residences, activity settles down, and beneath the veneer of commerce, everyday life has an unhurried pace and an almost mystical quality. During the past 50 years, dozens of European and American artists have succumbed to Ubud's lure, establishing permanent homes and developing the vibrant cross-cultural exchange that has guided the village's gradual growth. Arts and crafts are evident in every home, restaurant, temple, and shop.

Surrounded by patches of palm-studded jungle and vast expanses of rice fields in various stages of cultivation, Ubud is the best starting point for an exploration of Bali. The village itself warrants several days of investigation, and from here you can venture out to other points on the island.

Lodging

Because of the growing influx of tourists, all sorts of accommodations are available in Ubud, from economical losmen (homestays) to full-service hotels. We recommend beginning your stay at the **Hotel Tjampuhan**, P.O. Box 15, Ubud, Bali (tel. 0361-28871), gorgeously situated on a hillside overlooking a lush river canyon at the western end of town in the neighborhood of Campuhan. Although the rate of 55,000 rupiah ($32) per night, plus tax and service charge, is high by Ubud standards, the bungalows are clean and comfortable, have hot water showers, and are serviced by an attentive, friendly staff. A large breakfast of fruit, pancakes, omelets, toast, and coffee or tea is brought to your room in the morning. The hotel also features Ubud's best swimming pool, especially welcome after a long day of travel.

Somewhat farther out of town, up the Campuhan Ridge, the **Ananda Cottages**, P.O. Box 205, Denpasar, Bali, offer a variety of attractive rooms and houses in a garden setting surrounded by beautiful rice fields. The atmosphere is quiet, and the restaurant is an especially pleasant spot for a drink or snack. It, too, has a swimming pool. Rates range from 25,000 rupiah ($15) for one room to 100,000 rupiah ($60) for a house.

If you prefer to stay in the center of town, the **Hotel Puri Saren**, located on the main road in the middle of Ubud, puts you in the lap of traditional Balinese luxury. It is the home of Prince Corkorda Agung, and the immaculate bungalows, situated in a private garden courtyard and appointed with antiques, reflect his royal taste. The rates, 46,000 to 60,000 rupiah ($27-$35) including breakfast, are at the high end of the Ubud scale.

Moderately priced cottages and bungalows abound in Ubud. The **Homestay Karyawan**, where the sign reads, "Accommodation in Beautiful Garden," is located on Monkey Forest Road about a quarter of a mile down from the main road on the right-hand side. It has several large, clean cottages in a neatly landscaped setting surrounded by rice fields and is overseen by an especially friendly hostess who also runs a small shop out front. Breakfast is included in the 20,000 rupiah (about $12) rate.

Budget housing is available in dozens of modest losmen throughout Ubud. Here you can get a feel for everyday family life and be treated to the essence of Balinese hospitality. Our favorite is the **Homestay Campuhan Indah**, operated by I Gusti Nyoman Darta and his extended family. Located at the western end of the main road, next to Ibu Dewi's warung and behind a wall display of traditional masks, the Campuhan Indah has four sparsely furnished but very clean rooms. They are set behind the main house, and each has an individual front porch facing a quiet stream. The Balinese-style bathrooms, with cold-water showers and manual-flush toilets, are constructed as grottoes behind the rooms. The family is gracious and generous, sharing stories and information, serving tea or coffee, and providing a fine breakfast every morning, all for 6,000 rupiah (about $3.50) a day for two.

Getting Around
For short trips between villages on Bali, bemos (covered trucks with benches for seats) are the economical way to travel. They are not always comfortable. Drivers will load in passengers, including Balinese carrying goods to or from market, to the bursting point. Be sure to ask the going rate, as tourists are sometimes charged more than locals. A two- or three-mile trip should cost no more than 200 rupiah (about $.12) per person. The transportation hub of Ubud is Bemo Corner, the village's one main intersection, where Monkey Forest Road meets the main street. Public bemos, which drive along set routes, park here to recruit passengers to various destinations. Privately operated bemos with negotiable fares to the destination of your choice are available for hire here as well.

For your afternoon excursion, find a driver at Bemo Corner and tell him you want to stop first at Yeh Pulu and then Mas. The road from Ubud turns right at Peliatan, continues for 1 mile, and turns left toward Mas. About 1½ miles due east on this road is a major T-junction. Turn right toward Gianyar. About 100 yards south, the road turns left. Stop here at the sign for Yeh Pulu. To reach Mas, retrace the route to the T-junction at Peliatan and turn right (south). To return from Mas to Ubud, just stand on the left side of the road and flag down an oncoming bemo.

Sightseeing Highlights
▲▲▲ **Campuhan Ridge**—The early morning hours in Bali are perfect for walking, typically cool and misty, with sunlight filtering down through the palm trees. Rise with the dawn and the crowing of roosters for an invigorating walk along the crest of grassy Campuhan Ridge. You can pick up the trail below the swimming pool at the Hotel Tjampuhan or immediately off the left of the dirt road that passes to the left of the Homestay Campuhan Indah. The hard-beaten dirt path leads north. You will see children walking to school, women carrying baskets of goods on their heads on their way to market, and duck herders

guiding their flocks to the rice fields. The ridge leads into great plains of rice paddies in various states of cultivation. About 3 miles north, you encounter the small village of Kliki, where children are likely to be flying homemade kites up and down the dirt roads. At a leisurely pace, you can walk to Kliki and back to Ubud in two hours.

▲▲▲ Arts and Crafts Shops—As soon as you start walking from your hotel, you will begin encountering the myriad arts and crafts of Ubud. Although painting is the local specialty, shop owners gather masks, wood carvings, fabrics, jewelry, baskets, and clothing from all over the region. Shopping here takes on the added dimension of cultural education as you are exposed to an astounding array of handicrafts. Generally, the prices in Ubud are comparable to those in other villages and only slightly higher than in Denpasar and Kuta. Across the street and to the right of the Tjampuhan Hotel, an American named Simon has set up his For Earth Only design shop and gallery, featuring wild and futuristic prints hand-silk-screened by local youth. Just down the hill toward town, Murni has added shops selling the latest in Balinese and Indonesian fashions alongside her riverside restaurant. Once into the central section of Ubud, it seems like every other building is a shop of some kind. Here you will find batik, intricately woven ikat fabrics, silver and mother-of-pearl jewelry, and examples of all the other crafts. Browsing is welcome, and bargaining is expected, unless a "Fixed Prices" sign is posted. A good starting point for bargaining is half the initial asking price. The shops continue all the way down through Ubud to Peliatan, as well as down Monkey Forest Road. The quality of goods is similar from one place to the next, so don't feel pressured to buy the first things you see. Caveat emptor: there are very few authentic antiques available in these shops, but contemporary craftspeople frequently paint and scuff their pieces to give an antique appearance. From Murni's, turn right (east) and walk up the gradual grade into Ubud. You'll pass under a small aqueduct and come to the beginning of Ubud's main commercial strip. Browse through shops on your way to the Puri Lukisan Museum.

▲▲▲ Puri Lukisan Museum (Palace of Fine Arts)—Located on the left-hand (north) side of the road, the museum's entrance is set back from a small parking area next to the Mumbul Inn and leads to a path that crosses a stream in a spacious garden.

Nearly every village in central Bali is associated with a particular art or craft. Since the 1930s, when German and Dutch painters such as Walter Spies and Rudolf Bonnet settled here and encouraged local artists to develop new styles out of ancient traditions, Ubud (along with nearby Batuan to the

south) has been a vital center of Balinese painting. Taking off
from the rigid conventions of traditional, narrative *wayang*
styles (based on *wayang kulit*, shadow puppet theater),
painters began creating individualistic styles. Mythical themes
and everyday life in the villages and rice fields are portrayed in
meticulous detail. The Puri Lukisan opened in 1956 and has
built up a large collection of painting, sculpture, and wood
carvings from such masters as Gusti Nyoman Lempad of Ubud
to members of the contemporary "young artists" movement of
nearby communities such as Pengosekan and Penestanan. The
galleries are organized to provide a historical survey of the evolution of regional arts. They are open daily from 10:00 a.m. to
4:00 p.m., admission is 200 rupiah (about $.12).

▲▲ **Puri Saraswati**—From the museum, turn left and continue east about 100 yards on the main road. On the same side
of the street, past the Lotus Cafe, you will find Ubud's main temple. Every Balinese village has at least three temples: the Pura
Puseh, honoring village ancestors; the Pura Desa, for Brahma,
where current ceremonies are held; and the Pura Dalem, honoring the dead and the deities of the afterlife. In addition, each
family has a small temple in the household compound, and
numerous other temples and shrines are placed throughout the
community. They are open-air mazes of walls, courtyards, gar-
goylelike stone carvings, thatched pavilions, multitiered merus
(towers), platforms, and shelters. Ubud's main temple, located in
the center of town near Bemo Corner and next to the lotus
pond, is not as spectacular as many others around Bali but is
nonetheless a fascinating construction, a calm, introspective
place, central to the spiritual life of the villagers. Proper dress—
sarongs and sashes for women, long pants or sarongs and sashes
for men—is required in all temples.

▲▲ **Puri Saren**—After leaving the temple, turn to your left and
continue east on the road for about 50 yards. At Bemo Corner,
on the northeast side of the intersection, you will see the palace
of Ubud's historical royal family. Here you can still meet a real
prince, the Cokorda Agung, and catch a glimpse of the opulent
life-style enjoyed by the privileged classes of the raja era.
Located in the center of Ubud, the palace is a walled complex of
neat gardens, handsome bungalows, and ancient stone carvings.
Today, the bungalows are rented out to visitors at daily rates
ranging from 20,000 to 40,000 rupiah (about $12-$24).

▲▲▲ **Yeh Pulu**—There are thousands of temples and holy
places on Bali, but few are as mesmerizing as these infrequently
visited ruins of a fourteenth-century hermitage. To get to Yeh
Pulu, you have to walk a quarter mile or so from the end of the
road, down a narrow path, turning right along the small path

that runs through a field and along a river. Frequently waiting at the head of the path are children or an occasional guide who will show you the way. Here you will find an ancient wall frieze carved into the stony face of a cliff. About seven feet high and eighty feet long, the frieze depicts men, women, deities, and animals in mysterious vignettes. Excavated in 1925, the carvings attract very few visitors, and you are likely to find yourself alone as you contemplate the images of Ganesa, Krishna, and assorted creatures.

▲▲▲ **Mas**—Each village around Ubud has its own special crafts and unique styles. The road east from Ubud passes through Peliatan to Mas, a prosperous village of wood-carvers and superb mask makers. Here, Ida Bagus Njana developed a singular style of almost surreal carving in the decades from the 1930s through the 1960s. Have your bemo driver drop you off at one end of the village, so you can walk along and peruse the many workshops and storefronts. In the middle of Mas, on the east side of the road, look for the studio of Ida Bagus Anom, a master carver of ceremonial and dance masks. His work is exquisite, often combining human forms with images from the plant and animal kingdoms. Many Westerners have migrated to Bali to apprentice with him and study mask making and dance.

▲▲▲ **Dance Performances**—On any given night you have a choice of several performances at various stages in and around Ubud. The tourist office, located across the street from the temple, posts schedules of the events with times, locations, and the types of dances. At your hotel, the staff is always aware of what dances are happening each evening. In addition, throughout the day, men sell tickets in the streets of Ubud for the same price as is charged at the door.

The highly stylized dances are staged to entertain and accommodate the curiosity of tourists, but they are founded on religious belief and still retain their spiritual aura. The oldest dances are nearly 1,000 years old, deriving from the ancient Gambuh, but most of the popular dances date from the last forty years. Most are performed to the music of the *gamelan*, the delightfully clanging orchestra of drums, cymbals, brass gongs, kettles, and metallophones (a resonant, xylophonelike bronze and bamboo instrument). The rhythmically complex, polyphonic music creates a hypnotic background for the dances.

Four of the most frequently performed Balinese dances are the Legong, the Barong, the Kecak, and the Topeng.

The Legong, the Heavenly Dance of Divine Nymphs, is performed by elaborately costumed girls, usually 14 years of age or younger. It dramatizes twelfth- and thirteenth-century stories about the King of Lasem and his battles to win the maiden Rag-kesari. Its merits hinge upon the graceful precision and elegant hand movements of the young dancers.

The Barong dance brings to life a mythical, white magic beast, called Barong, who defends the people against the black magic witch, Rangda. Their battle is danced in fantastic costumes and gigantic masks.

The Kecak, or Monkey Dance, takes place in firelight and involves a seated chorus of 150 men who chant and chatter in eerie counterpoint and in unison. Individual dancers act out mythical stories against the background of strange human sounds and swaying movements of the chorus. The best Kecak is performed in the nearby village of Bona.

The Topeng, or Mask Dance, is drawn from centuries of tales about the exploits of noble families and heroes. The masks, often worn in succession by one dancer, are archetypes that magically come to life through the exacting and highly animated movements of the dancer.

If you are in Ubud on a Saturday night, by all means catch a performance of the Peliatan Legong. This troupe dates back to the early twentieth century and was the first company to tour the West. Its young dancers and veteran musicians still represent the height of Balinese culture.

Food

You could spend a month eating your way through Ubud and still not have sampled everything. Several restaurants cater to Western tastes, with prices to match. A full meal might cost between 4,500 and 10,000 rupiah (about $3-$6) per person at any of them. **Murni's**, next to the Campuhan River bridge, is one of the most popular spots, serving hamburgers, milk shakes, lasagna, excellent desserts, and coffee as well as Indonesian dishes. Murni also stocks a fine bookshelf of material about Bali. The **Lotus Café**, in central Ubud, features pasta specials and a lovely view of the immense lotus pond in front of the temple. It is a good place to meet Western travelers. **Beggar's Bush**, on the other side of the bridge from Murni's, serves good steaks and deliciously spiced fish dishes. Upstairs, the coziest late night bar in town plays taped blues and R&B music and closes whenever the last customer leaves.

The more moderately priced restaurants, where you can fill up for $2, also serve more indigenous cuisine. **Griya**, on the main road in Ubud, serves superb tuna *sate, nasi goreng* (fried rice with egg and bits of meat and vegetables), avocado salad, *jaffles* (closed, fried sandwiches), and banana pancakes. **Nomad**, at the eastern end of town, has delicious beef kabobs

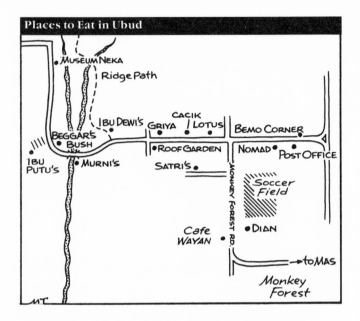

Places to Eat in Ubud

MUSEUM NEKA
Ridge Path
CACIK
IBU DEWI'S GRIYA LOTUS
BEMO CORNER
BEGGAR'S BUSH
ROOF GARDEN
NOMAD POST OFFICE
IBU PUTU'S MURNI'S
SATRI'S
Soccer Field
MONKEY FOREST RD.
DIAN
Cafe WAYAN
to MAS
Monkey Forest

and *mie goreng* (fried noodles). **Dian**, an extremely inexpensive Javanese restaurant down Monkey Forest Road, serves a wonderful chicken curry and exceptional black rice pudding. **Cacik**, not far from Griya, has the cheapest and tastiest *nasi campur* (steamed rice with assorted helpings of chicken, vegetables, tempeh, fish, and other tidbits) and chicken sate. **Satri's**, on Monkey Forest Road behind the Ubud performance stage, is operated by a delightful woman whom many consider the finest cook in Ubud. She makes wonderful tomato soup (prepared for each order), guacamole, mixed fruit *lassis* (yogurt drinks), and special Balinese dinners (about $4 per person) organized around your choice of two mouth-watering traditional dishes, banana chicken or smoked duck, either of which should be ordered a day in advance.

Even less expensive snacks and meals are available at any of the small roadside *warungs*, one- or two-person operations serving a variety of foods from fruit salads and juices to soups and rice dishes. Most serve the same types of foods, prepared with individual flare. **Ibu Dewi**, whose warung is beyond the western end of Ubud on the way to Murni's, makes excellent fruit salads and scrumptious black rice pudding, each for less than $1. The warung next door has delicious banana fritters.

Ibu Putu's small warung up the steps across the road from the Hotel Tjampuhan (look for the sign for Rasman's Houses) serves good noodle soups and fruit drinks.

SECOND DAY: LAKE BRATAN AND SINGARAJA

The volcanic mountains that separate northern and southern Bali create a fascinating cultural divide. Take a 100-mile round-trip through cool, highland croplands and jungles to the north-ernmost region of the island, where Dutch colonial rule began in the mid-nineteenth century and influenced the local way of life more strongly than in the south. Along the way, you can stop at a marvelous monkey forest, climb through the misty mountain range to a great volcanic lake, and descend again to the coast. The return trip includes a luxurious rest stop at a new resort with one of the most spectacular canyon views on all of Bali.

Suggested Schedule	
6:30 a.m.	Breakfast at your hotel or homestay.
7:30 a.m.	Ride to Lake Bratan, with stops at Monkey Forest in Sengeh, Pura Taman Ayun at Mengwi, and the Flower and Farmer's Market of Bukit Mungsu.
12:00 noon	Picnic lunch at botanical garden.
1:00 p.m.	Ride to Singaraja and Lovina Beach.
3:30 p.m.	Return trip to Ubud, stopping at Kupu Kupu Barong en route.
7:00 p.m.	Dinner in Ubud. Special Balinese dinner at Satri's.

Transportation

If you were staying in Bali for more than a week, it would be feasible to rent a car or Jeep for your personal use. Because the road markings can be hard to follow until you are familiar with the island's geography (and because driving in Bali is an art itself), we recommend hiring a driver for day trips. In either case, wait until you are in Ubud to make your arrangements, as the rates are lower there than in Denpasar or any of the beach communities. Azman Sukman and his brother, Isunin, who can be found through the Homestay Campuhan Indah, are especially reliable and informative drivers with expertly maintained Jeeps and vans. They can arrange to drive you on day trips as well as to the airport for your departure. If Azman and Isunin are booked up, they can help you find other drivers. Otherwise, at Bemo Corner, you can find public and private bemos waiting for passengers as well as private drivers who can be hired for the day. Most drivers will charge 40,000 to 60,000 rupiah ($24-$36) per day for their services, depending on the length of the trip. For day trips, make arrangements with your driver the day before. Make sure they understand the route you want to take.

We don't recommend driving yourself in Indonesia. Most of Bali's main roads are fairly well paved, but they are narrow and can be a challenge to even the most defensive Western drivers. Traffic moves on the left, sometimes at surprisingly high speeds. Drivers use their horns constantly to signal their approach. Trucks often take up most of the roadway, motorbikes zip around everywhere, and some side roads are chock-full of pot holes. Foreigners are often assumed liable even in accidents that may not be their fault.

Sightseeing Highlights

▲▲▲ **Sangeh**—Here you can experience one of Bali's most intense encounters with wildlife. Hundreds of friendly, pestering monkeys follow you through the forest and temple at Sangeh, begging for the peanuts you can purchase at the entrance. They climb up your leg and perch on your shoulder, taking the nuts from your outstretched hand with their soft fingers. The mythical origins of this Bukit Sari, or Monkey Forest, lie in the legend of Hanuman, the heroic monkey. Part of his monkey army landed here when a section of the holy mountain, Mahameru, fell to earth. The temple, Pura Bukit Sari, was built in the seventeenth century, and its grounds now include a row of booths selling handicrafts. Young, smiling guides are available to keep the monkeys at bay or to help you feed them as you stroll through the forest of nutmeg trees. Beware: remove all money and valuables from your arms, neck, and clothing. The monkeys are notoriously swift pickpockets.

▲▲▲ **Bukit Mungsu**—This large outdoor market presents an eye-popping array of colorful fruits and vegetables of every variety. Women walk through the parking lot selling freshly cooked corn on the cob from the giant pans they carry on their heads. Behind the front stalls of neatly arranged produce is a row of plant and flower stands, where vendors sell potted and freshly cut flowers. Dazzling varieties of orchids are the specialties. Lush nurseries extend back from the stalls. Select an assortment of fruits and vegetables for a picnic lunch to take back 2 miles west to the botanical garden or just down the hill ahead to Lake Bratan.

▲▲ **Lila Graha Botanical Garden**—Beyond a spectacular split gate, its ornateness typical of northern carving, acres of trimly cultivated gardens roll gently into the dense woods that cover the nearby hills. This vast forest expanse, visited by relatively few tourists, is dotted with special flower beds and greenhouses. Brilliant arrays of mountain orchids are a major attraction. The garden provides a tranquil setting for a picnic lunch.

▲▲▲ **Lake Bratan**—Filling an ancient crater of volcanic Mt. Bratan, this large lake provides a surprising alpine vista above the jungle line. The sometimes sun-drenched, sometimes mist-shrouded lake, surrounded by dark forested mountains, is used for fishing, canoeing, and waterskiing. The Ulu Danu Temple, honoring the goddess of the lake, is located on the western shore. There is a small guest house and restaurant on the southern side. After crossing the 1,220-meter mountain pass at Bratan, you will pass the world-class Bali Handara Golf Course and descend into the region of Buleleng, heading for Singaraja.

▲▲ **Singaraja**—Founded in 1604 by Raja Panji Sakti, this cosmopolitan seaport became the Dutch capital at the end of the nineteenth century. Its ethnically diverse population of 25,000 reflects the various waves of immigrants who populated the city, including Chinese, Europeans, Javanese, and the Bugis of Sulawesi. The town is quiet. Its main cultural institution is the Gedong Kirtya, a historical library of Balinese manuscripts, located on Jalan Veteran. The Hindu temples around Singaraja, at Jagaraga, Sangsit, Sawan, and Kubutambahan, reveal the differences between northern and southern styles. Here the carvings are even more ornate and fantastic, some incorporating scenes from everyday life—cars, bicycles, lovers—alongside wild, mythical creatures.

▲▲ **Lovina Beach**—Seven miles to the west of Singaraja, you will find this quiet and uncrowded beach resort. The waves are usually gentle, and while the beach is not spectacular, the snorkeling is very good in the clear waters. A refreshing dip in the sea is just the thing to perk you up for the drive back to Ubud.

▲▲▲ **Kupu Kupu Barong**—The perfect place to stop at the end of the long drive down from Batur is this luxurious new resort tucked into the hills at Kedewatan, about three miles northwest of Ubud. Although its bungalows were expensive and its restaurant was only mediocre the last time we visited, Kupu Kupu Barong boasts one of the most spectacular views on Bali. The Agung River has cut a deep, winding canyon through the hills, and rice farmers have terraced the land up from the water, creating a complex, multihued relief of blue water, green and yellow paddies, and tangled, palm-studded jungle. Grab a window table in the beautiful restaurant perched high above the river, and enjoy a cool drink as the sunset transforms the landscape into a magical pink and orange vista.

THIRD DAY: GUNUNG KAWI, BATUR, AND BESAKIH

Today, visit the heart of Bali's spiritual world. The second main route into northern Bali takes you to a breathtaking overlook of the island's largest lake, through the foothills of its highest peak, and to the temple that is the "mother" of Bali's religious life. Along the way, you will visit one of Bali's most unusual temples. The daylong, 110-mile trip ends with a refreshing swim in the soothing waters off Bali's finest southeastern beach.

Suggested Schedule	
7:00 a.m.	Breakfast at your hotel or homestay.
8:00 a.m.	Check out. Drive to Gunung Kawi, Batur overlook, and Besakih.
12:30 p.m.	Lunch at the warung at Besakih entrance.
1:30 p.m.	Tour Besakih.
2:30 p.m.	Drive to Candi Dasa.
4:30 p.m.	Check into homestay or hotel. Late afternoon swim in ocean.

Sightseeing Highlights
▲▲▲ **Gunung Kawi**—Some 300 steps lead down the steep hillside into the valley of the Pakrisan River, where, according to myth, the giant Kebo Iwa used his fingernail to carve this magnificent "Rocky Temple" out of the side of the mountain in the eleventh century. The enormous *candis* (monuments) are sculpted into deep, arching niches more than 20 feet high. Five are located on one side of the small Pakrisan River, four on the other. A tenth stands alone at the southern end of the narrow valley. A set of monks' cells is also carved into the canyon walls.
▲▲▲ **Lake Batur**—Resting in a broad, 12.5-mile-wide caldera between Mt. Batur and Mt. Abang, Lake Batur offers one of the most dramatic views on Bali. From the overlook on the road at Penelokan, you stand high above the huge lake, with the slopes of both mountains sweeping down from misty peaks to the silvery reflecting surface of water. The vast lava flows from the devastating eruptions of 1917 and 1926 are easily visible. A narrow road winds down to Kedisan on the shore. Across the lake from Kedisan lies Tunyan, one of the last original Balinese villages, where the inhabitants still live according to ancient traditions such as allowing the dead to disintegrate in the open air.

▲▲▲ **Pura Besakih**—The "mother temple" of Bali, also
known as Pur Panataran Agung, is situated on the eastern slope
of towering Mt. Agung, an active volcano that last erupted in
1963. A complex of more than 30 temples, Besakih has been
developed over the course of 1,000 years and represents the
highest spiritual unity of the entire island. During festival
periods, thousands of Balinese make pilgrimages to the temple,
the site of holy purification ceremonies. Before making the dramatic ascent to the temple, you can stop for an inexpensive
lunch of *nasi campur* at one of the warungs that line the parking lot. Then walk up the hill through the split gate and tour the
terraced towers and shrines of Pura Panataran Agung, often fes-
tooned with bright, colorful banners.

Candi Dasa
Developed specifically as a tourist area, Candi Dasa is a strip of
hotels, losmen, and restaurants along a narrow beach of soft
white sand. The atmosphere is very casual and relaxed. It
attracts a crowd of young Australian, European, and American
travelers. Despite the contrary wishes of the local population,
foreign women often sunbathe topless along the beach. Fishermen with outriggers will offer to take you for rides to the giant
rocks off the southern end of the beach. Every restaurant has a
beachside patio just above the waves. Candi Dasa is a perfect
place to wind down after a long day trip.

Lodging
The closest thing to a resort in the Candi Dasa area is the **Balina
Beach Hotel** (Buitan, Manggis, Karangasem, Bali, Indonesia)
near the tiny fishing village of Nalayan, about one mile west of
Candi Dasa's main strip. Built in 1987, the hotel has a variety of
attractive bungalows, cottages, and suites, ranging in price from
20,000 to 85,000 rupiah ($12-$50) per day. Some rooms overlook a rice field, and the deluxe upstairs accommodations have
fine views of the ocean. It offers an isolated setting with its own
beachfront, a good restaurant, a bar, a fine diving operation,
and beautifully groomed gardens.

In Candi Dasa, the **Puri Pandan** and the **Pondok Bamboo**,
under one ownership, offer clean, pleasant bamboo cottages
along lush garden walks just a few yards from the beach. Rates,
from 17,000 to 27,000 rupiah ($10-$16) per night, include breakfast. For the budget traveler, **Kelapa Mas Homestay**, toward
the eastern end of Candi Dasa, has small, spartan, but comfortable cottages facing the beach for about 10,000 rupiah ($6) per
night.

Food

The two best restaurants in Candi Dasa are **Puri Pandan** and **Pondok Bamboo**. They overlook the ocean and serve Indonesian dishes—nasi campur, nasi goreng, fish, squid, chicken, fruit drinks—at reasonable prices. A full dinner costs about 4,000 rupiah ($2.40).

FOURTH DAY: CANDI DASA

This is a day to rest, recuperate from your busy schedule of touring, and relish the pleasures of the sea. In contrast to the crazy commerce and nightlife of the Kuta and Sanur beach areas, Candi Dasa remains relaxed and hassle-free. The southeastern coast of Bali has numerous sites for scuba diving, snorkeling, and swimming in warm, gentle waters. If you are ready for more sightseeing, ride to the nearby ancient Balinese village of Tenganan and the palatial sites of Balinese kings.

Suggested Schedule

8:00 a.m.	Breakfast at your hotel or homestay.
9:30 a.m.	Scuba diving or snorkeling trip from Balina Beach. Or set out on a tour of southeastern historical sites.
1:00 p.m.	Lunch in Candi Dasa.
2:00 p.m.	Relax on beach. Scuba dive or snorkel.

Getting Around

You can arrange for daily transportation at your homestay or at the Balina Beach Hotel. If you are staying in Candi Dasa, you can catch a public bemo heading west and be dropped off at the hotel's driveway. The parking lot is a regular gathering spot for drivers. You can also make arrangements at the hotel desk. Expect to pay 40,000 to 50,000 rupiah ($24-$30) for an all-day trip.

Sightseeing Highlights

▲▲▲ **Tenganan**—Very few villages of the Bali Aga, the original Balinese, have endured into the late twentieth century. Only three miles north of Candi Dasa, Tenganan is one of the last outposts of this old culture. Protected as much by a strong sense of custom, a tradition of communal landownership, and a rigidly maintained isolationism as by the thick wall that surrounds the village, Tenganan is the home of double ikat weaving, the ancient Redjang dance, and an annual festival, Usaba Sambah. The weaving, which brings Tenganan its greatest fame, is a fastidiously intricate process using patterned threads on both the warp and the weft, resulting in the rare "flaming" cloth of dazzling patterns and intense colors.

▲▲▲ **Amlapura**—Formerly known as Karangasem, this village was the center of the Karangasem Kingdom, the most powerful regency of late eighteenth- and early nineteenth-century Bali. At the turn of the twentieth century, the raja cooperated with the Dutch colonialists and survived with a modicum of power. The strangely eclectic palace, the Puri Kanginan, combines European, Chinese, and Balinese styles. The last king, Anak Agung Anglurah Ketut, spent much of his late life building water palaces for his royal retreats.

▲▲▲ **Ujung**—The Karangasem king's first palatial construction, the famous Floating Palace, was completed in 1921. Severely damaged by a great earthquake and the devastating eruption of Mt. Agung in 1963, the arrangement of pools, pavilions, moats, and royal bungalow stands in ruins on the beach five miles south of Amlapura, a fascinating monument to the king's fantasies.

▲▲▲ **Tirta Gangga**—In 1946, the king undertook a second water palace nine miles north of Amlapura. It was a series of connected pools shaded by a giant banyan tree, where the king and his family could relax and enjoy the view of mighty Mt. Agung above the rolling hills. When the temperamental volcano blew its top in 1963, the elaborate compound and exotic statuary were damaged, but it is still possible to appreciate the pastoral setting and sense of escape that brought the king to this site.

Scuba Diving and Snorkeling—At the Balina Beach Hotel, Abdi Padingga runs a scuba diving operation that supplies equipment, air, transportation, and dive guides for seven different dive spots around the southeastern and northern coast of Bali. Prices ranges from $25 to $50 for scuba trips, $5 to $20 for snorkeling. Prime locations include the coral gardens around Kambing Island, the "Blue Lagoon," Nusapenida Island, and a sunken U.S. Liberty Ship from World War II at Tulamben. Abdi can also arrange to take you on a special night dive at the shipwreck. The comfortable temperatures and marvelous visibility of the Indonesian waters and the abundant undersea life—immense rainbows of hard and soft coral, hundreds of species of exotic fish—make underwater exploration a must, even if you only paddle along on the surface gazing through a mask at the world below.

FIFTH DAY: TANAH LOT

Although the Balinese seek spiritual sustenance in the mountains, their life by the sea is equally fascinating. All over the island, the Balinese live in harmony with their environment. Here on the shoreline, they have built a magnificent temple that blends gracefully into the rocky silhouettes of the coast. At the other end of the cultural spectrum, in Kuta, you can witness what happens to a sleepy beach area when tourists and entrepreneurs join hands across the pocketbook.

Sightseeing Highlights
▲▲▲ **Tanah Lot**—Located on the coast due west of Denpasar, about 18 miles on the main road that loops north and then down to the coast, this sixteenth-century temple is built on a huge rock in the shallow sea waters. Under the guidance of the priest Nirartha, the people of the local fishing village built the temple to honor the spirits of the sea. One of the most popular vistas of Bali, the temple and rock create ethereal patterns at sunset. You can sit on the beach and watch the shapes and shadows merge into the enfolding dusk.

▲▲ **Kuta and Legian**—Less than 30 years ago, Kuta was a quiet coastal village, home to fishermen and metal workers. Now, this bustling beach town, which merges inseparably into Legian at the northern end, is bursting with activity, from the nonstop bartering that goes on in the hundreds of boutiques to the busy beach scenes of surfing and sunbathing. The streets are narrow and frenetic; the shops are small and jam-packed; the restaurants sell pizza, hamburgers, and Mexican food as well as Indonesian dishes; the beach is full of people insistently hawking everything from sarongs to massages. Compared with the inland villages, rice fields, and temples, Kuta is the "future shock" of Bali. In an hour or two of browsing the shops, you can find almost unbelievable shopping bargains, especially hand-tailored clothes of native fabrics and leathers. Made's Warung, on Jalan Pantai Kuta, is a popular gathering spot for locals and Westerners.

SIXTH DAY: LOMBOK

Travel to the neighbor island of Lombok, where you'll enjoy the lush retreat of Tetebatu at the foot of one of Indonesia's highest volcanic peaks. Hike through the monkey forest and relax at a fine resort known for its excellent bird-watching and fine meals.

Suggested Schedule	
8:30 a.m.	Taxi from Candi Dasa to Padang Bai.
10:00 a.m.	Catch the morning ferry from Padang Bai to Lembar.
1:30 p.m.	Arrive in Lembar.
3:30 p.m.	Arrive in Tetebatu. Check into your inn.
4:00 p.m.	Hike local trails on the slopes of Rinjani volcano.
6:00 p.m.	Dinner.
	Evening at leisure.

Lombok
Just 3 ½ hours away by ferry or 40 minutes by air, Lombok is separated from Bali by a deep channel often characterized as an oceanic continental divide. You'll see why as soon as you step onto the shores of Lombok, an island that appears to have more in common with Australia's outback than with the lush world of Bali. While there are verdant volcanic uplands and rice terraces on Lombok, you'll also find stark landscapes, particularly on the southern end of the island. In addition, Lombok offers some exceptional white sand beaches. Shaded by coconut palms, these uncrowded retreats have the feel of a remote coral atoll.

Most of Lombok's 2 million residents live in the central east coast villages of Ampenan, Mataram, and Cakranegara. Nearly 80 percent are dark brown-skinned Sasaks, mainly hill tribe people who have maintained their Islamic customs and animist practices without developing dances and festivals geared to the lucrative tourist industry. The balance of the population is Balinese, with a sprinkling of Javanese, Chinese, and Arabs. Everyone speaks Bahasa Indonesia and their own dialect. You'll find that English is not spoken as widely or as well as it is in the tourist centers of Bali.

Getting There
The ferry from Padang Bai, Bali, takes 3 ½ hours to sail the channel to idyllic Lembar Harbor. We recommend taking the 5,000 rupiah ($3) early morning boat, arriving about 1:30 p.m., and then connecting by bemo to Mataram. You can also take one of three daily flights from Denpasar to Mataram, a 40-minute trip on Merpati Air which runs $18 each way (if you're prone to sea-sickness, you will find the plane preferable to the ferry during the winter rainy season, October to March, when storms make the channel crossing rough). In Mataram, you can continue by

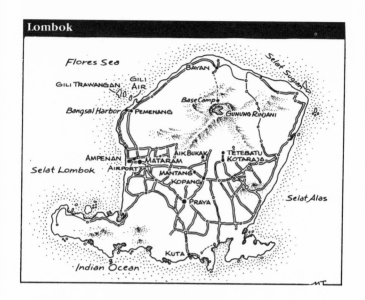

bemo for the 50-kilometer trip to Tetebatu, a tiny village at the end of a road on the southern slope of Gunung Rinjani, or charter a minivan taxi by the day or half-day for about the same rate you paid in Bali.

Lodging and Food

Just outside the village of Tetebatu, you'll find the colonial Wisma Sudjono. The two-story bungalows scattered on spacious grounds have superb vistas and a large swimming pool. These rooms, complete with showers and Western toilets, run about 10,000 rupiah ($5.65) a night. We do not recommend the less expensive units nearby, because they are not well ventilated and have no view. At Wisma Sudjono, you'll also enjoy the Javanese and Dutch food offered in the charming open-air restaurant. During the predictable early afternoon rain, guests gather for hot tea and watch the showers descend on the pool, pet geese, and giant fig trees. Box lunches are also available here for your day hikes. Remember that in this Moslem land the call to prayer, via very loud cassette music that slides all over the scale, takes place at 5:00 a.m. Grin and bear.

Sightseeing Highlights

▲▲ **Rinjani Volcano**—Ask the hotel to arrange a guide to show you some of the trails and paths leading through the rice fields and what remains of Rinjani's flanks. As you ascend the foothills, expect to attract plenty of friendly attention from workers in the fields and children bathing in irrigation canals. Along the Rinjani hiking trails, you'll also have an easy time photographing the ubiquitous black monkeys. It's also possible to tour the rough back roads by a minivan or bemo charter. Your hotel can help make the necessary arrangements. Ascending all the way up Rinjani, a popular religious pilgrimage on Lombok, takes four days. This difficult trek, attempted only in the dry season, begins at Bayan on the north side of the island.

▲▲▲ **Sunset at the Wisma Sudjono**—A perfect moment for fans of Hitchcock's *The Birds*. Watch great flocks of fantail pigeons circling overhead in hypnotic patterns as they make eerie harmonic whistling sounds. Each bird produces a different tone. It's not a call, not the wind in their wings, but tiny carved flutes attached by the owners to one of each bird's legs. The discordant experience peaks when 50 or 60 birds sweep across the twilight sky.

SEVENTH DAY: LOMBOK

In the morning, relax on the volcanic slopes of Tetebatu. Then head down to Ampenan and Bangsal harbor to pick up an outrigger en route to Gili Trawangan, a coral atoll with some of the best snorkeling in Indonesia.

Suggested Schedule	
8:00 a.m.	Breakfast at your hotel.
9:00 a.m.	Take a Tetebatu walk, explore Rinjani.
1:00 p.m.	Take a bemo or minivan taxi to to Ampenan Museum.
3:00 p.m.	Continue to Pemenang and Bangsal Harbor.
5:00 p.m.	Catch a prahu (outrigger) to Gili Trawangan.
6:00 p.m.	Check into your hotel, dinner.
	Evening at leisure.

Sightseeing Highlights
▲▲ **Tetebatu Walks**—With the help of a guide, you can return to the realm of the mountain people on the lower Rinjani trails. Or, if you prefer, take a peaceful walk (about three hours) through the uplands to the village of Pomotong. From here, you can catch a bemo back to Tetebatu. Another possibility is the walk to Lendang Nangka, about four miles from Tetebatu. With

the help of a local guide and map, it's possible to see a beautiful waterfall and spring, visit blacksmiths, or hike through the forest. Pak Radiah, a schoolteacher, accommodates guests in his home and can guide you through this region. You can ask for him at the village school, or locals will guide you to his house.

▲ **Ampenan Museum**—On your trip across Lombok, it's worth stopping off to see the masks, weaving, basketry, krises, and other handicrafts sold here. It's located on Ampenan's Jalan Banjar Tiler Negara Street.

Gili Trawangan
Off the northwest coast of Lombok are three idyllic coral atolls. The largest and most distant is Gili Trawangan. It has fine white sand beaches, transparent waters, and snorkeling that feels like floating around inside a *National Geographic* special on marine life.

Getting There
A 90-minute bus or charter minivan ride takes you through mountainous jungle en route to the coastal village of Pemenang. A short *dokar* (donkey cart) ride completes the trip down a 2-kilometer road to Bangsal Harbor. If you prefer, hike this last trail down to the sea. Here, you'll arrange for the 45-minute *prahu* (outrigger) ride across to Gili Trawangan. Expect to pay about 17,000 rupiah (a little under $10) for the ride out to Gili Trawangan, the island with a crocodilelike profile. It's best to wait for a scheduled crossing, as a charter can run several times the regular fare.

Lodging and Food
Homestay Makmur and **Holiday Inn** are our favorites. You'll pay about 8,500 rupiah ($5) a day for modest bamboo bungalows. This price for country living, Lombok-style, includes all three daily meals. If you're staying more than one day, it's easy to buy fish off the early morning prahu. This will make a fine contribution to lunch or dinner prepared by your hosts. A few convenience items are sold at these spartan inns, but don't count on being able to find much more than toiletries, tobacco, and sweets.

EIGHTH DAY: GILI TRAWANGAN

Enjoy this idyllic coral atoll, swimming, snorkeling, and beachcombing.

Suggested Schedule

8:00 a.m.	Breakfast at your homestay or inn.
9:00 a.m.	A morning stroll on the island.
11:00 a.m.	Swimming and snorkeling.
12:00 noon	Lunch and rest.
2:00 p.m.	Another leisurely walk.
4:00 p.m.	Swim and snorkel.
7:00 p.m.	Watch sunset from "Crocodile's" shoulder.

Exploring Gili Trawangan

It takes about five hours to stroll all the way around the island, pausing whenever you like to take a dip. If you're feeling lazy in the heat, settle for shorter morning and afternoon strolls. Sunsets are best observed from the Crocodile's shoulders, a small hill on the island's interior easily reached by a footpath branching off the main trail just south of the Holiday Inn. From this elevated vantage point, the sun sets behind Bali. Your hotel can easily guide you to this chosen spot.

If you have more time, catch a prahu over to Gili Air, the smallest of the coral atolls, offering excellent beaches and snorkeling. The foliage here is lusher and more tropical than on Gili Trawangan; it is also quieter. One of southeast Asia's greatest bargains is Hans Bungalows: good food, friendly owners, and clean, spartan accommodations just steps from the beach. The price is right, just 8,500 rupiah ($5) a day including meals. After completing your visit to Lombok, you'll want to return to Bali by sea or air (there's a 35-minute flight from Mataram to Denpasar at 7:55 a.m. or 12:15 p.m.).

Denpasar Airport

To rejoin the main around-the-world itinerary on Day 11, you have several options. Take the 10:15 a.m. or 3:15 p.m. nonstop to Jakarta, arriving an hour later. In Jakarta, you can catch a 6:30 p.m. flight to Singapore, where you'll connect to the 10:15 p.m. Singapore Airlines flight to Cairo. You'll arrive in Egypt the following morning at 5:35 a.m.

The food at the Denpasar Airport is mediocre and dreadfully overpriced, and flights are often delayed an hour or more. If you have a long layover, you may want to eat at the Depot Barito, on Jalan Raya Puputan Nitimandala, across from the Department of Justice on the outskirts of Denpasar. It is operated by a Javanese family who also run a fine restaurant—the Bundo Kanduang—in Denpasar. You might take a bag lunch of *rendang* (meat simmered in spices for 24 hours), *perkedel* (fried, spicy mashed potatoes), *sambal goreng udang* (shrimp, potatoes, and chilis), or other Sumatran and Javanese delicacies. Savor them on the plane.

Stopover Option: Yogyakarta

Yogyakarta is the spiritual and cultural capital of Java, located in the broad, central plain that spreads out below Mt. Merapi. Usually called "Yogya," it is a busy metropolis of 500,000, teeming with bemos and *becaks* (three-wheeled taxi carts) and dotted with batik galleries, silver workshops, leather factories, *wayan kulit* (shadow puppet) theaters, and gamelan stages. During a three-day side trip, you can explore the historic sites of the sprawling city, the nearby ancient temples of Prambanan and Borobudur, and the quieter twin court city of Solo (Surakarta).

Garuda Indonesian has nonstop one-hour flights daily between Denpasar and Yogyakarta leaving at 7:15 a.m., 11:15 a.m., and 3:15 p.m. Upon your arrival, be sure to walk across the street from the airport and visit the gallery of Sapto Hudoyo. The dashing, white-haired artist is like the Gucci of Java, a renowned batik designer and a collector of Indonesian artifacts. His gallery is actually a splendid home organized into showrooms and a spectacular museum.

In Yogya, visit the royal Kraton, the 200-year-old palace at the heart of the city, the dazzling Taman Sari (royal pleasure gardens), and the fascinating bird market. In the surrounding area, see the ancient temple complex of Borobudur (26 miles northwest of Yogya), which includes the world's largest Buddhist monument; Prambanan, a Hindu temple complex featuring some of Java's most spectacular temples (17 miles east of Yogya); and Solo (38 miles east of Yogya), which offers a chance to appreciate the fine arts and crafts of central Java in a less frenetic setting than bustling Yogya.

Accommodations in Yogya range from the first-class Ambarrukmo Hotel, about 127,500 rupiah ($75) a night on Jalan Adisucipto (tel. 8848-8), and the historic Hotel Garuda, about 85,000 rupiah (about $50) a night Jalan Marlioboro 72, tel. 2113-4, to budget losmen along the railroad tracks. We recommend the centrally located, midrange guest houses along Jalan Prawirotaman, such as the Duta Guest House at about 25,500 rupiah ($15) a night on Jalan Prawirotaman 20 (tel. 5219). The Duta, the Metro, and others offer free transportation from the airport and organize excursions to Prambanan and Borobudur.

From Yogyakarta, there are frequent one-hour flights to Jakarta, where you can connect to Egypt and rejoin the main around-the-world itinerary.

CAIRO: GATEWAY TO THE MIDDLE EAST

You're midway through your trip, and now that you have enjoyed some of Asia's most fascinating cities and exotic backcountry, your itinerary shifts to the Middle East. Cairo, gateway to the pyramids, the Sphinx, and the treasures of the Nile Delta, is famous for its art, artistry, and monuments. After settling into your hotel, you'll have a chance to see all three. Highlights include Byzantine mosques with soaring minarets, a walk through the very old "Old City," and a stop at the eclectic home of an eccentric British major.

Suggested Schedule

7:00 a.m.	Arrive at Cairo Airport.
9:00 a.m.	Arrive at your hotel. Relax.
1:00 p.m.	Ibn Touloun Mosque.
2:00 p.m.	Gayer-Anderson Museum.
3:00 p.m.	Mosque and School of Sultan Hassan.
4:00 p.m.	The Citadel/Mohammed Ali Mosque.
	Evening at leisure.

Cairo

For more than 1,000 years, Cairo has been the center of Egyptian life. Africa's largest city, with a population of more than 11 million, Cairo presents some very special opportunities to the visitor. Here you'll be able to see the Pyramids of Giza, the only one of the Seven Wonders of the World still standing. Gone, but not forgotten, are the Hanging Gardens of Babylon, the Artemision at Ephesus, the Mausoleum at Harlicarnassus, the Colossus of Rhodes, the Olympian Zeus statue by Phidias, and the Pharos at Alexandria (some lists substitute the Walls of Babylon). You'll have a chance to tour the overwhelming collection of the Egyptian Museum. And, with a little luck, your hotel might be able to arrange a moonlit horseback ride in front of the Pyramids.

Located in the flat Nile Delta 120 miles south of the Mediterranean, Cairo is a city of 1,000 minarets which also boasts Africa's tallest skyscrapers. Best known for its pyramids dominating the Giza Plateau, the city has some of Islam's finest art and architecture as well as many treasures of Christendom. Although Cairo is a hectic and at times frustrating city, you will find Egyptians courteous and helpful. Modest prices make it easy to visit the city comfortably and tour with reputable guides and drivers. In

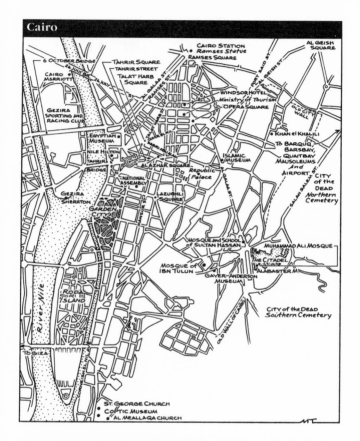

Cairo

short, this is a city where you can relax and focus your energy on enjoying the region's antiquities, ancient neighborhoods, and traditional way of life. While Arabic is Egypt's official language, most Egyptians understand and speak English, particularly in major tourist centers. And if your image of an Islamic nation is a place where the sidewalks roll up at 6:00 p.m., you'll be delighted to know that Cairo boasts excellent nightlife.

Arrival
Arrival at Cairo Airport's new international terminal is smooth. If you're on Egyptair, lines can be long because this carrier uses a very busy terminal. If you make your hotel reservations through a tour company such as Naggar or Wagon Lits, company representatives will meet you at the airport and expedite

your arrival. In some cases, companies may be able to arrange
early hotel check-in during the morning. After proceeding
through passport control, baggage claim, and customs, you can
take a taxi to your downtown hotel for about 12 pounds
(roughly $5).

Getting Around
Taxis are convenient and inexpensive. The trip from your hotel
to Old Cairo runs 2 pounds (about $1), and the journey to the
Pyramids is only about 5 pounds (about $2). Be sure to agree on
a price when you get in. Alternatively, you may prefer the convenience of a car and driver, arranged by you hotel. Expect to
spend 5 to 8 pounds (about $2 to $3) an hour. It's a good idea to
book your driver the night before. Tipping is recommended.

Lodging
Overbooking can be a problem at Cairo hotels. One way to protect yourself is to reserve through a tour operator. A complete
list of tour companies is available through the Egyptian General
Authority for the Promotion of Tourism, 630 Fifth Ave., New
York, NY 10111 (tel. 212-246-6960). If you choose to book
independently, be sure to arrive with confirmed reservations.

All the major chains such as Marriott, Hilton, and Sheraton
can be booked through 800 numbers in the United States. An
early arrival time should help you avoid being bumped.

Hotels in the "expensive" category charge about 312 to 440
pounds ($125 to $175) a night double. Our top hotel choice is
the **Cairo Marriott** on Saray el-Guezira Street, Zamalek (tel.
340888). Built around a nineteenth-century palace, this is a real
oasis with acres of gardens and pools on an island adjacent to
downtown. Ask for a top-floor room to enjoy the best view of
the Nile or the city. On the same island and with many similar
amenities is the **El Gezirah Sheraton** (tel. 411333). In the
downtown Tahrir Square area, convenient to many of the city's
leading tourist destinations, is the **Nile Hilton**, Corniche el-Nil
(tel. 750666). Or try the **Semiramis Intercontinental**, Corniche el-Nil (800-327-0200 for reservations in the United
States).

If you'd prefer to sleep by the Pyramids, which are seven
miles away at the Giza Plateau, consider the Mena House-
Oberoi on Sharia el-Ahram (tel. 855444, or in the U.S.,
800-223-6800). By spending one night here during your stay,
you'll be able to see the sound and light show, walk back to
your room, and then rise at dawn to see the Pyramids before the
crowds arrive. This is a good way to beat the traffic hassles
between downtown and the Giza Plateau the following morn-

ing. You may find the site so romantic you'll want to spend all your Cairo nights here. Created from a nineteenth-century palace, this hotel charges about 112 to 275 pounds ($45 to $110) a night. Higher-priced rooms are located in the older palace section. The pool overlooks the Pyramids. Ask for a view room. This spot is ideal for those who want to be out of the busy downtown area.

In the moderate price range, try the **Windsor Hotel**, 19 Alfy St. (tel. 915810). A double runs about 68 pounds ($27) a night. In the Tahrir Square area, **Shepheard's Hotel**, Corniche el-Nil (tel. 3553800), offers rooms from 66 to 90 pounds ($25 to $36). Another possibility is the **Delta Bel Air Hotel**, Mokkatam (tel. 916177). Located near the Citadel, this French-run hotel charges 112 to 255 pounds ($45 to $100).

Food
Due to health considerations, we prefer to eat in hotel restaurants (or on board ships when cruising the Nile). We do recommend two inexpensive nonhotel restaurants that are safe to try: **Felfela**, 15 Hoda Sharawi, Cairo (off Talaat Harb St.), where you can enjoy *taamiya*, the chickpea dish known in our country as falafel (tel. 740521), and **Abou Shakra**, at 69 Kasr el-Ainy (tel. 848860), where the specialty is *kofta*, a spiced minced meat. Bottled water is sold everywhere in Egypt, and in the marketplaces, you'll want to try the round brown bread available at bakeries.

The Old City
Like the Persians, Romans, and first Islamic settlers who once lived here, you'll find this neighborhood the place to begin a visit to Cairo. The Old City has been Cairo's traditional crossroads for warriors and merchants, farmers and clerics, sultans and craftsmen. Five centuries before the American Revolution, Cairo was the biggest city in the world, the Middle Eastern capital of business, politics, and culture. The Old City's famous mosques, palaces, bathhouses, convents, and mausoleums were the heart of that world. Although some of the best have disappeared, Cairo has been working to preserve this splendid Islamic architecture. Archaeologists, volunteers, and even foreign governments are now busy restoring the Old City, your introduction to the land of the Nile.

Sightseeing Highlights
▲▲▲ Mosque of Ibn Touloun—The oldest mosque still used for Islamic services is also the first one to see in Cairo. Incredibly, many guided Cairo tours omit this gem due to time con-

straints. It is easily reached by taxi (if the driver looks confused, simply show him the location on your map). Built in A.D. 879 during the reign of El-Emir Ahmed Ibn Touloun, this simply designed, red-brick mosque—one of the largest in Egypt—has an open courtyard surrounded by four loggias and is highlighted by 128 latticed windows. The prayer niche is surrounded by marble and gold mosaic pointing toward Mecca. The wooden pulpit has some of the finest inlays in Islamic art and impressive stucco patterns on the inner courtyard arches. If you're feeling adventurous and are not prone to vertigo, climb the 131-foot-high spiral staircase that winds around the outside of the minaret. Hours are 8:00 a.m. to 4:00 p.m., admission 1 pound ($0.39). Be sure to take your shoes off before entering this and all other mosques.

▲▲ **Gayer-Anderson Museum**—Located immediately to the right of the mosque, this sixteenth-century home shows how the well-to-do lived during the colonial era. Actually two houses joined together, the museum features English, French, and Islamic furniture as well as Egyptian antiquities. Tip the caretaker and he'll guide you through the labyrinth of corridors and passageways linking up these houses. Incidentally, that painting of a gentleman with a startling resemblance to the Sphinx is Major Gayer-Anderson himself. Hours are 8:00 a.m. to 4:00 p.m. The house is closed from 11:15 a.m. to 1:30 p.m. Fridays. Admission is 1 pound ($0.39). After visiting the mosque and museum, you can explore the old town area before heading to dinner.

▲▲ **Mosque and School of Sultan Hassan**—From the Gayer-Anderson Museum, turn east to Sharia Saliba Street and Salah el-Din Square. At the junction of Citadel Road, you'll see this fourteenth-century landmark, one of the finest examples of Islamic architecture in the Middle East. Built for Sultan Hassan en-Nasir, the mosque/school consists of four halls built around an open courtyard paved with blue and gray mosaic. Kufic scripts decorate the walls of the southern hall, and the dome is inlaid with marble as well as carved and gilded woodwork. The sultan, who took the throne at age 13, was murdered in 1361 while the mosque was being built. He is buried in the mausoleum located directly behind the prayer hall. At the back of the mausoleum, you'll find an excellent view of your next destinations.

▲▲▲ **Citadel and Mohammed Ali Mosque**—In 1176, Saladin began building this medieval fortress with stone taken from the small Giza pyramids. Little of the original Citadel remains, because the Ottomans made over this landmark in their own image while occupying Egypt. After Mohammed Ali conquered this site in the early nineteenth century, he began this Byzantine-style mosque, a domed complex with soaring minarets. Known as the Alabaster Mosque, it is one of the city's grandest religious monuments. Completed by Mohammed's successor, the mosque includes a clock tower donated by France's King Louis Philippe. Be sure to enjoy the panoramic view of Cairo from the mosque's west corner. Admission to the Citadel and the mosque is 2 pounds ($0.78).

Nightlife

Our first choice is the Sound and Light Show at the Pyramids/ Sphinx. This hour-long performance, staged twice nightly, runs 20 pounds ($10). Confirm show time and purchase your tickets at the hotel. Then catch a taxi to the performance and ask the driver to pick you up afterward for your return trip. Expect to pay about 5 pounds ($2) an hour for his services.

For entertainment, try the **Siag Pyramids Night Club**. The doors open at 8:30 p.m., and the Hassan Afifi folk dancers are featured in the show beginning at 10:30 p.m. (tel. 856022). You might also enjoy the Reda Folklore Troupe, which performs from October to March at the **Balloon Theater** in the Agouzia district on Sharia el-Nil (tel. 811718).

CAIRO SIGHTSEEING

Home of the vast King Tut collection, the Egyptian Museum should be visited early today to beat the crowds. From here, you'll proceed to the City of the Dead, the ancient necropolis that includes several of Egypt's best-known mausoleums. There will also be time to shop at Cairo's time-honored answer to K Mart, the 12,000-stall Khan el-Khalili bazaar. After dinner, travel out to Giza for a romantic nighttime look at the Pyramids.

Suggested Schedule	
9:00 a.m.	Egyptian Museum.
12:30 p.m.	Lunch.
2:00 p.m.	City of the Dead.
3:30 p.m.	Khan el-Khalili bazaar.
Evening	Pyramids Sound and Light Show.

Sightseeing Highlights

▲▲▲ **Egyptian Museum**—A taxi will take you to this museum spread out across several buildings on the northwest side of Midan el-Tahrir (Liberation) Square. The museum is open 9:00 a.m. to 4:00 p.m. daily except Friday, when it is open 9:00 to 11:00 a.m. and 1:00 to 4:00 p.m. Admission is 3 pounds ($1.40). Confirm the hours by calling 754310, and arrive when the door opens to avoid the crowds that descend on this spectacular collection each day.

In the 1970s, many Americans flocked to see the touring King Tut exhibit at museums across our country. That impressive show displayed only a small portion of the treasures to be seen here. We suggest taking in some of the highlights this morning and then returning on Day 14 if you'd like to follow up. The world's finest museum of Egyptian archaeology, this 250,000-piece collection spans 5,000 years of Egyptian history. We suggest beginning in room 48, the rotunda, and then proceeding clockwise around the first floor. Here are some of the highlights you won't want to miss:

Akhnaton colossal statues and El Amarna period objects (room 3) are musts because of their historical and artistic importance. In room 24, you'll see statues of gods and pharaohs, including King Taharqa. You'll also want to see the wood statue of village headman Sheikh el Balad (room 42), the alabaster head of King Mycerinus (room 36), and the statues of Tuthmosis III, Amenophis III, and the God Khons (room 12).

The second floor is nirvana for Tut buffs. Considered Egypt's greatest collection of funerary objects, Tut dominates galleries on this level. The treasures of Tutankhamen discovered by Howard Carter in the Valley of the Kings are spread across rooms 4, 7-10, 15, 20, 25, 30, 35, 40, and 45. Rooms 7, 8, and 9 feature the gold-leaf shrines from Tutankhamen's tomb. In room 10, you'll see photographs of Tut's tomb at the time of its discovery by Carter. Also in this room are the king's beds adorned with gilded hippo, crocodile, and lion figures. Rooms 7 and 8 have superb wooden shrines decorated with stucco figures of the gods that enclosed the Tut sarcophagus. Room 4 has Tut's famous gold mask, his coffins, jewelry, gold sandals, and scepters.

Also on the second floor: room 3 displays gold jewelry through the ages, including bracelets from King Djer's tomb, a golden falcon's head, and Queen Ahhotep's treasures; room 2 features Queen Hetpheres' furniture and funerary pieces. Her son, Cheops (the Great Pyramid you'll see tonight was built for him), moved these pieces to Giza after her tomb was raided; room 53 has animal mummies.

▲▲ **City of the Dead**—Take a taxi to this necropolis that begins on the southeast side of the the Citadel. Even better, ask your hotel to arrange a guide to show you some of the Islamic tombs here. From the Citadel, follow Sharia Salah Salem Road northeast to the main entrance. Your first stop, the fifteenth-century Mausoleum of Barquq, is easily identified by the two domes and a pair of minarets on top. The northern minaret offers an excellent overview of the City of the Dead. A marble pulpit is a highlight of the sultan's resting place. Above the mausoleum is a Dervish monastery. One block southeast of Barquq is Bars Bey, another fifteenth-century tomb. Inside this domed monument, you'll want to see a prayer niche ornamented with fine mosaics and stained glass. A few blocks south of Bars Bey is the Mausoleum of Qait Bey. Renovated in 1898, this fifteenth-century tomb is a Cairo landmark depicted on one-pound notes. Decorated with carved floral patterns, minarets, marble mosaics, and striped walls, Qait Bey's dome is exceptional even by Egyptian standards. Climb to the roof and you'll enjoy a great view of Cairo.

▲▲▲ **Khan el-Khalil**—With more than 12,000 shops, this labyrinth of alleyways and courtyards is your introduction to Egyptian mercantilism. Here you'll find gold and silver jewelry, copper, wooden art, textiles, and needlework. Founded in the fourteenth century, the bazaar is divided into districts specializing in such products as textiles, spice, copper, leather, and other goods. Most shops open by 10:00 a.m. and don't close until 10:00 p.m. The entire district shuts down on Sunday, and many shops close for prayer at noon Friday. Before bargaining for objects, it makes sense to compare prices. Leave yourself plenty of bargaining room by offering no more than half the price you're initially quoted. You'll be surprised how walking away from a shop persuades the owner to come down in price. Jewelry, semiprecious stones, and papyrus drawings all make excellent gifts. In this marketplace, you'll also see ivory items offered for sale. We urge you to follow the advice of numerous conservation groups and not purchase elephant products. Undocumented import of ivory products may also give you problems at customs at the end of your trip.

▲▲▲ **Sound and Light Show**—You'll want to check the schedules at your hotel for this one-hour performance at the Pyramids and then arrange for a taxi to take you to the Giza Plateau. Be sure to ask the driver to wait for you after the show. If you don't want to return to Cairo after the performance, you may want to spend the night at the Mena House-Oberoi adjacent to the Pyramids. That way, you'll be able to easily enjoy sunrise on the Giza Plateau. See the hotel section for additional details.

CAIRO: THE GREAT PYRAMIDS

Today, you'll see the only one of the Seven Wonders of the World that still stands, the Great Pyramids of the Giza Plateau. In addition to offering you the opportunity to explore inside at least one of these tombs, this world-famous site embraces the Sphinx and the Solar Boat, one of the great archaeological finds of modern Egypt. The story behind the boat's discovery rivals the best fantasies of Indiana Jones. In the afternoon, you'll have a chance to visit one of the best craft centers in the Middle East.

Suggested Schedule

7:00a.m.	Depart for the Giza Plateau.
8:00 a.m.	Cheops Pyramid.
9:30 a.m.	Solar Boat/Museum.
10:30 a.m.	Chephren Pyramid.
11:30 a.m.	Cheops Pyramid.
12:30 p.m.	Lunch at Mena House-Oberoi.
1:30 p.m.	Pyramid of Mycerinus.
3:30 p.m.	Visit to craft center of Harrania.
Balance of afternoon and evening at leisure.	

Sightseeing Highlights
▲▲▲ **The Pyramids**—The best time to begin a visit to the Pyramids is dawn. If you're not staying across the street at the Mena House-Oberoi, catch a taxi from your hotel to the Giza Plateau nine miles west of Cairo. Built 45 centuries ago, the three pyramids and smaller tombs are understandably popular with tourists. An early start will put you ahead of the tour buses and offer a chance to explore the Giza monuments without standing in lines. Take an hour before the pyramid inner sanctums, tombs, and temples open at 8:00 a.m. to explore the plateau. Then pick up one of the great bargains in the world of tourism—a 3 pound ($1.20) admission ticket—and begin your visit. You can set a leisurely pace because the doors don't close until 4:30 p.m.

▲▲▲ **Pyramid of Cheops**—Built from more than 2 million blocks of limestone for this powerful pharaoh. An oppressed work force estimated at 100,000 built this 480-foot-high monument. You can explore the pyramid's tomb chamber via a long passageway. During your visit, you may see some visitors climbing the pyramid's exterior. Don't follow their example. They are

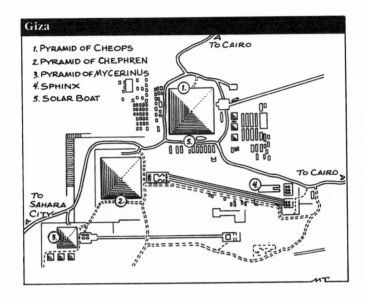

Giza

1. PYRAMID OF CHEOPS
2. PYRAMID OF CHEPHREN
3. PYRAMID OF MYCERINUS
4. SPHINX
5. SOLAR BOAT

TO CAIRO

TO CAIRO

TO SAHARA CITY

breaking the law and risking their necks. Three smaller pyramids located on the east side were built for the pharaoh's queens and daughters. Also worth a stop is the royal cemetery on the west side.

▲▲▲ **Solar Boat and Museum**—In the 1950s, a young Cairo employee of the government's Antiquities Service, Kamal el-Mallakh, heard a story that a boat had been used to bring the pharaoh's remains from the capital at Memphis to Giza. After learning that the southern portion of the boundary wall was nearer the Great Pyramid than the north or west walls, he theorized that it was covering something up. Initial excavation proved promising, but the Antiquities Service was skeptical. Finally, in May 1954, after a nationalist revolt died down and Gamal Abdel-Nasser had replaced King Farouk, the government office decided to let Mallakh open up a portion of the pyramid foundation. Some senior members of the Antiquities Service laughed at Mallakh's "dig we must" enthusiasm, until one day he found a 4,600-year-old piece of Lebanese cedar. Like John Sutter hitting gold in California's American River, the crews paused to rejoice and then continued digging. Soon they found the intact solar boat encased in limestone. The vessel was in excellent condition. The 143-foot-long wooden vessel was meticulously reassembled right down to the oars and ropes.

You can visit this exhibit and related displays in the museum behind the Cheops Pyramid.

▲▲ **Chephren Pyramid**—Built for the son of Cheops, this pyramid is slightly smaller than his father's tomb. But because it has a higher base, it looms larger. The interior of this tomb is less impressive than the Cheops Pyramid. The pyramid's interior was first explored in 1881 by Giovanni Belzoni. Unfortunately, the burial chamber he discovered has been defaced with graffiti.

▲▲▲ **Sphinx**—While building his pyramid, King Chephren's crews found their right-of-way blocked by a big limestone rock. Their first instinct was to move it out of the way. But the pharaoh had a better idea. He brought in sculptors and had them create a recumbent man/lion figure immortalizing his own face. Like the Mona Lisa, this enigmatic sphinx has become one of mankind's best-known images. Today he appears to be a sentry guarding the entire Giza Plateau. Although several groups of invaders couldn't resist the temptation to give the Sphinx a nose job, he has aged well and continues to hold his head high.

▲▲ **Pyramid of Mycerinus**—The third Pharaonic generation is represented here by the tomb of Chephren's son, a pyramid half the height of the Cheops and Chephren. Reaching the interior is an ordeal. To the rear are three unfinished pyramids built for the pharaoh's queens.

▲ **Harrania**—Located just 20 miles south of Giza, Harrania is famous for its museum-quality pottery, textiles, woven crafts, and rugs. Many excellent shops with first-class handicrafts are found in this community. If you're looking for rugs, be sure to have your driver or a taxi take you here.

CAIRO: CITY OF FAITH

On your final day in Cairo, visit museums and synagogues that embrace the story of the region's three great religions. Although not as large or famous as the Egyptian Museum, the Islamic and Coptic museums display superb collections of art, artifacts, monastery doors, and Nubian frescoes. The Synagogue of Ben Ezra is one of the few buildings in the world that has served both Christian and Jewish congregations. You'll also have a chance to leisurely explore the city, revisit your favorites, and sample other sights before preparing to continue to Greece.

Suggested Schedule

9:00 a.m.	Islamic Museum.
11:00 a.m.	Coptic Museum.
12:00 noon	Lunch.
1:00 p.m.	Synagogue of Ben Ezra.
Balance of afternoon and evening at leisure.	

Sightseeing Highlights
▲▲ **Islamic Museum**—Perhaps the world's finest collection of Islamic art, this museum on Ahmed Maher Square provides a wonderful introduction to classic prayer rugs, illuminated manuscripts, stained glass, ceramics, mosque lamps, and many other treasures. We don't see how any visitor to Cairo can pass up a visit to this Moorish building with its russet and off-white stripes. Formerly the National Library, this nineteenth-century structure is divided into 23 exhibition rooms that trace the evolution of Islamic art. Don't miss the stained-glass windows and mosaic fountain in room 5. You'll also want to see the Persian miniatures upstairs in the Egyptian Library. Open 9:00 a.m. to 4:00 p.m., the museum is closed Friday from 11:15 a.m. to 1:30 p.m. Admission costs 2 pounds ($0.78).

▲ **Coptic Museum**—Descendants of the first Christians, the Copts ruled Egypt from A.D. 300 until the Arab conquest in A.D. 641. Christian art flourished during this relatively brief period in Egyptian history, and many remarkable examples of Coptic art are found in this museum. Rare collections dating back to the first century A.D. are found in this Old Cairo building on Mari Girgis Street. The story of this Christian interlude in Egypt's Islamic history is beautifully told through this museum set around a lovely garden. Limestone choir screens, Nubian frescoes, textiles, weaving, manuscripts, and tombstones are just a few of the rare objects on display here. Beautiful Coptic fabrics, frescoes, monastery doors, jewelry, candelabra, and bronze oil lamps are also on display. The museum is open 9:00 a.m. to 4:00 p.m. daily except on Friday, when it closes from 11:00 a.m. to 1:00 p.m. Admission is 2 pounds ($0.78). The guards can direct you to the Church of St. Sergius around the corner and the Church of St. Barbara a short walk from the museum.

▲ **Synagogue of Ben Ezra**—Go left coming out of St. Barbara's, pass the next intersection, and turn in the gate to this Jewish temple built on the site of Cairo's first synagogue. Originally a church, this building was renovated into a Jewish sanctuary in the twelfth century. Once it was the hub of the city's Jewish community. Although most of their descendants now live in another modern neighborhood, this temple remains an important landmark.

Option: Luxor-Aswan Nile Cruise

This is the best way to see life on the Nile as it was centuries ago. Many companies offer extended cruises down the Nile. The typical four-night, five-day itinerary stops at many of the important landmarks and is a relaxing and informative way to tour this region. With the boat as your hotel, you can focus on seeing Luxor treasures like the Karnak Temple, seat of Amun, the imperial god. The Karnak Temple also contains the obelisks of Queen Hatshepsut and statues of Tuthmosis I.

On Luxor's west bank, you'll see the Valley of the Kings—the tombs where the pharaohs buried their offerings to the gods—and ancient wall paintings. In this area, you'll also descend to the tombs of Seti I, Ramses VI, and Tut. Other cruise highlights include the Colossi of Memnon and the temple of Deir el Bahri. A short one-hour drive from Luxor takes you to the superb temples of Abydos and Dendera. With a taxi, you can easily arrange to see them both on your own. Your tour will end in Aswan, home of the world's largest rock-fill dam. While in this area, you'll see Philae, the Temple of Isis, goddess of the Nile. If you'd like, your cruise line can arrange for you to take a short side trip on the Nile by traditional *felucca* (a small sailing vessel picked up anywhere along the shore).

The Nile cruises can also be extended with a one-day side trip to Abu Simbel, where you'll see the Ramses II Great Temple and the smaller Queen Nefertari temple. Many of the hotels as well as Naggar Tours, Club Med, and Abercrombie and Kent operate the top five-star-rated boats. A complete list is available from the Egyptian Tourist Authority. Depending on the operator and the length of your cruise, expect to pay about $80 to $325 per

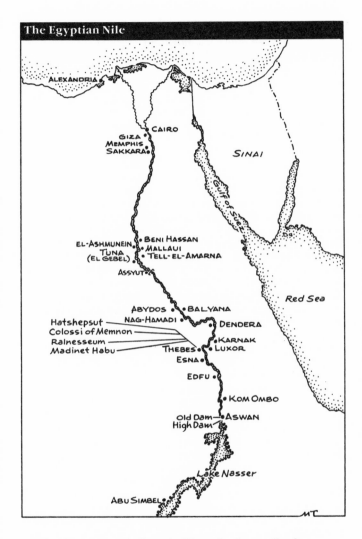

The Egyptian Nile

day for the cruise and all meals. We prefer the smaller five-star boats carrying less than 50 people, because they don't take as long to load and unload at the various stops along the way. But the larger five-star ships often have more amenities such as swimming pools and elaborate buffets. It is crucial to book your Nile cruise as far in advance as possible, particularly during the winter months. You can take the cruise in either direction, from

Luxor to Aswan or from Aswan to Luxor. In either case, you'll
reach the ship and return to Cairo by air.

Alternatively, train buffs looking for an adventure can connect to the Nile boats in Luxor via an overnight 12-hour trip
from Cairo. Delays are not unusual on this train, which will give
you another perspective on the river. You'll ride in a sleeper and
share the bath. If you don't have time for a Nile cruise, consider
taking a $20 felucca ride on the river in the Cairo area. Your
hotel can make arrangements. Although we do not recommend
biking in Cairo, it is practical in less-congested Luxor. The rental
price is right, just $1 a day. Your hotel front desk can help you
arrange a bike rental. Begin with the pleasant two-mile ride to
the Karnak Temple.

If you'd like to spend more time in Luxor, we recommend
two hotels. **The Winter Palace**, located on a small lane off
Sharia Nefertiti (tel. 82222), is a nineteenth-century classic with
rooms running about 200 pounds ($80) per night. The less
expensive Savoy, on El-Nil Street (tel. 82200), charges 68 to 100
pounds ($27 to $39). In Aswan, the **Pullman Cataract** on Abtal
el-Tahrir Street (tel. 23510) offers rooms from 145 to 175 pounds
($57 to $69). The garden rooms are less expensive.

CAIRO TO ATHENS

Today you depart Egypt for Greece. No trip around the world could be complete without visiting a Mediterranean country, and Greece is our favorite choice. It is a land known for its ancient ruins, sun-drenched islands, brilliant light, and endless vistas of blue sea. Watching the sunrise from an Aegéan island is an experience unmatched almost anywhere else on earth, and there is no more perfect island from which to do this than Santorini. On this volcanic island, you will wander through ancient white-washed villages perched atop vertical cliffs that plunge into the sea, swim in quiet coves, and sail through a volcano's crater.

But first, you must pass through Athens, a city abounding in history but suffering from unchecked modern development. It is still possible, however, to sip a cup of Turkish coffee or a glass of ouzo in an outdoor café in the Plaka (Old City Center) and gaze quietly on the 2,500-year-old Parthenon. In the evening, the *volta* (promenade) is a national pastime; teenagers, families, and black-attired widows amble happily through the streets at night in a city with the lowest crime rate in the West.

Suggested Schedule

Early a.m.	Depart for Athens.
8:00 a.m.	Arrive at Athens.
9:00 a.m.	Check into your hotel.
10:30 a.m.	Walk through the Plaka (Old City Center).
1:00 p.m.	Outdoor lunch in the Plaka.
2:00 p.m.	National Archaeological Museum.
4:00 p.m.	Acropolis walking tour.
8:00 p.m.	Dinner.
	Evening at leisure.

Athens
Few cities have had as much influence on Western thought and civilization as Athens. As the "birthplace of democracy," the city-state of Athens achieved glorious accomplishments in architecture, sculpture, philosophy, mathematics, drama, poetry, and government. Although Athens sprawls across the plain to the sea, most of the ancient monuments cluster around the Acropolis. This makes sightseeing relatively easy, and it is possible to see much of Athens on foot in just a few hours, sav-

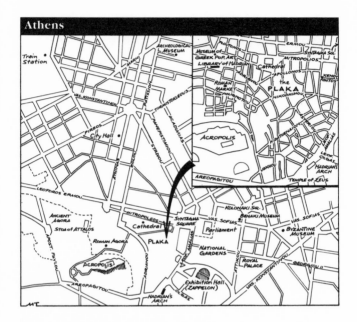

ing a side trip to the National Archaeological Museum for an inexpensive taxi ride.

Arrival

Your flight from Cairo to Athens takes less than two hours, and you'll arrive at the Athens International Terminal just six miles from the heart of the city. (Note: the domestic airport, across the runway, will be your departure point for Santorini tomorrow morning.) You will need small-note drachmas for the taxi to your hotel, so exchange money at the bank as you deplane. For a quick mental conversion from drachmas to dollars, multiply the drachmas by 6 and then move the decimal point three places to the left. For example, 1,000 drachmas equals $6. Greek customs and immigration are efficient; they want you to be on your way as quickly as possible. Just outside the terminal, across the street, is the taxi kiosk. There are always plenty of taxis, and though the line may look long, it moves quickly. Taxis are metered, and drivers are generally very honest. The ride to your hotel will be inexpensive, less than 850 drachmas ($5) including a 15 to 20 percent gratuity.

After you have unpacked, stretch your legs and explore the area immediately around your hotel. Syntagma (Constitution) Square is a busy plaza bordered on the east side by the former royal palace, now the Parliament House. It is easy to locate because of its rose-tinted ocher plaster. On the north stands the large, neoclassical Hotel Grand Bretagne. Airline and tourist offices are located here, as well as numerous outdoor cafés, restaurants, and taxi and bus stands. Enjoy a late morning coffee or tea at any of the cafés in Syntagma Square or on quiet side streets in the Plaka. You'll then be ready to explore the highlights of the National Archaeological Museum before your afternoon visit to the Acropolis.

Helpful Hints
The Greeks are very hospitable and friendly; they respond positively to the slightest effort to speak their language. Learning to say "good morning" (kal-i-MER-a), "good afternoon" (kal-e-SPER-a), "thank you" (ef-are-ese-TOE), or "please" (para-ka-LO) will bring an immediate smiling response. The Greek alphabet is used nearly everywhere and adds to the exotic flavor of Athens, but menus are written in English as well as Greek. Street signs and numbers are in English, and rest rooms use pictures rather than words. Nearly every hotel, restaurant, or café has someone who speaks English.

Lodging
If you plan to be in Greece between May and October, we recommend that you telephone for a room reservation as soon as possible, as written responses can take months. Dial directly by accessing Europe (011), then the country code (30), and city code (1), followed by the number. All the hotels we recommend have English-speaking staff to confirm your room. The city code for Santorini is 286 and for Samos is 273.

For a short stay in Athens, you will want to be near the Plaka, so that you can walk to most of the major sites. Within a fifteen-minute walk of the Plaka can be found distinguished luxury hotels and pleasant budget accommodations. Rates quoted are high season (May-September) and may be 20 to 30 percent less at other times of the year. Some hotels add a 10 percent one-night stay surcharge to cover the cost of changing linen.

The **Grand Bretagne** at One Constitution Square (better known by its Greek name "Syntagma") is a favorite because of its grand, Old World style and gracious service (tel. 323-0251, Fax 322-8034). Built in 1862 and refurbished in 1981, it is one of the few remaining examples in Athens of nineteenth-century neoclassical architecture. Top-floor rooms, including the dining room, have views of the Acropolis. It is only a ten-minute walk from the Grand Bretagne to the Plaka. Double rooms start at 28,000 drachmas ($160).

The **Elektra Palace Hotel** at 16 Nicodimou Street (tel. 324-1401) is a very comfortable, moderately priced hotel on the edge of the Plaka. Each top-floor room has a private balcony facing the Acropolis, but they can be noisy at night during the summer months. If you opt for the quiet rooms facing the back basket-ball court (playing stops before dinner), you need not give up the view. On the roof of the Elektra Palace, you'll find a garden with a swimming pool, a bar, and a view of the Acropolis. It is worth staying here for the sunsets alone. All rooms are air-conditioned and 13,700 drachmas ($80) for two. (There are two Elektra Palace hotels. Make sure the driver knows you are going to the one in the Plaka.)

A little farther into the Plaka and a little less expensive is the new and modern **Hermes Hotel** at 19 Apollonos (tel. 323-5514). All the small rooms have private showers and toilets, and nearly all are air-conditioned. Doubles are 9,800 drachmas ($58) without air-conditioning to 10,800 drachmas ($63) with air-conditioning. Our favorite budget hotel inside the Plaka is the charming **Hotel Nefeli** at 16A Agios Hatsimihali (tel. 322-9044). Rooms are small but faultlessly clean, and a continental breakfast is served in the lounge. Bed and breakfast for two is 6,300 drachmas ($37).

Outside the Plaka, just beyond Syntagma Square in fashionable Kolonaki, is the **Athenian Inn**, 22 Haritos Street, Kolonaki (tel. 723-9552). The staff speaks fluent English and is very helpful. The 6,170 drachmas ($36) nightly rate for two includes fresh fruit and cereals in addition to the usual toast, jams, and coffee.

Food

From May until mid-October, the most popular way to dine is outdoors in a garden taverna or at tables along the sidewalk of a narrow street in the Plaka. If you are in an adventurous mood, try the traditional aperitif ouzo, a strong spirit with an aniseed flavor. It is acceptable to add water to make it less strong. With your ouzo, try some typical Greek appetizers: *taramasalata* (a delicious preparation of fish roe), *tzadziki* (cucumber with yogurt and garlic), or *dolmades* (grape leaves stuffed with rice and nuts).

At most tavernas, it is the custom to go into the kitchen to greet the cook and see what you wish to order. Traditional favorites include *keftedakia* (small spicy meat balls), *lemonato* (veal in light lemon sauce), *moussaka* (a layered pastry with aubergine, chopped meat, cheese, and spices) and tomatoes or peppers stuffed with rice and ground meat. As there is little marine life left in the Mediterranean, fish is very expensive. But Greek "peasant salads" are rarely more than 500 drachmas ($3).

Cucumbers, tomatoes, and onions are sliced only after you've ordered; then feta cheese, olives, and oregano are added to complete the very fresh meal. At your table you add olive oil and vinegar to suit your taste. Nearly every taverna restaurant in Athens also serves spaghetti and pizza.

Our favorite restaurant in the Plaka is **Tavern Xinos**, located on a quiet lane off Angelou Geronta Street, off Iperidou Street. (You'll need dinner reservations in the high season, tel. 322-1065.) You'll see Greek families dining here next to tourists from every nation. The Greeks know this is one of the best restaurants in the Plaka for excellent cuisine at very moderate prices.

Eden is a vegetarian restaurant in a renovated villa at 3 Flessa Street (tel. 324-8858), open from noon to midnight. One can eat well here for 850 to 1,200 drachmas ($5-$7).

The **DeProfundis Tea Room 850** (tel. 721-4959) at 1 Hatzimichali is a very tastefully decorated café owned by a French-speaking Greek couple who have lovingly restored an old mansion. Natural juices, herbal teas, imported coffees, and a liquor bar are available as well as spinach and cheese pies.

Gerofinikas at 10 Pindarou Street (tel. 363-6710) is in the fashionable Kolonaki area and has an elegant atmosphere. Reservations are required in summer as the chef prepares only a limited number of dishes.

Sightseeing Highlights
▲▲ Plaka (Old City Center)—On the northern slopes of the Acropolis, medieval Athens still survives in the narrow streets and alleys opening out into tiny squares and terraces. Conservation of old buildings and the exclusion of traffic make this an ideal area for walking.

Syntagma Square is a good place to begin. Start with your back to the Public Gardens on the east side of Syntagma and the Grand Bretagne Hotel on your right; Mitropoleos Street with its airline offices will be on your left. Walk straight ahead on Mitropoleos for five minutes until you reach Platia Mitropoleos. In this square, the New Metropolitan Orthodox cathedral (eighteenth-century) dwarfs its neighbor, the marvelous Old Metropolitan.

▲▲ The Old Metropolitan—Dedicated to the Virgin who answers prayers swiftly, this is a charming twelfth-century Byzantine church built on the Greek cross plan with a dome. Incorporated in the external walls are many decorative pieces from an earlier age; between the Corinthian capitals flanking the facade stretches an unusual ancient frieze (fourth century B.C.) showing the months and signs of the Zodiac together with their corresponding festivals or activities. There are also several tenth-century A.D. low reliefs of Christian motifs: peacocks drinking at the source of eternal life, griffins feeding on holy grapes, and lions flanking a cross. To leave the square, face the Acropolis and take the streets going south and west, Odos Paleologou Venizelou, Odos Erehtheos, and Odos Kristou, to reach Tower of the Winds.

▲ **Tower of the Winds**—This 42-foot-high octagonal building of white marble dates from the reign of Julius Caesar (first century B.C.) It takes its name from the eight winged figures carved on the eight faces of the tower, representing the winds that blow in Athens. The tower was built to house a hydraulic clock invented in Syria or Macedonia. The water supply came from a spring on the north slope of the Acropolis Hill. The semicircular tower attached to the south face was the reservoir from which the water flowed in a steady stream into a cylinder in the main tower. The time was indicated by the water level in the cylinder, and the northwest tower door stood open so that people could consult the clock. In the sixth century, the Tower of the Winds was converted into a chapel, and under Turkish rule, it became a Muslim convent. Open 8:00 a.m. to 3:00 p.m., admission 200 drachmas.

The streets here are narrow. Turn into less-visited alleys. If it is warm, doors and windows will be open and you will get glimpses of Greek home life that most visitors never see.

You can retrace your steps back to Syntagma or return via Odos Pandrossou, a narrow street thronged with busy crowds. It resembles a market, with awnings and pavement stalls where the proprietors stand enticing the pedestrians to buy their Turkish slippers, gold and copper work, carpets and embroidery, belts, religious articles, and ceramics. Odos Pandrossou ends in Monasteraki Square, a lively area with open-air stalls selling souvenir items of every description.

If you get lost, all roads head north back to Ermou Street (with the Acropolis behind you to the south). Turn right on Ermou Street and head back to Syntagma.

▲▲▲ **The National Archaeological Museum**—Located at 1 Tossitsa Street (tel. 821-7717), the museum is open from 8:00 a.m. to 7:00 p.m. (Sunday until 6:00 p.m.), closed Mondays. It is a short taxi ride from any of our recommended hotels or a #1 or #3 trolley ride from Syntagma Square. Admission is 500 drachmas ($3).

The museum has one of the most extensive collections of antiquities in the world. You could easily spend days here, but an overview of the highlights is possible in an hour or two; it will be the perfect introduction to your afternoon walk and the trip tomorrow to Santorini.

Room 4, the Mycenaean Room, includes gold jewelry, artifacts, and masks from the chamber tombs discovered by Schliemann. The famous "Mask of Agamemnon" brings to life Homer's words from the Iliad: "He was the King of Men . . . distinguished amongst many and outstanding amongst heroes."

Room 6, the Cycladic Room, contains marble figurines from 3000 B.C.

Rooms 7-11 contain archaic sculpture that once filled the great temples. Room 40, the New Bronze Room, contains the Marathon Boy, a bronze Hermes from the school of Praxiteles, found in 1926 off the coast of Marathon. His eyes are limestone with pupils of glass; his nipples were inlaid with copper. Room 48 (top of stairs) is the Fresco (Thera) Gallery, which displays the marvelous reconstructed frescoes found in the 1970s on the island of Santorini. The magnificent, undamaged frescoes are a valuable source of information about life on the island before the volcanic eruption of 1600 B.C. Various aspects of Cycladic civilization depicted are two boys engaged in fisticuffs, a fisherman with his catch, antelopes, young women, and a naval expedition. The ceramics reflect the influence of Minoan Crete and yet are highly original. A graceful pitcher with a spout in the shape of a bird's beak is marvelous.

The museum gift shop has an excellent collection of items for sale.

▲▲ **Museum of Cycladic and Ancient Greek Art**—If you are in Athens on a Monday, when the National Archaeological Museum is closed, this is another museum well worth visiting which is open that day. It is located above the National Gardens at 4 Neophyou Douka Street off Vass. Sophias Street. Open 10:00 a.m. to 4:00 p.m., Saturday until 1:00 p.m., closed Thursday and Sunday, tel. 72-28-321. Admission is 350 drachmas ($2).

Housed in a simple, elegant building, this new museum (1986) traces the development of Greek art over a period of 5,000 years. On the first floor, you will see 230 objects produced by the Cycladic island civilization (3000-2000 B.C.) that traded with mainland communities: marble and pottery vessels, some with herringbone decoration, and a collection of Cycladic marble idols with folded arms and lyre- or almond-shaped heads where only the nose was in relief, the other features being painted. These figurines are remarkable for their austere contemporary style and clarity of line.

On the second floor is a fine collection of vases with red and black figure decorations, household bronze vessels, and gold

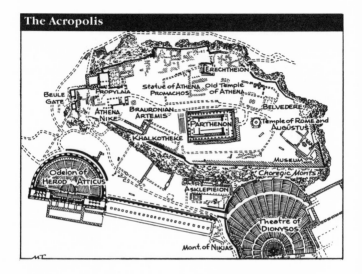

The Acropolis

and bronze jewelry. Note the bell krater (430 B.C.) showing a girl flautist and two male dancers.

▲▲▲ **Acropolis**—The artistic climax of Greek architecture, the Acropolis (meaning the upper town) stands on the summit of a steep rock platform covering an area just less than ten acres. The principal buildings—the Temple of Athena Nike, the Erechtheion, and the Parthenon—are all in white marble and belong to the Age of Pericles (fifth century B.C.). These unmatched examples of ancient architecture constitute our most tangible relic of the epoch that history has come to call the Golden Age. For over 200 years, this was the center of the civilized world. Plato, Aristotle, Sophocles, Euripides, and Aristophanes walked among these pillars and down these steps.

The #16 bus from Syntagma stops near the main entrance. From the Plaka, a path winds up to the north side of the hill. Open 7:30 a.m. to 7:30 p.m. (8:00 a.m. to 5:30 p.m. in winter), admission 400 drachmas ($2.40).

▲▲▲ **The Parthenon**—It is a miracle that this temple to honor the goddess Athena has survived. An immense gold and ivory statute of Athena that adorned the sanctuary was carried off to Constantinople in the Byzantine period and destroyed by the inhabitants in 1203, when the city was besieged by the Crusaders. For eight centuries, the Parthenon served as a church until plundered by the Franks.

The Turks converted the Parthenon into a mosque and built a minaret in the southwest corner and houses among the monuments. An explosion in 1687 destroyed the marble roof slabs and 28 columns, and, in 1801, Lord Elgin of Britain received permission from the Sultan (Greece was under Turkish rule until 1823) to remove marble statuary of his choice, which is now in the British Museum.

Neither the crane (here for restoration until the end of the century) nor the crowds can detract from the beauty of this ancient site. The Parthenon does not contain a single straight line of any length. Every one of its lines is subtly tapered to optically correct a straight line (which would otherwise recede or advance in viewing) into a graceful and slender perspective. There are curves everywhere. Stoop down to ground level and you will see a bulge in the center of the step! Each piece of this building was carefully ground and chiseled and polished to make a perfect fit with the preceding piece. No mortar or cement of any kind was used. Walk around the site; each viewpoint is different and equally astonishing.

▲▲▲ **Erechtheion**—This little temple, dedicated to Erechtheus, a mythical king, was completed in 407 B.C. It is unusual because of the sloping ground and because several existing shrines had to be incorporated in it. The most important of them were the shrines of Athena, Poseidon, and Erechtheus. The Porch of the Caryatids, on the southern portico facing the Parthenon, is supported by six statues of young women. Their garments are in vertical parallel folds that resemble the fluting columns they replace. One of the original statues was taken by Lord Elgin and ultimately sold to the British Museum, while the remaining five are in the Acropolis Museum just a few minutes walk away.

▲▲▲ **Acropolis Museum**—Skillfully recessed in a hollow in the rock, the Acropolis Museum contains the sculptures and other objects found during the excavation of the Acropolis. Room 5 contains four statues from the old Temple of Athena (c. 525 B.C.) and near the entrance to room 6 is the justifiably famous Mourning Athena, a fifth-century B.C. votive relief. Room 7 is devoted to reconstructions of the Parthenon pediments, room 8 contains sculptures removed from the temples (especially noteworthy is the figure of Nike undoing her sandal), and in the last room, the caryatids from the Erechtheion are displayed behind glass. On leaving the museum, walk along the southern edge of the Acropolis for a view of the theatres of Dionysos and Herod Atticus.

▲▲ **Temple of Athena Nike (Temple of Victory)**—Standing on a projecting bastion overlooking the Sacred Way, it is closed to the public, but there are a few original pieces of the exterior frieze on the east and south sides.

ATHENS TO SANTORINI

Today you will visit Santorini, the most spectacular island in Greece. Although cruise ships visit daily from May through October, and tourists crowd the capital, Thera Town, you will be visiting Ia, a village so quiet and peaceful that time seems to have stood still for over 2,000 years. You may swim in a hidden cove and dine on a quiet side street in Ia, where the bright night sky will be your entertainment. You will sleep well knowing that the magic of a Greek dawn is not far away.

Suggested Schedule

9:00 a.m.	Early departure from Athens Domestic Airport.
10:00 a.m.	Taxi from the airport to the village perched high above.
10:30 a.m.	Check into your Thera Town hotel.
11:00 a.m.	Visit Ia (pronounced "eeya").
1:00 p.m.	Swim in a quiet cove.
2:00 p.m.	Lunch.
3:00 p.m.	Afternoon siesta, at leisure.
8:00 p.m.	Dinner.
	Evening at leisure.

Santorini
From about 2000 B.C. to 1600 B.C., one of the most advanced societies in ancient Greece flourished on the soil of this volcanic island, also called Thira. The society was influenced greatly by Minoan Crete some 60 miles to the south. But around 1500 B.C., a massive volcanic eruption blew out the center of the island, destroying civilization and creating awesome formations. In the centuries that followed, fact and fiction have mingled. Some feel Santorini is Plato's lost Atlantis; others have uncovered impressive archaeological finds in an effort to prove it.

The village of Ia is one of the most beautiful and architecturally pure in the entire Aegean, yet tourists rarely make the effort to get there. Its caves, ancient churches, and winding streets are a joy to explore. The Greek government has done a marvelous job of preserving and rebuilding the village after a 1956 earthquake. The new houses, which look almost carved out of rock, are interspersed among the ruins of the old. The tourist accommodations are small clusters of traditional houses overlooking

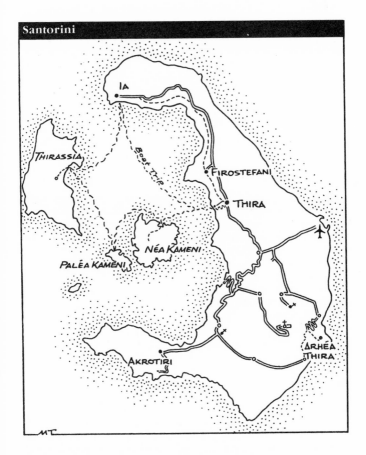

the sea; they blend perfectly with the village architecture and rocky landscape. A deep swimming lagoon awaits the intrepid hiker who makes the 30-minute trip down.

Arrival
Your flight from Athens to Santorini is a short one, approximately 30 minutes. You will land on a vast level plain near a long stretch of beach with several modern hotels. The real beauty of Santorini awaits you on the mountain rim, some 1,000 feet above the airport. Taxis meet arriving morning and late-night planes from Athens, and you will be on your way in minutes. (It is a good idea to reconfirm your return flight while you are waiting for your baggage.)

Lodging

There are no luxury hotels on Santorini, but there are some of
the most pleasant and interesting accommodations to be found
anywhere in Greece.

Hotel Atlantis, Thera Town, Santorini (tel. 22232) has the
most spectacular setting of any hotel we have seen in Greece.
Lawrence Durrell says the view from the Atlantis is "so much
the high spot of the Cycladean journey that even rhapsody is
out of place, as it must be when one is dealing with a real experience, an Event and not a mere Happening." Rooms with private verandas facing the sea are 16,280 drachmas ($97).

The **Hotel Galini**, in Firostefani, a ten-minute walk from
Thera Town (tel. 22095), is a modest 15-room white-washed
building on the cliff edge with sea views. There are two private
bungalows that rent for 10,280 drachmas ($60), but the small
rooms with private shower and toilet are 6,000 drachmas ($36).
The small budget **Fregata Hotel** in Ia (tel. 71221) will rent a
room for just one night.

Those who wish to linger for more than two nights can rent a
moderately priced villa, a tastefully restored traditional house
(living room, fully equipped kitchen, private yard with sea
view). In a village near Thera Town, the **Nefeli Villas** (Finikia-
la, Thera, Santorini, tel. 1391) are open from April to October,
while the Perivolas Villas in Ia (tel. 71308) are open from March
15 until December 15. Both run about 13,700 drachmas ($82)
per night.

Food

One of the advantages of Santorini's international popularity is
the wide variety of restaurants and good food there. At **Camille
Stefani** in Thera, you will find a sophisticated Greek-
continental menu and an excellent selection of Santorini's local
white wines. Outdoor dining on the veranda makes this an ideal
spot for lunch or dinner during the summer, but reservations
are recommended (tel. 22265). It is very difficult to get good,
fresh vegetables in Greece, but the owner of the **Galaxy Restaurant** (tel. 22717) at 25 Maritou grows all his own vegetables
and prepares delicious eggplant, tomato, and zucchini dishes.
To sample *fava*, an island specialty made from lentillike beans,
try **Nicola's** on E. Stavrou in the center of town (open daily
from noon to 12:30 a.m.). **Aresana**, on a side street between
the water and the town square, is a quiet art gallery/café with
good food. **Franco's** gets raves for snacks, pastries, coffees, and
drinks; classical music is the perfect accompaniment for the
extraordinary setting.

The **Lotza** is a good choice for lunch, but the ultimate dining experience is **Kyblos Restaurant**, built into the nearby caves and grottoes on the island's northern tip. Reserve a table with a sunset view for dinner and linger into the twilight to watch the Maxfield Parrish-colored sky. Then, when the sky has darkened and the stars appear, amble along the quiet streets to explore this Cycladic village at night.

Thera Town and Ia
Thera Town (also Thira or Fira), the island capital, perches precariously on the top of a precipitous cliff. The town (pop. 1,581) is a maze of picturesque streets, which are well worth exploring once you have seen enough boutiques and restaurants. Note especially the view from in front of the Orthodox cathedral.

The new district on the north side of town was rebuilt after the 1956 earthquake; the curved roofs are specifically designed to resist earth tremors. In the Dominican convent next to the cathedral, you will find a carpet weaving workshop open to visitors. It has an excellent store where you will be tempted to buy a small handmade rug typical of the island.

Between 11:00 a.m. and 3:00 p.m., Thera is crowded with cruise passengers and tourists up from the beach to shop. For those visitors lucky enough to be spending the night here, the early evening is a quiet, ideal time to explore the town on foot.

Ia, missed by most visitors to the island, is just six miles beyond Thera. You can walk (3 hours), but buses and taxis will give you more time to explore the village. From the northwestern end of the village, you'll get a view of the crescent shape of the island, the caldera, and the volcanoes at its center.

The new church at Imerovigli contains a beautiful screen in carved wood, the only piece rescued from the old building destroyed in the 1956 earthquake. The architecture is being carefully restored, and life moves quietly in this traditional village. Explore the side streets and enjoy lunch at any of the few Greek tavernas that may be open.

SANTORINI

"The Greek dawn puts words to flight and throws painters out of business," said Lawrence Durrell. No doubt he had Santorini in mind, because this was one of his favorite islands. The broad expanse of sea and changing light makes dawn here a unique experience. After the sunrise and a leisurely outdoor breakfast, there is only one more experience that can compare: a boat trip in the crater with lunch on the island of Thirassia. There is time for another swim or walk in the late afternoon before your last dinner in Greece.

Suggested Schedule

Early a.m.	Homage to the rising sun.
10:00 a.m.	Museum in Thera Town.
11:00 a.m.	Boat trip in the crater.
12:00 noon	Visit center of volcano.
1:00 p.m.	Boat stop at Palea Kameni.
2:00 p.m.	Lunch at beach taverna on Thirassia Island.
4:00 p.m.	Return to hotel for afternoon at leisure.
8:00 p.m.	Dinner and evening stroll.

Sightseeing Highlights
▲▲▲ **Dawn** as seen from the site of ancient Thera—The light and expanse of a Greek dawn can be enjoyed from the balcony of your hotel or from a nearby vista point. But the best location for this experience is from the ruins of ancient Thera in the southwest part of the island. Founded in the nineteenth century B.C., it was once a substantial city of 5,000 inhabitants, then declined under the Romans and was abandoned in the thirteenth century A.D. The ruins of Byzantine fortifications and chapels blend with the meager remains of what were once the Temple of Apollo, the Agora, a gymnasium, and the sacred enclosure of Artemidoros. Allow 30 minutes for the taxi ride to the saddle below the site and another 15 minutes for the walk up the path. For a nominal charge, 800 drachmas ($5), the driver will wait an hour before the return trip to your hotel. The departure and return time will depend, of course, on the time of the year.
▲▲▲ **Boat Trip in Crater**—Apply to one of the tourist agencies (a day in advance in high season) to arrange this boat excursion for about 1,200 drachmas ($7.20). Allow 20 minutes for the

walk down to the waterfront. The view of the towering cliffs from the deck of a small boat is impressive. Beneath the villages, the cliff is composed of many layers of volcanic debris laid down after successive eruptions: bands of black lava, rust-colored slag, purple gray ash, and at the top, a light-colored layer of pumice stone.

The first stop is at Nea Kameni, where you will walk for 30 minutes over the old cinders to the center of the volcano, which emits wisps of sulfurous smoke. Here you will have a panoramic view of the outline of the original Round Island. As the boat approaches the next stop in Palea Kameni, the water becomes warmer and is colored red by the soft volcanic mud of the inlet; bubbles of gas erupt on the surface of the sea. There is a lunch stop on the island of Thirassia and time for a refreshing swim before a hearty meal at the beachfront taverna. If you prefer lunch in a quiet village of white and blue houses, hire a donkey for the climb to the top of the island's cliffs, where you will find several small taverna restaurants.

▲ **Museum in Thera Town**—In this small museum, you will see the ceramics and sculptures that have been found on the island, particularly at ancient Thera. Also on display are artifacts from the excavations at the southern end of the island at Akrotiri. Open 8:45 a.m. to 3:00 p.m., 9:30 a.m. to 2:00 p.m. Sundays and holidays, closed Tuesday. Admission is 100 drachmas ($0.60).

TURKEY

Turkey, the world's most underrated country, is well worth visiting if you are traveling between March and November. The beaches and archaeological sites are some of the best in the world, and the local food is a marvelous combination of French and Middle Eastern cuisines. Forget what you've seen in the movies or read in books; the kindness and friendliness of the Turkish people will overwhelm you. The spectacular ancient city of Ephesus is just ten miles from the picturesque harbor town of Kusadasi.

Getting There
Ferry service from Piraeus (the port city of Athens) leaves at 9:00 a.m. and arrives in Samos at 9:00 p.m.

Daily Olympic Airways flights take only 50 minutes and cost $47 each way. We allow an overnight on Samos to arrange for the ferry and hotel in Turkey. There are numerous excellent travel agencies along the waterfront in Pythagorion where you can reserve the ferry (regular service March-November) and complete customs formalities. Your passport is kept overnight for a routine police check (we've never heard of one not being returned the following morning). The boat trip is 10,200 drachmas ($60) round-trip and takes approximately 2½ hours in each direction. It will seem much longer should a sudden squall appear and the boat start to rock. We've found that standing toward the bow with fresh sea air blowing in your face helps prevent seasickness, but your doctor may recommend other preventatives.

Getting Around
The Samos airport is just 2 miles (250 drachmas or $1.50 by taxi) from Pythagorion, our favorite harbor town and the starting point for the ferries to Turkey. To explore the mountain villages or the main towns of Samos, hire a taxi at about 3,000 drachmas ($18) for a 3-hour excursion. If you want the freedom to linger and explore on your own, you will find several car agencies in Pythagorion or at the airport. Driving is a pleasant experience, as there are no traffic jams. In fact, there is virtually no motor traffic once you leave Samos town.

In Kusadasi, Turkey, it is a ten-minute walk from the pier to the center of town and the exotic Karavanserai Hotel. You can easily explore Kusadasi on foot, then travel the 10 miles to Ephesus by minibus or taxi.

Lodging
On Samos, our favorite hotel is the **Samaina** in Pythagorion.
The English manager is very hospitable, and a double room
with private bath was just 4,800 drachmas ($28) in August 1989
(tel. 61024). Other choices in picturesque Pythagorion are the
Hotel Labito (tel. 61572), a two-story inn with balconies and
an inviting garden at 5,400 drachmas ($3) double, and the
Polixeni (tel. 61590). All of the rooms at the friendly Polixeni
have balconies with a view of the ports, beach, and sea and are a
very modest 4,400 drachmas ($26) for two.

In Samos town, our favorite is the **Hotel Samos** (tel. 28377)
with spotlessly clean rooms and a restored classic facade. The
rooms in the back of the hotel are quieter and have larger balconies. Expect to pay about 5,000 drachmas ($30) for two. Do not
come to Samos during the summer without a room reservation,
or you may spend the night on a park bench as a friend of ours
did two years ago. From the United States, it is easy to dial any
hotel on Samos, ask for an English-speaking person, and confirm your room. (Remember to take into account the time
difference—7 to 10 hours later than the United States).

Food
In Pythagorion, we always dine outdoors at a harborside café.
For a good view and a tasty meal, the **Samaina** is again our
favorite. Both the **Trovas** and **Athena** are good second choices
for Greek peasant cooking along the waterfront. In Samos
town, the excellent food at the **Samian Restaurant** (tel. 285) is
served beneath the shade of a large palm tree in a romantic,
enclosed garden.

FIRST DAY: SAMOS

We recommend an early arrival by plane from Athens, as it is
usually calm in the morning, and there is less chance of a delay
due to strong winds. Leave your baggage in the lobby of your
hotel until the usual afternoon check-in, arrange for the Turkey
excursion at any of the efficient travel agencies along the waterfront, then sit back and enjoy a leisurely coffee or tea at a har-
borfront café. Then you'll be ready to explore this beautiful
island.

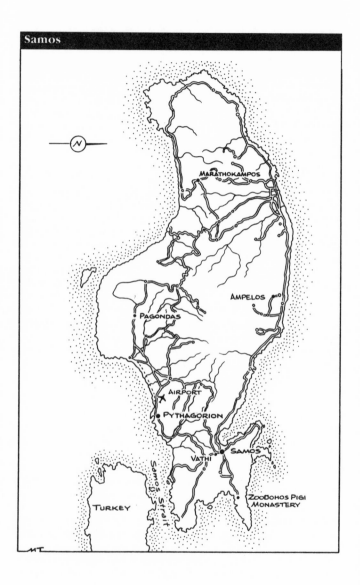

Suggested Schedule

Early morning	Depart Athens for Samos.
9:00 a.m.	Arrive at Samos.
10:00 a.m.	Check into your hotel.
11:00 a.m.	Walk through Pythagorion.
1:00 p.m.	Lunch in Samos town.
2:30 p.m.	Explore Samos town.
4:00 p.m.	Monastery of Zoodohos Pigi.
7:00 p.m.	Dinner along Pythagorion waterfront. Evening at leisure.

Sightseeing Highlights

▲ **Pythagorion**—Named after the island's most famous son, the ancient philosopher Pythagoras, this harbor is justifiably popular for fishing and pleasure boats. The foundations of the jetty are the ancient tunnel built by Polycrates. Above the town is the Castle of Logothetes, which was built in the nineteenth century on the site of the ancient acropolis. On the hillside are traces of the sixth-century B.C. walls, which were reinforced by towers. The ruins of a theater and the famous aqueduct Evpalinio add to the charm and historic ambience of this small town (population under 1,500).

▲ **Samos Town (Vathi)**—The picturesque island capital has a waterfront promenade and pastel-colored houses that climb the hillside. There is a shady park frequented by the locals behind the waterfront Xenia Hotel. Here you'll find a small museum (open 8:45 a.m. to 3:00 p.m., closed Tuesday, admission 100 drachmas [$0.60]), which is worth visiting for its ivories of Perseus and Medusa and the collection of archaic sculpture. There is excellent regular bus service between Pythagorion and Samos.

▲ **Monastery of Zoodohos Pigi**—Four miles east of the town toward Kamara. The views of the Samos Strait and Turkish coast are well worth the effort to get here.

SECOND DAY: SAMOS TO TURKEY

Leave Samos by ferry at 9:00 a.m., and 2½ hours later, enter Turkey at Kusadasi, a charming port of exotic minarets, open-air markets, cafés, and friendly vendors. Shop, swim, eat, and meet the townspeople. Then, in the late afternoon, head out to Ephesus, Turkey's most extraordinary archaeological ruins.

Suggested Schedule

9:00 a.m.	Depart Samos for Turkey.
11:30 a.m.	Arrive Kusadasi.
12:00 noon	Check into your hotel.
12:30 p.m.	Begin walking tour of Kusadasi.
2:00 p.m.	Lunch in waterfront café.
3:00 p.m.	Swim.
4:30 p.m.	Depart for Ephesus.
5:00 p.m.	Arrive Ephesus.
7:00 p.m.	Return to Kusadasi.
	Evening at leisure.

Turkey

Spanning two continents and with a 10,000-year-old cultural heritage, Turkey is one of the world's most exotic destinations. Like ancient Greece and Rome, the Ottoman Empire was an early world power extending from Africa through the Middle East and into central Asia. You can find important remnants of that empire throughout the Aegean and Mediterranean. But the only way to fully appreciate the Turkish contribution to art, architecture, science, medicine, and religion is to visit here. With more than 4,890 miles of coastline, many tourists come to enjoy some of the beaches that Mark Antony gave to Cleopatra as a wedding present. Turkey's cultural heritage, the focus of today's itinerary, is equally compelling. Ancient ruins line the coast. On the Aegean side is Homer's Troy, site of the epic *Iliad* struggle. To the south is Pergamon, the cultural center that was home to one of antiquity's great libraries, which housed more than 200,000 books. And near Pergamon's Acropolis are the ruins of the Asclepion, one of the most important medical centers in ancient times. For a cultural experience, a relaxing vacation, a chance to enjoy some of the world's finest cuisine, and explore an unspoiled Old World village, Turkey is an ideal extension to your around-the-world itinerary.

Arrival

After docking in Kusadasi, you'll want to stop by the Tourist Information Office (tel. 1328) for background information. They can direct you to a bank, where you'll change your money for Turkish liras. For a quick mental conversion from lira values to dollars, multiply the lira amount by 4.5 and then move the decimal four places to the left. For example, 22,000 liras is roughly $10. From the bank, take a taxi to your hotel. You can also change money at your hotel.

Lodging

There are several excellent hotels in Kusadasi. The **Karavan-serai** (tel. 2457) is certainly the most unusual. Originally built as an Ottoman caravansary, this fortlike building has been taste-fully refurbished, and the central courtyard is now a luxurious garden with outdoor dining. Expect to pay around 99,000 liras ($45) for a room at this well-located hotel in the center of town. Our other favorite choice is the **Kismet** (tel. 2005) set in a lush garden on a promontory that juts into the aqua-clear sea. The walk to town takes 30 minutes, but you can always hop one of the minicabs that regularly plies the promenade for passengers. A swim in the clear water below the hotel is as sensual as a Turk-ish bath. Double rooms run 110,000 liras ($50). Other hotels we've enjoyed are the **Ci Dem**, with sea views from the roof ter-race or private verandas at 57,000 liras ($26) for two with break-fast (tel. 1895), and the **Mini Tusan** in the town center, with views toward the port at 57,000 liras ($26) double (tel. 2359).

Food

Turkish cuisine is one of the finest in the world. We know American chefs who vacation in Turkey for the food alone. What makes eating special is the freshness, variety, and blend of flavors, and the intensive labor that goes into its preparation. Try the *patlican salatasi* (puréed eggplant mixed with yogurt); *coban salatasi* (chopped tomatoes, cucumbers, parsley, olives, and spicy peppers); *borek* (pastry rolls filled with white cheese and parsley, then deep fried); and dozens of fancy kebabs. The waterfront cafés don't expect you to be an expert on Turkish cuisine; they have a sample order of most dishes on display behind glass counters. On our first trip, we just pointed to many items and tried as many as we could. You can afford to experi-ment, as prices are very reasonable: in fact, they get lower and lower the farther you are from the waterfront. You can't go wrong anywhere in Kusadasi (although the Karavanserai Hotel is a disappointment for the high prices). Restaurants we've fre-quented include the **Ali Baba** and on the waterfront, the **Toros Canh Bali**, **Kazim Usta'nun**, and **Diba**.

Sightseeing Highlights

▲ **Kusadasi**—The name means "island of birds"; it was the port of ancient Ephesus. Today, this charming town is known for its slender, white minarets that poke up between the palm trees, its variety of open-air shops, waterfront cafés, and deep, clear seas ideal for aquatic sports. On arrival, head toward the fifteenth-century caravansary, now the Karavanserai Hotel and the town center. Wander up the main street (Tayyare Caddesi) to see the vast assortment of rugs and handmade crafts for sale, then turn into the safe, less-trod backstreets. Have a Turkish bath, enjoy a cup of local tea, and watch the world go by. When the sun lowers in the sky, move on to Ephesus.

▲▲ **Kalamanaki National Park**—If you're already overburdened with bargains from Egypt, you may prefer an expanse of woodlands, glistening waterfalls, and deserted beaches 18 miles south of Kusadasi. Minivans marked "Milli Park" leave every half hour for 2,200 liras ($1); by private taxi expect to pay from 17,600 liras to 22,000 ($8 to $10).

▲▲▲ **Ephesus**—"Is there a greater city?" St. Paul once asked of Ephesus, the Roman capital of Asia. Throughout antiquity, Ephesus was the commercial and population center of the western Mediterranean. The region's leading port in the second century A.D., this metropolis was home to 300,000. Built in the imperial manner, the city has monumental temples, baths, public ways, commercial streets, and brothels. Within its boundaries was one of the Seven Wonders of the World, the Temple of Artemis.

The wealth of Greek- and Roman-era remains is only part of Ephesus' appeal; since medieval times, Christians have marked a visit to Ephesus among the holiest of pilgrimages. Today, you can also see the little chapel at the site where the Virgin Mary spent her final days.

Among those who rode in processionals on Ephesus' Arcadian Way were Mark Antony and Cleopatra. Here, too, St. Paul preached in the theater (there was seating for 25,000) against the Ephesians' goddess Artemis. A cool reception to his criticism, particularly from local merchants, persuaded him to leave town. Afterward, he sent epistles to the Ephesians.

Among the highlights of a visit to Ephesus are the Arcadian Way, library, Temple of Hadrian, Temple of Domitian, and the theater, which continues to host cultural events to this day. Just 45 minutes away by foot (or, if you prefer, take a taxi) is Selçuk. Protected by a fort built by Emperor Justinian, this is the site of the Temple of Artemis. While hardly anything remains of this 129-column marble monument that was several times larger than the Parthenon, you can find out more about it at the Selçuk Museum. On display here is a statue of Artemis and many other artifacts and art objects from this famous city's past. Don't miss it.

Ephesus, including the Selçuk Museum, is open from 8:00 a.m. to 7:00 p.m., slightly earlier in the off-season. Double check on the times at your hotel. Minivans make the 20-minute trip from Kusadasi for $0.80; taxis cost approximately 15,000 liras ($7). Allow at least two hours to explore the city, seen at its best in the early evening light.

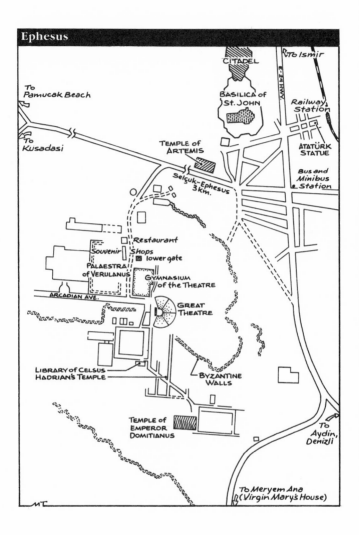

Ephesus

To Pamucak Beach

To Kusadasi

CITADEL

BASILICA of St. JOHN

To Ismir

E-24 HWY

Railway Station

ATATÜRK STATUE

Bus and Minibus Station

TEMPLE of ARTEMIS

Selçuk-Ephesus 3 km.

Restaurant

Souvenir Shops

lower gate

PALAESTRA of VERULANUS

GYMNASIUM of the THEATRE

ARCADIAN AVE.

GREAT THEATRE

LIBRARY of CELSUS
HADRIAN'S TEMPLE

BYZANTINE WALLS

TEMPLE of EMPEROR DOMITIANUS

To Aydin, Denizli

To Meryem Ana (Virgin Mary's House)

MT

SANTORINI TO PARIS

This morning, you'll fly back to Athens and connect to Paris, arriving in midafternoon. After settling into your hotel, there'll be time to try one of the city's popular bistros and explore the City of Light. Today's highlight is an evening Seine boat ride past some of the city's dramatically lighted landmarks.

Suggested Schedule	
7:20 a.m.	Fly from Santorini to Athens.
10:00 a.m.	Fly to Paris.
12:15 p.m.	Arrive in Paris.
3:00 p.m.	Check into your hotel.
6:00 p.m.	Dinner.
Evening	Bateau mouche ride down the Seine.

Paris
The best place we know to complete a world tour is Paris. It has something for every taste, and every arrondissement is worth visiting. Come to think of it, we've never met a traveler who was disappointed by Paris. In fact, the final days of your journey offer so many outstanding opportunities that all you have to do is simply sort through the seemingly endless choices. We're here to help.

Why do we love Paris? First, it's the kind of city every traveler dreams of. No tacky billboards or postmodern architecture clutters the inner city. No matter when you come, Paris is always electric, a city in the best sense of the word. You can count on dining at some of the best restaurants in the world, seeing some of the finest architecture and, of course, the world's preeminent museums. Although 9 million people live in the Paris area, the city functions on a human scale, inviting casual strolling, leisurely afternoons in grand parks, and a chance to sample the continent's most famous outdoor cafés. There may be a better place to watch the world go by, but we haven't found it.

The museums of this city number in the hundreds. We have included only our top choices. If you are an avid art lover, by all means spend several hours in each one. But feel free to just pop in and have a look around for an hour. The cavernous Orsay (a former train station), the classical lines of the Louvre with its controversial new glass pyramid, the fanciful colors and tubes of the Centre Pompidou, and the quiet elegance of the old man-

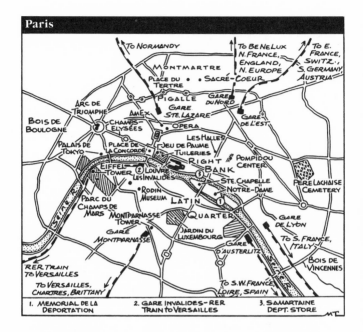

sion that houses the Picasso Museum are just a few of the high-lights you can enjoy. On our last visit, we spent a fine hour on a hot day propped up against a pillar in the Louvre courtyard, watching French schoolchildren touring with their teachers and tourists soaking their feet in the pools that flank the pyramid. All the while, a trio of young flutists under the shade of a nearby archway played Vivaldi for spare change. Moments like these are what you remember when the last painting has shrunk to post-card size in you mind's eye.

Go with the flow. No visitor who values peace of mind would drive in Paris. We have emphasized the smart ways to get around—walking tours and public transit. The best way to enjoy yourself is to slow down to a leisurely Paris stroll and see what Kenneth Clark calls "the city at the very center of civiliza-tion where pilgrims from Henry James downward have paused and breathed in the aroma of a long-established culture." This city is an excellent place to rest up before heading back home. If you have more than 22 days, we believe the first destination you should consider extending is Paris. No city we can think of is better suited to the casual life style. Lounge at a swimming pool by the Seine, take a park bench and watch the French children at play, or rent a bike and cycle through the Bois de Boulogne.

No matter how many days you spend in Paris, we're certain you'll want to come back.

After catching an Olympic Airways flight back to Athens, you'll connect on Singapore or TWA to Paris. Rick Steves, who pioneered the 22 Day Itinerary Planner series, has written *22 Days in France* (Santa Fe, N.M.: John Muir Publications, 1989) with Steve Smith. Here are their tips for getting oriented in Paris.

Airport Strategy
Both of Paris' efficient international airports have easy public transportation into the city and offer handy, uncrowded tourist information services. After clearing customs, visit the tourist office (open 7:00 a.m. to 11:00 p.m.) behind the "meeting point" at Charles de Gaulle. At Orly, get information at the ADP counter (Paris airport services, open 6:00 a.m. to 11:45 p.m.) near Gate H. Pick up two free city maps and tear the subway map out of one for your shirt pocket. Ask for directions to the airport post office (Bureaus de Poste), where you can buy a phone card (*telecarte*). Call to confirm hotel reservations or find a room. Be sure to get the nearest metro stop to your hotel. If you're having trouble, the tourist office or ADP can help.

Getting into Paris: From Charles de Gaulle, catch the free shuttle bus (called *navette*, gate 28) to Roissy Rail, where a train will zip you into the heart of Paris sans seat (26F, free with a rail-pass). Line B takes you right into Paris' subway system.

From Orly, several bus options can take you to different parts of the city. The Air France bus (28F) at Gate J will take you to Les Invalides Métro station (near rue Cler). The RATP bus (20F) at Gate F will take you to the nearest Métro station.

Parisian Public Transit: The Métro (Subway)
Europe's best subway is divided into two systems: the Métro covers the city, and the RER serves suburban destinations. You'll be using the Métro for almost all your trips.

Paris Métro stops are a standard aid in giving directions. If an address says "mo. Invalides," that's Parisian for "it's near the Invalides Métro stop." One ticket takes you anywhere in the system. Save nearly 50 percent by buying a *carnet* (pronounced "car-nay") of 10 tickets for about 32F at any Métro station. Study your Métro map before entering the station and figure out which line(s) you need to complete your trip. Find the first major stop (in bold lettering on your map) of each line you need. Your route will be indicated by the signs for that stop. Lines are also numbered, but I use the last-stop designations. Pass through the turnstile, reclaim and keep your ticket, and follow signs toward your last-stop designation. Transfers can be made at any station where lines cross. When you transfer, look for the orange *correspondance* (connections) signs when you exit your first train, than follow signs to the last stop of your next line. Keep your ticket; you may be inspected for proof of purchase. To exit, follow *sortie* signs. Before you leave the Métro, check the *plan du quartier* (map of the neighborhood) to get your bearings and decide which sortie you want. Most stops have several sorties, often hundreds of yards apart. Remember your essential Métro words: *direction* (direction), *correspondance* (connections), *sortie* (exit), and *carnet* (cheap set of 10 tickets). Parisian purse snatchers and pickpockets thrive in the Métro. Keep valuables in your money belt.

RER routes are the thick lines on the map. They work like the Métro, but they are much speedier. One Métro ticket is all you need for rides within Paris. To travel outside the city (to Versailles, for example), you'll need to buy another ticket at the RER station window.

Public Buses

The bus system is a bit tricker but worth figuring out and using. The same yellow tickets are good on both bus and Métro, though you can't use one ticket to transfer between the two systems. While the Métro shuts down about 12:45 a.m., some buses continue until late in the night. Schedules are posted at bus stops. Study the big system maps at each stop to figure out which route(s) you need. Then look at the individual route diagrams, showing the exact route of the line serving that stop, to verify you route. Major stops are also painted on the side of each bus. Enter through the front doors. Punch your yellow Métro ticket in the machine behind the driver or pay the higher cash fare. Get off the bus using the rear door. Even if you're not certain you've figured it out, do some joyriding. Lines 24, 63, and 64 run along Paris' most scenic routes and make a great introduction to this city. Remember: in Paris, you're never more than a ten-minute walk from a Métro stop.

Taxis

Parisian taxis are reasonable. A ten-minute ride costs about $4 (vs. 50 cents to get anywhere in town on the Métro); luggage will cost you more. You can try waving one down, but it's easier to ask for the nearest taxi stand. The rates are higher at night and on Sundays, and if you call one from your hotel, the meter starts as soon as the call is received.

Paris Information

Paris requires study and a good map. Two fine Paris guidebooks
are the *Michelin Green Guide* and the *Access Guide to Paris*.
While it's easy to pick up free maps of Paris once you've arrived
(your hotel will probably have them), they don't show all the
streets, and you may want to do a little planning before you go.
Consider picking up the huge Michelin #10 map on Paris. The
Pariscope weekly magazine (3F at any newsstand) lists museum
hours, concerts, musical festivals, plays, movies, nightclubs, and
special art exhibits. There are 11 English language bookstores in
Paris where you can pick up guidebooks. Try Shakespeare and
Company for used travel books (at 37 rue de la Boucherie,
across the river from Notre-Dame), the basement at American
Express (near the Opera at 11 rue Scribe), or W. H. Smith's at
248 rue de Rivoli. Avoid the Paris Tourist Information offices
(TIs)—long lines and little information. Still, if you feel you
need more information, call the TI (tel. 47-23-61-72, 127 avenue des Champs-Elysées, open 9:00-20:00), check your neighborhood TI office, or ask your hotelier.

Paris Orientation

Paris is circled by a ring-road freeway (the Peripherique), split in
half by the Seine River, and divided into 210 arrondissements
(governmental jurisdictions). You'll find Paris much easier to
negotiate if you know which side of the river you're on, which
arrondissement you're in, and which Métro stop you're closest
to. Remember, if you're above the river (look at a map), you're
on the Right Bank (*Rive Droite*), and if you're below it, you're
on the Left Bank (*Rive Gauche*). Arrondissements are numbered
starting at ground zero (the Louvre is 1èr) and moving in a
clockwise spiral out to the ring road. The last two digits in a
Parisian zip code are the arrondissement number. In Parisian jar-
gon, Napoleon's tomb is on the rive gauche in the 7ème, near
Métro: Invalides. Its zip code is 75007.

Helpful Hints

Most museums are closed on Tuesdays, half-price on Sundays,
and least crowded first thing in the morning and at lunch.

Carry small change for pay toilets, or walk into any café like
you own the place and find the toilet.

If you need cash on Sunday, go to 115 or 154 avenue Champs-
Elysées for banks with good rates, open 10:00-18:00. Paris
recently expanded its overworked phone system, adding a 4 to
the beginning of all old numbers.

For a quick mental conversion from francs to dollars, simply multiply the franc value by 15 and move the decimal two points to the left. For example, 100 francs is worth roughly $15.

Lodging

Paris offers a great variety of accommodations ranging from bed and breakfasts to houseboats on the Seine, studio and luxury apartments, pensiones, and the world's most luxurious hotels. Here are some of our favorite choices in all price categories.

The **Hotel Lancaster** at 7 rue Berri, Paris 75008 (tel. 359-9043, telex 640891), is a truly elegant and luxurious intimate hotel facing a quiet inner courtyard. A double room here starts at 1,680F ($258). The only French-owned luxury hotel left in Paris is the magnificent **Hotel Crillon** at 10 place de la Concorde, Paris 75008 (tel. 42-65-2424, Fax 47427210, U.S. rep. 1-800-223-6800). The elegant rooms have enormous bathrooms, many with huge windows. The entire hotel was renovated in good taste in 1985 (except for the red, white, and blue decor of the suites). Facing the place de la Concorde, the dining room is one of the most elegant places to enjoy even a simple breakfast of thinly sliced mangoes and papayas with coffee and croissants. If you can afford the best (2,400F or $370) you can't go wrong at the Crillon. Try the small and charming **Hotel Deux Iles** (960F, about $147 double) on the Ile St. Louis, the "heart of the heart of Paris." **Hotel Manchester** at 1 rue de Gramont (tel. 296-60-81) is in a convenient Right Bank location near the Opera, the boulevards, and famous shops. The rooms are slightly worn, but they overlook a little garden courtyard and are quiet. The price is right: 288F ($44).

Hotel Saints-Pères, at 65 rue des Saints-Pères, Paris 75006 (tel. 45-44-5000), is the best of the moderately priced small hotels. The building was designed by Louis XIV's architect and refurbished in 1985 with antique mirrors, tapestries, and old paintings. Most of the rooms overlook an interior garden. The best room is the Chambre à la Fresque with a seventeenth-century painted ceiling. Rooms for two start at 840F ($129). **Hotel de l'Université** at 22 rue de l'Université, Paris 75007 (tel. 42-61-0939), is a small, cozy place on a charming Left Bank street. The lobby has half-timbered walls and stone-tile floor, and there are fireplaces and beamed ceilings in some rooms. A room for two starts at 700F ($107).

The **Hotel Lenox** at 9 rue de l'Université, Paris 75007 (tel. 296-10-95), is our favorite inexpensive small hotel in Paris. The location is superb, the rooms are nicely decorated, and the baths are brand new. If it's sold out, they may put you in their sister establishment, the **Montparnasse**, a charming place but not as well located. Rooms start at 470F ($72). For a splurge, try the two-story suites with skylights at 900F ($138). **Hotel St. Louis** at 75 rue St. Louis-en-l'Ile (tel. 4634-04-80) offers rooms in a seventeenth-century home across the Seine from Notre-Dame. First-floor rooms have no view but are easier to reach. If you don't mind the climb, the fifth-floor top rooms have wonderful views of rooftop Paris. This island in the middle of the Seine is one of Paris' most elegant and historic neighborhoods. Car traffic is so light that you can hear the birds in the morning. Continental breakfast is served in a small and very charming lobby. Rooms without private bath or shower are 240F ($36); for a private bath, you'll pay 420F ($65). No credit cards. **Hotel le Pavillon**, 54 rue Saint Dominique, Paris 75007 (tel. 45-51-42-87), is located in a lovely neighborhood that includes the famous La Chaumieux restaurant and the Musée d'Orsay. From here, it's an easy walk to the Saint-Germain area and the Right Bank. The hotel is a little rough around the edges, but the courtyard removes you from street noise. Take rue Malar to reach the hotel by taxi. There's a laundromat one block from the hotel. A room for two is 400F ($62) including breakfast. **Hotel du Vieux Marais**, 8 rue du Plâtre, Paris 75004 (tel. 42-78-47-22), is a clean and comfortable choice on the Right Bank. The location in a Jewish/Chinese/Italian neighborhood is excellent. English spoken here. A room for two with continental breakfast runs 400F ($62).

Prince Albert, 5 rue Saint-Hyacinthe, Paris 75001 (tel. 4261-58-36), has a quiet location between the Opera, Louvre, and Tuileries. Small rooms for two start at 300F ($46).

Bed and breakfast accommodations and comfortable rooms on Seine barges can be arranged through Chez Vous, 220 Redwood Hwy., Suite 129, Mill Valley, CA 94941 (tel. 415-331-2535).

If you wish to extend your stay in Paris, consider renting an apartment. More spacious and often less expensive than a moderate hotel, this is the ideal way to enjoy the city. You have your own fully equipped kitchen and can shop in the open-air food markets. Rates start at $70 for a studio with kitchen and average $120 a day for a spacious two-room apartment (living room, kitchen, bathroom, and separate bedroom). Our favorite rental firm is Rothray. They speak English, are courteous and helpful, and put you immediately at ease. You can write, phone, or Fax them for reservations. Owner Ray Lampard prefers a one-week minimum but has rented to us for as little as four days. He is at 10 rue Nicholas Flamel, Paris 75004 (tel. 48-87-13-37; Fax 1-40-26-34-33).

Food

Breakfast in your hotel will invariably consist of very strong coffee or tea (*au lait* is half milk, half coffee), bread and/or croissant, butter, and marmalade.

Most restaurants start serving lunch at 12:00 noon and finish at 2:00 p.m., although a few keep going throughout the day. If you ate lunch in Paris like the Parisians used to, your palate would be happy, but your wallet and your tourist itinerary would be full of holes. Fortunately for the tourist, more and more restaurants now offer lighter fare such as mixed salads (*salades composées*) or quiche and salad combinations instead of or in addition to the traditional three-course meal. To eat in the more traditional way and still keep it simple, order le menu, a *prix fixe* offering of the day that usually will include appetizer, main course, and dessert, sometimes with several alternative choices. (To get what we call a menu, ask for *la carte*). Ordering *le menu* is usually cheaper than ordering à la carte; you know exactly what your bill will be, and you avoid wading through the long, mysteriously named and often handwritten choices on the regular menu.

For house wine, *une carafe* will bring you a liter, *un demi* a half liter, *un quart*, a quarter liter. For draft beer, order *une bière pression*. *Une carafe d'eau* calls forth water from the faucet.

The French love their food, and dining out is supposed to be leisurely. Service is attentive but never rushed, allowing you time to enjoy each course. Many restaurants don't begin dinner service until 8:00 p.m. *Le menu* sometimes disappears in the evening, leaving you adrift in flowery descriptions inscribed under plastic menu covers in curly script. Hang in there and you won't starve, although you may not get what you expected.

Don't mistake French waiters' abruptness for rudeness; that's just the way it is here. Of late, we've noticed more patience and tolerance in the service and a bit more English. Politeness on your part will help things go smoothly. Say please and thank you a lot and address the waiter as "monsieur," not "garçon" as in the movies. Smile steadfastly and do not let anyone intimidate you.

Café stops are essential: here's where you consult your map, write your postcards, and make critical decisions with your travel companions. The waiters and passersby are a study in themselves, confirming our conviction that the most delicious aspect of travel is the in-between moments. All drinks in cafés will be at least 6F ($1), often more. Look at it this way: you are not just drinking coffee or mineral water; you are renting expensive parking space for yourself. For a café snack, try a *croque-monsieur*, a grilled ham and cheese sandwich (eat it with knife and fork). Don't buy pastry in a café; go instead to a *patisserie. Salons de thé* serve pastries with tea and coffee; some serve light meals as well. Street stalls around the place St. Michel and rue de la Huchette sell crepes, sandwiches, and ice cream. Cheapest picnic food will be at street markets, or look for neighborhood grocery stores (*alimentation*).

All French restaurants are required by law to post their menus outside, so price and selection are never a mystery. No tipping is required or expected: a service charge is included in the bill.

Montparnasse: La Moule en Folie at 5 rue du Maine (tel. 43-20-03-42) offers moderately priced mussels and other seafood dishes in a friendly, nontouristy atmosphere. The owner is opening an inexpensive fish-and-chips room next door. **Tarte Julie** at 8 rue Jolivet (tel. 43-20-70-34) serves takeout quiche and other main dish and dessert pies and salads. There's a small sit-down restaurant next door. Other franchises are found around the city. **La Canaille** at 4 rue Crillon (tel. 42-78-09-71) serves good French food in an informal atmosphere at moderate prices. You'll also enjoy the art exhibits here. **Brasserie de l'Ile St. Louis** at 55 quai de Bourbon (tel. 43-54-02-59) offers Alsatian dishes at an excellent location popular with expatriates and tourists. Moderately priced, this is a good place to have a beer while looking over the river.

Left Bank, along the river: L'Ecluse Grands-Augustins, 15 Quai des Grands Augustins (tel. 46-33-58-74), is a pleasant, trendy wine bar in a great location, a good place for a drink or a light meal. The food is pricey but good. Next door, **A la Grignoterie** offers wonderful, moderately priced main dish salads served in an airy ladies' tearoom atmosphere with great views of the passing scene along the river. **Git le Coeur**, 14 rue Git-le-Coeur (tel. 46-33-02-06), is located on a little side street near the place St. Michel. This charming, expensive, and rather formal little restaurant is in an ancient building. Reservations advised. If you are a beef eater, the **Hippopotamus** chain is highly recommended for its moderately priced meal of steak and fries. One is on the boulevard des Capucines, near the Opera.

An Evening Seine Cruise

After exploring the neighborhood around your hotel, walk or taxi over to the Pont-Neuf for an evening ride aboard one of the *bateau mouches* (fly boats). This is the best possible introduction to Paris, a relaxing and inexpensive way to get an overview of the city's dramatically lit monuments and bridges. We believe this is the finest nightlife in town, far better than the tacky over-priced shows pushed at tour groups. The bateau mouche from the Pont-Neuf leaves every 30 minutes from 10:00 a.m. to 12:00 noon and 1:30 to 6:30 p.m. and 9:00 to 10:30 p.m. The trip lasts an hour and costs 30F, 15F for kids under age 10. Boats also leave from the Pont d'Alma and other spots along the river. Some serve lunch and dinner aboard. If you're planning to dine on board, reserve by calling 46-33-98-38.

THE HEART OF PARIS

Today's itinerary includes some of the best reasons to visit Paris.
You begin at Notre-Dame cathedral and then continue along the
Right Bank for a look at Sainte-Chapelle, the Palais de Justice,
and Palais Royale. After lunch at the department store Le Printemps, there's time to visit the Tuileries or stroll over to the Ile
de la Cité. The evening is reserved for a visit to the brightly lit
place de la Concorde.

Suggested Schedule

9:00 a.m.	Notre-Dame.
10:00 a.m.	Sainte-Chapelle.
10:30 a.m.	Right Bank stroll.
12:00 noon	Lunch at the Printemps rooftop restaurant.
1:00 p.m.	Grands magasins (department stores).
2:00 p.m.	Right Bank stroll.
4:00-5:00 p.m.	Café break.
5:00-6:00 p.m.	Finish your walk.
Evening	Visit place de la Concorde/Champs-Elysées/Arc de Triomphe.

Sightseeing Highlights

The best way to explore this changing city is on foot, but if if it
is too hot and muggy or too cold and rainy or your tourist legs
give out, just find a red Métro sign and let this all-encompassing
urban transportation system deliver you to your next destination.

▲▲▲ **Notre-Dame**—Begin at the true center of Paris, the
square (place du Parvis Notre-Dame) in front of Notre-Dame
cathedral. After marveling at the stained glass, you may want to
pay the fee to climb up into one of the towers (open from 10:00
a.m. to 5:30 p.m., admission 10F) for a view of the famous gar-
goyles and the city. There are 387 steps, but the expansive view
is worth it.

When you come out of the cathedral, step into the lovely
interior courtyard of the Hôtel-Dieu, the hospital to your right.
Walk behind the cathedral to get a good view of the flying buttresses supporting the structure. While you're there, pay a visit
to the Memorial de la Déportation, a tribute to those who died
in Nazi concentration camps. It's located at the very tip of the

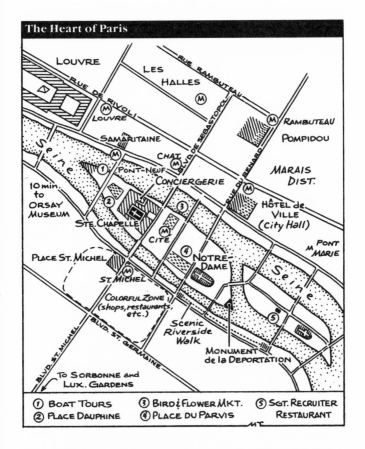

The Heart of Paris

LOUVRE

RUE DE RIVOLI

LES HALLES

RUE RAMBUTEAU

Ⓜ LOUVRE

SAMARITAINE

Seine

Ⓜ

BLVD. DE SEBASTOPOL

CHAT.

① PONT-NEUF

CONCIERGERIE

10 min. to ORSAY MUSEUM

②

STE. CHAPELLE

③

Ⓜ CITÉ

PLACE ST. MICHEL

④ NOTRE-DAME

Ⓜ ST. MICHEL

COLORFUL ZONE (shops, restaurants, etc.)

Scenic Riverside Walk

BLVD. ST. MICHEL

BLVD. ST. GERMAINE

To SORBONNE and LUX. GARDENS

Ⓜ RAMBUTEAU

POMPIDOU

MARAIS DIST.

RUE DU RENARD

Ⓜ

HÔTEL de VILLE (City Hall)

PONT MARIE

Seine

MONUMENT de la DEPORTATION

⑤

| ① BOAT TOURS | ③ BIRD & FLOWER MKT. | ⑤ SGT. RECRUITER |
| ② PLACE DAUPHINE | ④ PLACE DU PARVIS | RESTAURANT |

Ile de la Cité. You might want to buy a small guidebook in English describing the cathedral's history and architecture in detail.

▲▲ Sainte-Chapelle—Walk west along the quay next to the Préfecture de Police until you reach the boulevard du Palais. To your left is the huge nineteenth-century building that houses the Palais de Justice (Hall of Justice). Within it remain two of the medieval structures that formerly occupied the site, the Conciergerie and the Sainte-Chapelle. The Conciergerie was once a part of the royal palace and later a prison that housed Marie Antoinette and others.

The chapel was built by King Louis IX (who later became a saint) to house relics of the cross and crown of thorns of Jesus.

Two stories high, with a delicate Gothic spire, its red and blue stained-glass windows on the second level are spectacular. Watch how the dominant color changes as the sun goes behind a cloud. This is the same shade of blue found in the stained glass at Chartres, a color no one has ever been able to reproduce. Candlelight concerts are sometimes offered at Sainte-Chapelle in the evening. Open 10:00 a.m. to 6:00 p.m. every day, 9:30 a.m. to 6:30 p.m. in summer, admission 22F adults, reductions for children and seniors.

After leaving Sainte-Chapelle, walk around behind the Palais de Justice to the place Dauphine, a quiet residential square with a small park filled with chestnut trees. Pause here to see the beautifully proportioned stone and brick facades before exiting the square at the other side and crossing the Pont-Neuf. When you reach the Right Bank, turn right and detour along the Quai de la Mégisserie, where a lively plant and animal market lines the sidewalks. Or, if your prefer, go left until you reach the rue de l'Admiral de Coligny. Just around the corner from the Louvre (which we will save for another day) is the handsome Gothic facade of St. Germain-l'Auxerrois, the church of the royal family before the French Revolution. Next to it is a tearoom of the same name, quiet and reasonably priced, with a heavenly selection of pastries. After taking a break, walk under the arcades of the rue de Rivoli with its touristy shops until you reach the place du Palais Royale. (If you are interested in antiques, go from here to the nearby Louvre des Antiquaires, a pavilion of shops displaying furniture from all periods, paintings, and bibelots of every description.) Look straight up the avenue de l'Opéra to the monumental nineteenth-century Opéra. Note on the right the Comédie Française, the famous theater company that performs the French classics.

▲ **Palais Royale**—The Palais itself is a government office building, closed to the public, but the interior gardens are splendid. One section is an updating of a classical French site almost as controversial as I. M. Pei's pyramid—the Colonnes de Buren. Installed in the early 1980s, these small, round, black and white pillars have outraged some Parisians who believe architectural sites should be inviolate. We find them a light and whimsical addition to this classic seventeenth-century site.

▲▲ **Place Vendôme**—Take the rue St. Honoré (high fashion row), to the place Vendôme. Designed in the seventeenth century by the famous French architect Mansart, this elegant square is highlighted by a black and green column that Napoleon made from bronze cannons captured at the Battle of Austerlitz. Place Vendôme is the site of the famed Ritz Hotel, where the term "understated elegance" must have been coined. Nearby is W. H.

Smith, corner of rue Cambon and rue de Rivoli, an English bookstore with an upstairs restaurant serving English teas, scones, and little sandwiches.

▲ **Opéra, Le Printemps, and Fauchon's**—From the place Vendôme, follow the rue de la Paix to the Opéra. You can tour the interior of the building, which includes a view of the Chagall painted ceilings and the world's largest stage. Directly behind the Opéra on the left, you'll find the boulevard Haussmann, where the department store Le Printemps is located. At the information office on the ground floor, pick up an English-language brochure about the store which includes a free Métro map and an excellent, manageably sized map of the city. Have lunch at the rooftop cafeteria, which has reasonable prices, an outdoor terrace, and a 360-degree view of the rooftops of Paris. Another restaurant in the two-building complex is located beneath a vast blue and yellow art deco glass dome. After lunch, you may want to browse through the store. Brightly colored, high-quality cotton print *tissu de Provence* tablecloths or placemats (brand name Soleado) found in the household goods departments make good gifts or souvenirs. (For serious shoppers, the nearby, more upscale Galeries Lafayette is also a must.) As you leave Printemps, find the rue Tronchet on your map and head down it toward l'Eglise de la Madeleine, noting as you pass 22 rue Tronchet one of the last practitioners of an ancient profession, a woman sitting in a shop window darning stockings.

On place de la Madeleine, be sure to check the window at Fauchon's, certainly the most elegant and costly display of prepared foods, as handsome as many a still life in the Louvre. Across the square, Chez Hediard is reputedly the only place in France where chocolate chips can be found. Also on this square is one of the city's many lovely flower markets.

From the Madeleine, walk down the rue Royale to the place de la Concorde and one of the most famous boulevards in the world, the Champs-Elysées. We suggest saving this destination for a memorable evening visit. Instead, why not take the rest of the afternoon off? Walk over to the Tuileries gardens, a formal park that offers you the shade of handsome chestnut trees. Or if you prefer, take a stroll across the Pont-Neuf, the quintessential Paris bridge. As you cross over the Ile de la Cité in the middle of the bridge, walk down the stairs to the tiny Square du Vert Galant, an oasis of calm and green at the tip of the island.

▲▲▲ **Champs-Elysées, Arc de Triomphe, Place de la Concorde (at night)**—Bright lights add to the grandeur of these three landmarks. During the French Revolution, the place de la Concorde was the site of over 1,000 deaths by guillotine, including Marie Antoinette. The Champs-Elysées, the spine of the city, was orginally designed as a garden extending from the Tuileries. Today, it is the street for official state processions. The Arc de Triomphe was built by Napoleon to celebrate his military victories. Beneath it, a flame is lit nightly to honor France's Unknown Soldier. Twelve streets radiate out from the surrounding traffic circle known as l'Etoile (The Star) at place Charles de Gaulle. There are underground passageways for pedestrians to reach the Arc de Triomphe.

PARIS: RIGHT BANK

Today, you'll have a chance to see some of the city's best-known museums as well as some of its finest neighborhoods, churches, and parks. Mainstream tourist highlights include the Picasso Museum and the Centre Pompidou. There's also time to enjoy less touristed spots like the yacht harbor's rose arbor and the place des Vosges. The jazzy new Halles district and beautifully restored Marais quarter showcase Parisian adaptive reuse.

Suggested Schedule

9:00 a.m.	Stroll through Ile St. Louis-Bastille-place des Vosges.
11:00 a.m.	Picasso Museum.
1:00 p.m.	Lunch.
2:00 p.m.	Stroll through Marais.
3:00 p.m.	Centre Pompidou and surroundings.
5:00 p.m.	Return to your hotel.
7:00 p.m.	Return to Les Halles area for dinner.
After dinner	Stroll past beautifully lit nearby buildings and monuments.

Sightseeing Highlights

▲▲ **Ile St. Louis**—Take the Métro to Ile de la Cité (St. Michel or Cité) and walk behind Notre-Dame. Cross the bridge to Ile St. Louis and meander down the central corridor of this quiet, exclusive, but also densely tourist-haunted enclave, the rue St. Louis en L'Ile. Looking down the ivy-covered walls of the side streets, you can see the river Seine in both directions. You could try the famous ice cream at Berthillon (31 rue St. Louis en L'Ile).

▲▲ **Place de la Bastille and Opéra de la Bastille**—At the eastern tip of the island, turn left and cross over the Pont Sully. Negotiate some heavy traffic here and walk up the boulevard Henri IV to the place de la Bastille. This is the site of the famous prison destroyed by revolutionaries on July 14, 1789, now celebrated as the major French national holiday. The July Column in the center of the square, however, commemorates a rebellion against a later monarchy. To one side stands the new Opéra de la Bastille, built to coincide with the 200th anniversary of the French Revolution. Nearby is the Paris yacht harbor. With its adjacent rose arbor, this makes a pleasant, untourist spot for a pause, and from here you have the option of a peaceful three-hour canal boat ride through the city waterways, an unusual and restful slant on the city. (Departures at 9:15 a.m. and 2:30 p.m., 70F.)

▲▲ **Place des Vosges**—From the place de la Bastille, go down the rue St. Antoine and turn right on the rue de la Biraque, which ends in the place des Vosges, the oldest and quite possibly the handsomest square in Paris. Planned in the seventeenth century by King Henri IV, this square includes a quiet, formal park. The bronze statue of Henri IV goes unnoticed by the neighborhood toddlers at play. The home of Victor Hugo, who once lived here, is now a museum. This is a must-see for getting a sense of old, ongoing, untouristy Paris. Sit in the park and watch Parisian children at play or have an espresso in one of the cafés under the arcade. Here you'll enjoy the view of the beautifully restored brick and stone houses with their steep slate roofs.

▲▲▲ **Picasso Museum**—Follow the rue de Turenne to the rue du Parc Royal, which becomes the rue de la Perle just as the rue Thorigny veers off to the right. There you'll find the Picasso Museum at 5 rue de Thorigny. (To avoid getting lost in these streets, be sure to consult your map.) This museum, opened in 1985, offers a panoramic look at Picasso's career along with art by Matisse, Renoir, Braque, Cézanne, and many others. Here, Picasso's personal collection of his own work is arranged chronologically according to the periods of his development as a painter and is juxtaposed with photographs of himself, his friends, and various female companions in his studio. The changes in his painterly "periods" and their dramatic coincidence with shifts in his personal life are amply described in the exhibit, which is housed in a restored seventeenth-century mansion called the Hôtel Salé (Salted Hotel), because it was paid for by the taxes on salt collected by the proprietor. The contrast between this most modern of painters and the quiet classicism of the setting is startling. Admission is 21F. Open Wednesday 9:45 a.m.to 10:00 p.m., Thursday through Monday 9:45 a.m. to 5:15 p.m.

▲▲ **Centre Pompidou**—Head south on rue de Thorigny to rue des Francs-Bourgeois and turn right to rue Beaubourg and the Centre. Known to Parisians as Beaubourg, this is the busiest museum in the world. Inside, you'll find an excellent collection of modern art as well as a library and film archives. Go up to the fourth floor on the exterior escalator (terrific view of rooftops) and have a look at the modern stuff, including an installation by Los Angeles artist Ed Kienholz. Admission is free. Open Wednes-

day through Monday 12:00 noon to 10:00 p.m., weekends 10:00
a.m. to 10:00 p.m., closed Tuesday. After you have explored the
collection, see the living theater that plays on the large, sloping
square outside. Here all manner of street performers vie for
your attention and francs. Later, you might want to return to
your hotel or remain here for dinner and an evening of people-
watching.

▲▲ **Beaubourg/Les Halles Neighborhood**—A curious mix-
ture of old and new, this was once one of the roughest areas of
Paris. The old central markets have been replaced by a large
public garden and a glassed-over underground shopping complex called le Forum des Halles. Nearby is the Gothic classic, St.
Eustache Church, perfectly illuminated at night. Three or four
blocks down the rue du Renard will take you to the place de
l'Hôtel de Ville, where the gracious old City Hall building is now
complimented by rows of fountains that have been recently put
into place. From here you can see the Tour St. Jacques, where
pilgrims in the Middle Ages set out toward the Spanish monastery of Santiago (St. Jacques) de Compostello. While you're in
the neighborhood, cross the river and check out Notre-Dame
by night. The brilliant lighting makes the bas-reliefs stand out.

PARIS: LEFT BANK

If your hotel is situated on the Left Bank, you'll already have a bit of a feel for this part of the city. Explore it further today on a relaxed schedule that includes the Musée d'Orsay, the charming Musée Cluny, and the mandatory ride up the Eiffel Tower. There's also time to stroll the secondhand bookstalls along the river and enjoy life in the sidewalk café society.

Suggested Schedule

10:00 a.m.	Musée d'Orsay.
12:00 noon	Lunch.
1:00-4:00 p.m.	Leisurely explore the Left Bank.
Evening	Eiffel Tower.

Sightseeing Highlights

▲▲ **Musée d'Orsay**—This building, once a train station, has been converted into a home for nineteenth-century art (most notably the Impressionists) which bridges the classical work found in the Louvre and the modern agenda of the Beaubourg. The divisions of space are designed so that the interior still seems like one vast hangarlike hall. Bring patience and a sense of humor: viewers are often three deep in front of the most popular paintings. The rooftop has an excellent view. Located at 1 rue de Bellechasse. Admission is 21F, 11F on Sunday. Open Tuesday through Saturday 10:00 a.m. to 6:00 p.m., Thursday 10:30 a.m. to 9:45 p.m., and Sunday 9:00 a.m. to 6:00 p.m.

After leaving the museum, take an hour or two to explore some of the nearby streets depicted by the Impressionists. Rue de Lille and rue de Verneuil have fine antique shops, and the area around the Ecole des Beaux-Arts (School of Fine Arts) is a hub for art galleries. You might want to stop for lunch at the **Restaurant des Beaux Arts**, on the rue Bonaparte across the street from the art school, before moving into the more heavily touristed area of St. Germain des Prés.

Once the center of French bohemian and intellectual life, the St. Germain neighborhood takes its name from the oldest church in Paris, l'Eglise St. Germain des Prés. After you've stopped to have a look at the church, you might want to indulge in a coffee (if you can get a table) at the **Café des Deux Magots**, a great place to watch passersby from the glass

enclosed terrace, or the **Café Flore**, once a haunt of Camus,
Sartre, and de Beauvoir. Another café worthy of note is
Procope, 13 rue de l'Ancienne Comédie, purportedly the oldest
café in Paris. Once the hangout of Voltaire and, later on, Victor
Hugo, the place now has a slightly snobby feel to it. There is an
excellent street market on the nearby rue de Buci. If it's a picnic
day, pick up your bread and cheese and take it to the Luxem-
bourg Gardens, a leafier, greener, more relaxed park than the
Tuileries. On your way there, a small detour will bring you to
the place St. Sulpice, a lovely square dominated by the St. Sulpice church.

From here, you can head up the rue de Rennes to Montparnasse. Take the elevator up to the top of the Tour Montparnasse
to enjoy the grand view. There is also a rich selection of places
to eat around the Montparnasse train station, including many
creperies. Crepes are a specialty of Brittany, and the trains to
Brittany leave from here. Be sure you choose a place where the
crepes are made to order and not warmed up from a precooked
stack visible next to the grill. Another nearby lunch alternative
is **Tarte Julie**, 8 rue Jolivet, which, in addition to a vast and lus-
cious array of dessert pies, sells quiches and other savory pies
whole or by the slice for takeout. (Eat in the quiet little park
across the street.) Their restaurant is a few doors down. Across
the square is the **Moules à la Folie**, where mussels and other
seafood are the specialty. These places do not cater particularly
to tourists. The prices are reasonable and the quality generally
high.

▲ **Musée Cluny**—Now walk back down the length of boulevard St. Michel, known locally as the boul' Miche, the broad
avenue central to Parisian student life. Look for the massive
stone building that is the Sorbonne, the great French university,
on your right as you go toward the river. Just beyond it is the
Musée de Cluny, with its famous medieval tapestry, *Lady with
Unicorn*. A tapestry collection and decorative arts from the
Middle Ages are also found in this fifteenth-century monastery
built on the site of old Roman baths. Admission 15F, 8F on Sunday. Open Wednesday through Monday 9:45 a.m to 12:30 p.m.
and 2:00 to 5:15 p.m. Just before you come to the river, you will
hit the place St. Michel, a large square crammed with cafés and
restaurants. The central fountain is a gathering place for drunks
and punks, and the restaurants are strictly for tourists; nevertheless, this is a place with a certain charm. Take time to stroll along
the river, browsing in *les bouquinistes*, the stalls that sell
secondhand books and watercolors and etchings of the city. If
you want to meet English speakers or are out of things to read,
drop in at Shakespeare and Co., 5 rue de la Bucherie, which has a

good selection of secondhand books, including travel guides, in English. A little farther along is the Square Rene Viviani, with the small romanesque Church of St. Julien le Pauvre, now Greek Orthodox. Go into the park here for the best possible view of the spires and buttresses of Notre-Dame. The ancient acacia here is supposed to be the oldest tree in Paris. Back a bit from the river are the pedestrian-only rue St. Severin and rue de la Huchette, full of Greek, North African, and Chinese restaurants that serve honest, if not inspired, meals.

▲▲▲ **Tour Eiffel**—Take the Métro to this landmark built by engineer Gustave Eiffel in 1889 to celebrate the centennial of the French Revolution. This massive structure, like many subsequent bold architectural additions to the city, was at first decried as ugly and out of harmony with its surroundings. It's here to stay for a while, though, having just seen the celebration of its own centennial in 1989. Best seen at night when its girders are illuminated; the view from the decks is terrific. Take the elevator and the prices rise with it: second floor, 12F; third, 28F; fourth, 44F. You can walk to the second and third floors—7F and a lot of stairs. Open every day 10:00 a.m. to 11:00 p.m. In July and August, the hours are extended to midnight on Friday and Saturday.

PARIS SUPERLATIVES

A visit to the world's most famous art museum is followed by a trip to either one of the world's finest cathedrals or grandest palaces. No matter how hard you try, you won't be able to exhaust superlatives on the last day of your global tour. In the evening, you can go up to Montmartre and see the famed Bohemian quarter. If you're up for a big splurge at dinnertime, we know just the place.

Morning	The Louvre.
Afternoon	Chartres or Versailles.

Dinner and evening in Montmartre or area of your choice.

Sightseeing Highlights

▲▲▲ **Louvre**—From the Mona Lisa to the *Winged Victory of Samothrace*, this museum embraces what millions of people come to Paris for—great art. Take an English-speaking guided tour, a self-guided recorded tour, or pick and choose carefully on your own. Resist the temptation to overdo it. Save some rooms for your next visit. It will all still be here. Before it became an art museum, the Louvre was the Paris palace—but usually not the major residence—of several generations of French royalty. While it appears to have a unified classical style, the Louvre was constructed over several centuries. The buildings are centered around several courtyards, including the relatively small, perfectly proportioned Cour Carré, enclosed on four sides, and next to it, the vast rectangle of the Cour Napoleon, which contains the recently finished glass pyramid, the entrance to the museum. The work of the Chinese-American architect I. M. Pei, the pyramid has met with much resistance from the French due to its marked contrast with the classical style. We find it an uplifting counterpoint to the buildings surrounding it, the lines of which can be seen through the glass. Together with the new fountains and pools that flank it, the pyramid gives focus and a cooling effect to what was once a rather empty, arid space. On a hot day, it's like encountering an unexpected block of ice cubes. The tubular structure that supports the glass from the inside looks like cracks in the ice. The west side of the Cour Napoleon opens onto a still larger space, the Jardin du Carrousel. Here stands the Arc du Triomphe du

Carrousel, an echo of its larger cousin straight up the Champs-
Elysées. When you enter the pyramid and go downstairs to the
new museum lobby, don't miss the extensive bookstore, which
stocks a vast and inexpensive selection of prints, posters, and
postcards. Although the museum doesn't open until 10:00 a.m.,
get there early to look around the outside and to be among the
first inside, so you don't have to look over shoulders to see the
paintings. Admission is 25F, 18- to 25-year-olds 13F, under 18
free; free admission on Sunday. Open Thursday through Sunday
9:00 a.m. to 6:00 p.m., Monday and Wednesday 9:00 a.m. to
9:45 p.m., closed on Tuesday.

▲▲▲ **Chartres**—The famous Gothic cathedral was built in the
twelfth century on the site of several previous churches, the last
of which burned to the ground. It is particularly noted for its
stained-glass windows, especially the "Chartres blue." Guided
tours are given, frequently in English. Tip the guide at the end
of the tour, then wander through the narrow streets of the
lovely medieval town.

Trains from the Montparnasse station leave hourly and take
about an hour to get there (round-trip costs 100F).

▲▲▲ **Versailles**—Built in the seventeenth century for Louis
XIV, this massive, stately palace and its surroundings are heavily
visited by tourists, so get here early and avoid going on Tuesdays, when there is an extra rush because the major art
museums in Paris are closed.

The palace is fronted by an impressive wrought iron and gilt
fence. Beyond it lies a vast cobblestone courtyard, through
which you can imagine carriages rushing up to the palace
entrance. Visit the royal apartments for a glimpse of the Sun
King's (Louis XIV) tiny bed. Here, too, is the dazzling Hall of
Mirrors, a long, sumptuous room that has been the scene of
many historic events, including the signing of the Treaty of Versailles that concluded World War I. Admission to the chateau is
21F, Sunday 11F. Open Tuesday through Sunday 9:45 a.m. to
5:00 p.m.

Behind the palace lies an immense formal garden, including
two tree-reflecting canals that intersect each other. Wander here
for a while among the box hedges and formal floral plantings,
then find your way to the royal retreats from court life: the classic Grand Trianon, built by the famous architect Mansart; the
later Petit Trianon, designed for Louis XV; and the Petit
Hameau, the charming, elaborate dwelling where Marie
Antoinette played at being a simple country girl. If you've taken
the trouble to come out here, don't miss them. Because you
have to walk a bit from the palace to get there, you will find
them less crowded than the main event. Tickets for visits to

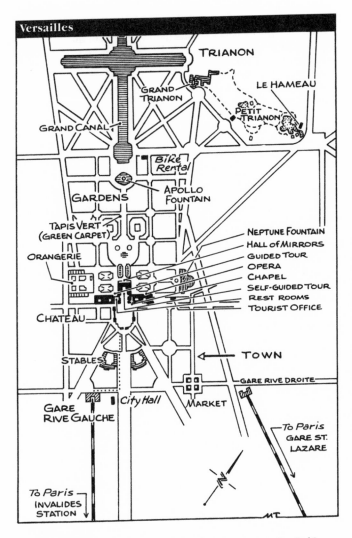

both Trianons cost 11F. Open Tuesday through Sunday 9:45 a.m. to 12:00 noon and 2:00 to 5:00 p.m.

▲ **Montmartre-Sacré-Coeur**—The century-old domed white basilica of Sacré-Coeur, postcard familiar, dominates the city from its hill. Montmartre streets were once painted by Utrillo, and its jumping nightlife was recorded in the posters of

Toulouse-Lautrec. Now the place du Tertre, center of the neighborhood, is the biggest tourist trap in Paris, full of quick-sketch artists and overpriced restaurants. Nevertheless, the view from Sacré-Coeur is fine, and the warren of streets and stairs surrounding it are charming.

▲▲▲ **Le Grand Vefour**—Why not celebrate the last night of your around-the-world journey at the ultimate restaurant, Le Grand Vefour? If you've ever wondered where visiting restaurant chefs flock to when they visit Paris, look no further. The mirrored dining room offers traditional haute cuisine. The restaurant is located at 17 rue de Beaujolais (tel. 42-96-56-27), closed Sundays and during the month of August. Reservations are a must, and men must wear a tie and jacket. Expect to spend at least $100 a person.

Tomorrow you will depart Paris, catching your flight back to the United States. Have a great trip home.

VENICE

A memorable train trip from Paris takes you across the Alps to this city built on more than 100 islands. We recommend Venice as an extension from France for several reasons. As discussed in the introduction, many popular around-the-world fares limit the number of hops you can make within Europe. To add a Venice stopover to our recommended Athens-Paris routing on the primary itinerary would add significantly to your airfare. More to the point, a trip through the south of France, Switzerland, and northern Italy by train is one of Europe's great adventures. Even if you're not a rail buff, you'll love the high level of service and comfort and, above all, the scenery. The train is also a great way to relax; some travelers insist they actually sleep better to the rhythm of the rails. Although it only adds a few days to your travel time, this Venice option makes the perfect coda to your global journey.

Located in an Adriatic lagoon about half an hour from the mainland, Venice has a history as romantic as its setting. Descended from refugees who moved into these coastal marshes in the tenth century to escape invaders, the Venetians adapted well to their island world. Within a few centuries, their fleet dominated the Adriatic and eastern Mediterranean and enjoyed a monopoly on trade routes to the Orient.

Exotic imports from the East were channeled through Venice's trading houses, and the city rapidly gained wealth and prestige. When Venetian fleets were sent to the Holy Lands during the Crusades, the Venetians took the opportunity to capture the body of St. Mark from the Alexandrians and bring him home as the Republic's holy protector. Venice's power peaked when routes opened across the Atlantic. As the city-state lost her control of the seas, she looked to the west for expansion, bringing the inland regions of both Padua and Verona within the shadow of the lion's wings.

While a visit to Venice is a good idea any time of year, May to October is the big tourist season. July and August are hot, humid, and crowded. There is talk among the Venetians of charging tourists an entrance fee to restrict the number of day-trippers, who arrive in overwhelming droves, bringing little profit. While winters tend to be cold and damp, accommodations are much easier to come by, and you'll never have to stand in line. It may also be the most romantic time of year to visit. Gondolas slide in and out of the thick winter mist, and during Carnival, you'll share the stone streets with cloaked, masked figures.

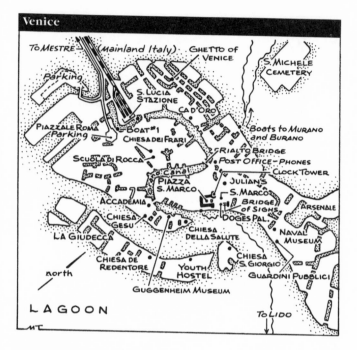

Getting There

While there is convenient air service on British Airways and Air France between Paris and Venice, we recommend the train. If you leave Paris late in the evening aboard train #10 (Pullman accommodations are very expensive; you may find sharing a berth in one of the couchettes a good way to save money), you'll still have a chance to enjoy the scenery of northern Italy before your morning arrival. At Mestre, train cars bound for Venice will be detached from the main consist. What's left of your train leaves the mainland and heads across the bridge to the islands, where the dream sequence begins.

Getting Around

After you arrive, you'll want to buy some lire. For a quick, rough conversion from lire into dollar values, multiply the lire amount by 7 and then move the decimal point four places to the left. For example, 10,000 lire is roughly $7. Leave any excess baggage that you didn't already check in Paris at the Deposito Bagagli. For only 1,000 lire ($0.75) a day, you'll save both money and aggravation en route to your hotel. Checking your bags will also save you the cost of a Venetian taxi. While these private motor launches offer a romantic way to arrive, they are very expensive. We recommend walking over to the Grand Canal platform and catching one of the *vaporetti*, the black-bottomed boats that leave every ten to twenty minutes. There are several routes. Each is numbered, as are the stops. The vaporetti will be your public transit system for the next few days, and with a lighter load, you can take one from the station to St. Mark's Square and walk to your hotel.

From the railway station (stop FS), take the number 2 heading to the left toward San Marco. Tickets are purchased for 2,000 lire ($1.40) at the window before reaching the waiting platform. To avoid buying tickets for every trip, ask about two-day and three-day passes. After disembarking at San Marco, you'll pay about 5,000 lire ($3.75) plus tip for porterage to your hotel.

Additional ferries (*traghetti*) connect St. Mark's with the Lido and other outlying islands. Of course, the gondola remains Venice's best known form of transportation. Built in the traditional manner by a team of artisans, each gondola is constructed from several kinds of wood. The overall shape is asymmetrical to compensate for the gondolier's position to one side. Originally painted in bright colors and lavishly decorated, gondolas are now all painted in Henry Ford's favorite color—black. The change, legend has it, was dictated by city leaders, who decided this was the appropriate color to mourn victims of the Black Death.

Not long ago, wealthy Venetians such as Peggy Guggenheim kept private gondolas at the docks to their palaces. You can still see wedding parties in elegant gondolas with polished brass fittings and plush brocade cushions. You may also spot groups of Japanese tourists floating down the Grand Canal at dusk, accordion player and tenor in tow. The performers will likely be playing Neapolitan songs, despite the mayor's edict banning non-Venetian music during gondola serenades. Incidentally, every Venetian's last ride is a gondola trip to an island cemetery.

Lodging
Do not leave your Venice hotel arrangements to the last minute. Accommodations are very tight during the high season and can also be dear during special events. Although many hotels on the mainland absorb the overflow, the commute distance will reduce your time in Venice.

If price is no object, the super-deluxe 400,900-lire-a-night ($280) **Gritti Palace** on the Grand Canal at San Marco, S. Maria del Giglio 2467 Venice (tel. 794611), and the similarly priced **Cipriani**, on Giudecca Island, 10 Venice (tel. 5207744), are both good choices. Popular with performers and *appassionati*, the expensive **Hotel La Fenice et des Artistes** is located at San Marco, Campiello Fenice 1936, Venice (tel. 5232333). Rooms here run 130,000 lire ($91) a night.

Also on the Grand Canal is the moderately priced **Hotel Carpaccio**, S. Polo, Calle Corner 2765 Venice (tel. 5235946). A room here runs 90,000 lire ($63) a night. Another good choice is the **Hotel Flora** at 158,000 lire ($105) a night . It's at San Marco, Calle Bergamaschi 2283-A, Venice (tel. 5205844), and features a lovely garden overlooking the Grand Canal. On the Lido, far from the madding crowd and close to the beach, is the small, chalet-style **Hotel Quattro Stagioni**. It's a bit removed from the tourist scene, which may be an asset in the busy summer season. Rooms cost 200,000 lire ($140) a night.

Less expensive accommodations include the 80,000-lire-a-night ($56) **Pensione Accademia**—Villa Maravegie, Fondamenta Bollani 1058 (tel. 5210188), and the **Hotel Bisanzio** at 150,000 lire ($105) a night, located at Riva degli Schiavoni, Castello, Calle della Pietà 3656, Venice 30122 (tel. 5203100). The rock-bottom **Pensione Bucintoro** is located near the train station at Castello, Riva S. Biago, 2135A (tel. 5223240). It runs 60,000 lire ($42).

Some Venice visitors consider the outer islands a good alternative to the busy tourist hubs. Queen Elizabeth's choice is Torcello, reached via public steamer. You can stay here at the six-room pensione **Locanda Cipriani**, Isola di Torcello 29 (tel. 730150). Rooms run 220,000 lire ($154) per person, including breakfast and dinner. A favorite of Ernest Hemingway's (the owner kept this hotel open during the 1948 winter to help the writer finish *Across the River and into the Trees*), you can also dine at the hotel's excellent terrace restaurant. Closed mid-November to mid-March.

Food

At **Do Forni** on Calle Specchieri (tel. 523-2148), a vast menu offers excellent shellfish, fish soup, and risottos. Ask for a table in the narrow room that resembles the Orient Express dining car. Expensive. **Trattoria La Madonna**, near the Rialto Bridge, is another good choice. Look for the Hotel Marconi and Milano along the canal downstream from the Rialto Bridge. On the left, just past the hotel, is an alleyway where a yellow and black sign directs you to the restaurant. Here, amid art-lined walls, you'll be able to order some of the promising fish you spotted at the morning market. Moderate. **Ristorante All'Angelo**, beneath and to the right of the clock tower, is also recommended. In warm months, you can sit outside beneath the maroon awning; in the winter, choose a table close to the ceramic stove. **La Corte Sconta**, Calle del Pestrin (tel. 5227024), is a good place to try mussels and other seafood. This inexpensive trattoria offers courtyard dining and is very popular with locals. On Torcello Island, try the **Locanda Cipriani** restaurant.

A good wine bar with sandwiches and snacks is **Enoteca Al Volto**, Cala Cavalli S. Luca (tel. 5228945). **Harry's Bar**, a Venice legend, is at Calle Vallaresso 1323 (tel. 5236797). It's named for American Harry Pickering, who borrowed money from bartender Giuseppe Cipriani and then, in a brilliant stroke of venture capitalism, paid the Italian back by funding his start-up. Many of the popular drinks are named for Venetian artists. Today, Cipriani's son Arrigo (Harry) operates this expensive establishment frequented by celebrities and readers of our book.

Sightseeing: First Day
▲▲▲ **Piazza San Marco**—Begin by observing the square with your back to the water. This is the way Venetian architects wanted visitors to first see the city as they disembarked from their ships. Under the porticos on the far side of the square is the tourist office, where you can pick up a map of the city as well as a schedule of special events and museum exhibitions. Begin by visiting the church and the Doge's Palace (open summer 8:30 a.m. to 6:00 p.m. daily; winter 8:30 a.m. to 2:00 p.m. daily; tel. 5224951), the pink and white building that graces the 1,000-lire note. Then take the 4,000-lire ($3) elevator ride up the brick tower to get a panoramic view of the city. With map in hand, orient yourself before heading out into the labyrinth of canals and alleyways spread out across 120 islands. Look across the Grand Canal to see Palladio's church of San Giorgio, the gold ball of the customs building, and the white domes of Santa Maria della Salute, built by eighteenth-century Venetians in gratitude for their salvation from the Black Death.
▲▲▲ **San Giorgio Church**—After getting an overview of the city, head to the vaporetto station behind the Doge's Palace for a short trip out to San Giorgio to visit Palladio's beautiful church. His classic designs were widely admired and copied not only in Europe but also the United States. Among others, he influenced Thomas Jefferson, who designed Monticello along Palladian lines.
▲▲ **Il Burchiello**—After visiting the San Giorgio church, you may want to book a daylong boat trip from Venice to Padua through the Veneto, a mainland region where Palladio designed

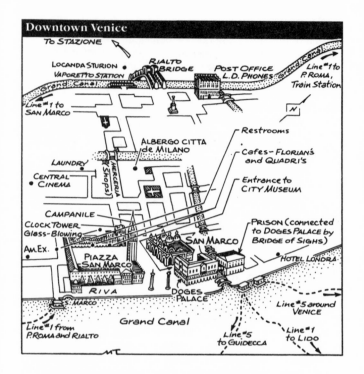

Downtown Venice

To STAZIONE

LOCANDA STURION
VAPORETTO STATION
RIALTO BRIDGE
POST OFFICE L.D. PHONES
Line #1 to P. ROMA, Train Station

Grand Canal

Line #1 to SAN MARCO

N

Restrooms

ALBERGO CITTA de MILANO

Cafes — FLORIAN'S and QUADRI'S

LAUNDRY

MERCERIA (Shops)

Entrance to CITY MUSEUM

CENTRAL CINEMA

CAMPANILE

CLOCK TOWER
Glass-Blowing

SAN MARCO

PRISON (connected to DOGES PALACE by BRIDGE OF SIGHS)

Am.Ex.

PIAZZA SAN MARCO

HOTEL LONDRA

RIVA

DOGES PALACE

S. MARCO

Line #5 around VENICE

Grand Canal

Line #1 from P. ROMA and RIALTO

Line #5 to GIUDECCA

Line #1 to LIDO

such classics as Villa Maser and Villa Malcontenta. You can visit
some of these majestic estates via Il Burchiello, an authentic
reproduction of a historic vessel that takes you through a net-
work of rivers and canals. Il Burchiello leaves in the morning
from San Marco with a stopover in Padua. The return trip is via
motor coach (tel. 854480).

▲▲▲ **Accademia and Scuola Grande di San Rocco**—On
your first day in Venice you'll want to take a leisurely pace,
allowing time to explore museums like the Accademia (open
daily 9:00 a.m. to 2:00 p.m., Sunday, 9:00 a.m. to 1:00 p.m.,
closed Mondays; tel. 5222247), where you can see paintings by
masters like Bellini, Titian, and Tintoretto. For more Tintorettos,
continue to Scuola Grande di San Rocco (open summer daily
from 9:00 a.m. to 1:00 p.m. and 3:30 to 6:30 p.m., winter daily
10:00 a.m. to 1:00 p.m., Sunday 10:00 a.m. to 1:00 p.m. and 3:00
to 6:00 p.m.; tel. 5234864). In addition to the legendary
museums and buildings, you'll want to take time to explore the
Venetian neighborhoods and enjoy outdoor restaurants such as
Caffè Quadri or Caffè Florian. Prices here are no bargain, but
there is no better place in Venice to relax. Perhaps you'll want to

return after dinner to watch the passing parade. This is Italian people-watching at its best. Take a comfortable seat, order a Bellini made from peach juice and champagne or a seasonal cocktail like a Carpaccio, and toast the night sky.

Sightseeing—Second Day
▲▲▲ **Scuola degli Schiavoni**—In the morning, walk east from San Marco along Riva degli Schiavoni to Fondamenta dell' Arsenale and turn left to Calle dei Furlani and Scuola degli Schiavoni (open summer daily 9:30 a.m. to 12:30 p.m. and 3:30 to 6:30 p.m., Sunday 9:30 a.m. to 12:30 p.m.; winter daily 10:00 a.m. to 12:30 p.m. and 3:30 to 6:00 p.m., Sunday 10:30 a.m. to 12:30 p.m., closed Monday; tel. 5228828). This is the former guild hall of the Dalmatians, who hired Vittore Carpaccio in 1502 to decorate their building with nine wonderful paintings. Among them is the famed portrait of St. Jerome and his terrier in the study. This small building is one of Venice's great treasures; don't miss it. From here, return to the Riva degli Schiavoni and catch a vaporetto upstream to the Rialto Bridge.
▲▲▲ **Rialto Bridge Area**—After disembarking, pass under the clock tower to the left of the church and follow the yellow signs. Located at high tide point along the Grand Canal, the Rialto is adjacent to an outdoor food market selling fish that may be destined for your dinner plate. Stroll through this area, enjoy lunch, and then cross the bridge to board vaporetto #1 downstream toward San Marco. Disembark at Ca' Venier dei Leoni, the Peggy Guggenheim Museum.
▲▲ **Peggy Guggenheim Museum**—It was originally called Ca' Nonfinito, because construction halted after the ground floor was completed in 1749. Ms. Guggenheim purchased this unfinished building in 1951 to display her modern art collection, which includes pieces by Picasso, Klee, Chagall, and Braque (open daily 2:00 to 6:00 p.m. April to October, closed Tuesday; tel. 706288). After seeing her collection, take a quiet walk along the Giudecca and the Zattere.
▲▲ **Lido**—If the weather is good, head to the Lido in the late afternoon. After disembarking from the vaporetto, walk along Via Santa Maria Elisabetta, take the second left, and you'll arrive at a bike rental stand. With your own wheels, you'll be able to explore the grand southern beachfront hotels favored by visitors like Thomas Mann and Evelyn Waugh. Along Via Santa Maria Elisabetta, you'll find Venetians and vacationing Italians people-watching and window-shopping. If you have a passport and a tie, you might want to visit the Lido casino, which opens at 2:00 p.m. Far more businesslike than Las Vegas or Atlantic City, European casinos like this one are great fun.

Sightseeing: Third Day

Buy some picnic fare and then take a public steamer to the outer islands of Murano, Torcello, and Burano. Because you're traveling independently—not with an organized tour—you can explore at your own pace.

▲▲ **Torcello, Murano, and Burano**—Torcello is an ideal spot for lunch. While here, you may want to visit the churches of St. Mary Genetrix and St. Fosca. A museum in the former Palazzo del Consiglio includes bas-relief sculpture, tombs, and sarcophagi. Murano is famous for its glassmaking. There's a fine glass museum located in the former home of a local bishop. It displays more than 4,000 glass pieces from both contemporary and ancient times. Plan on stopping for dinner at one of Burano's restaurants. Raspo de Ua on this island's main commercial street is a good, moderately priced choice.

After dinner, you can join one of Italy's greatest rituals, the evening stroll or *passeggiata*. You'll find mothers and daughters, fathers and sons, and entire families casually strolling the neighborhood and visiting with friends. This is Venice at its best, a place where you'll find men busy mending their nets and women sitting in the doorways of their pastel-colored homes doing lacework and gossiping. If our experience is any indication, you may be one of the few outsiders here enjoying an evening in Burano. Before the shops close, be sure to pick up

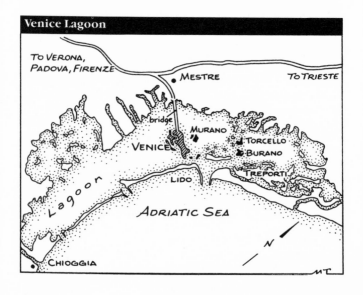

Venice Lagoon

Buranelli, special ring-shaped cookies that will be perfect for eating with tomorrow morning's cappuccino.

In addition to Murano, Torcello, and Burano, you may also want to take a public steamer to the island of San Patrizio. Italy's residents will be pleased to show you the monastery established by St. Francis, who bought this island for a very good reason. He purchased slaves in North Africa and then brought them to San Patrizio, where they were set free.

Option: Ghetto of Venice

If you have more time, visit the Ghetto of Venice, where the Jewish community lived from the fifteenth to eighteenth centuries. In this quiet neighborhood, away from the more heavily trodden tourist routes, you can visit three of the city's synagogues as part of a tour. In the summer season, 1,300 lire ($1) tours operate on the hour from the Museum in Campo del Ghetto Nuovo. To reach the museum, take the vaporetto to the railway station, disembark, and walk to the right along Lista di Spagna. Cross the bridge, turn left, and you will soon see an alleyway on the right with an inscription above the entrance. Continue straight and cross a little iron bridge into the Campo del Ghetto Nuovo, also called Museo Communita Israelitica (open daily 10:00 a.m. to 12:30 p.m.; tel. 715012). On the right, across the empty square, is the entrance to the museum. Here you'll learn the story of the Jewish refugees who came here in the late fifteenth century after being expelled from Spain. Segregated in this neighborhood, they were forbidden to own land and charged outrageous rents by the Venetians. After several centuries of harassment, the entire Jewish colony went bankrupt in 1735. The doors of the ghetto, opened by Napoleon in July 1797, were closed again during the Austrian occupation. Finally, in 1866, the ghetto doors were torn down when Venice was annexed to Italy. The museum, founded in 1953, is located inside a German synagogue. The collection includes prized textiles, Venetian silver, and rare books. On the far side of square, under a symbolic piece of barbed wire, the city has hung seven bas-reliefs that depict the story of the ghetto and the World War II concentration camps.

After completing your visit to Venice, you'll want to catch a train back to Paris to pick up your flight home.

INDEX

Other Books from John Muir Publications

Asia Through the Back Door, Rick Steves and John Gottberg (65-48-3) 336 pp. $15.95

Buddhist America: Centers, Retreats, Practices, Don Morreale (28-94-X) 400 pp. $12.95

Bus Touring: Charter Vacations, U.S.A., Stuart Warren with Douglas Bloch (28-95-8) 168 pp. $9.95

Catholic America: Self-Renewal Centers and Retreats, Patricia Christian-Meyer (65-20-3) 325 pp. $13.95

Complete Guide to Bed & Breakfasts, Inns & Guesthouses, Pamela Lanier (65-43-2) 512 pp. $15.95

Costa Rica: A Natural Destination, Ree Sheck (65-51-3) 280 pp. $15.95

Elderhostels: The Students' Choice, Mildred Hyman (65-28-9) 224 pp. $12.95

Europe 101: History & Art for the Traveler, Rick Steves and Gene Openshaw (28-78-8) 372 pp. $12.95

Europe Through the Back Door, Rick Steves (65-42-4) 432 pp. $16.95

Floating Vacations: River, Lake, and Ocean Adventures, Michael White (65-32-7) 256 pp. $17.95

Gypsying After 40: A Guide to Adventure and Self-Discovery, Bob Harris (28-71-0) 264 pp. $12.95

The Heart of Jerusalem, Arlynn Nellhaus (28-79-6) 312 pp. $12.95

Indian America: A Traveler's Companion, Eagle/Walking Turtle (65-29-7) 424 pp. $16.95

Mona Winks: Self-Guided Tours of Europe's Top Museums, Rick Steves (28-85-0) 450 pp. $14.95

The On and Off the Road Cookbook, Carl Franz (28-27-3) 272 pp. $8.50

The People's Guide to Mexico, Carl Franz (28-99-0) 608 pp. $15.95

The People's Guide to RV Camping in Mexico, Carl Franz with Steve Rogers (28-91-5) 256 pp. $13.95

Preconception: A Woman's Guide to Preparing for Pregnancy and Parenthood, Brenda Aikey-Keller (65-44-0) 236 pp. $14.95

Ranch Vacations: The Complete Guide to Guest and Resort, Fly-Fishing, and Cross-Country Skiing Ranches, Eugene Kilgore (65-30-0) 392 pp. $18.95

The Shopper's Guide to Mexico, Steve Rogers and Tina Rosa (28-90-7) 224 pp. $9.95

Ski Tech's Guide to Equipment, Skiwear, and Accessories, edited by Bill Tanler (65-45-9) 144 pp. $11.95

Ski Tech's Guide to Maintenance and Repair, edited by Bill Tanler (65-46-7) 144 pp. $11.95

A Traveler's Guide to Asian Culture, Kevin Chambers (65-14-9) 224 pp. $13.95

Traveler's Guide to Healing Centers and Retreats in North America, Martine Rudee and Jonathan Blease (65-15-7) 240 pp. $11.95

Undiscovered Islands of the Caribbean, Burl Willes (28-80-X) 216 pp. $12.95

22 Days Series
These pocket-size itineraries are a refreshing departure from ordinary guidebooks. Each author has an in-depth knowledge of the region covered and offers 22 tested daily itineraries through their favorite destinations. Included are not only "must see" attractions but also little-known villages and hidden "jewels" as well as valuable general information.

22 Days Around the World by R. Rapoport and B. Willes (65-31-9)
22 Days in Alaska by Pamela Lanier (28-68-0)
22 Days in the American Southwest by R. Harris (28-88-5)
22 Days in Asia by R. Rapoport and B. Willes (65-17-3)
22 Days in Australia by John Gottberg (65-40-8)
22 Days in California by Roger Rapoport (28-93-1)
22 Days in China by Gaylon Duke and Zenia Victor (28-72-9)

22 Days in Dixie by Richard Polese (65-18-1)
22 Days in Europe by Rick Steves (65-63-7)
22 Days in Florida by Richard Harris (65-27-0)
22 Days in France by Rick Steves (65-07-6)
22 Days in Germany, Austria & Switzerland by Rick Steves (65-39-4)
22 Days in Great Britain by Rick Steves (65-38-6)
22 Days in Hawaii by Arnold Schuchter (65-50-5)
22 Days in India by Anurag Mathur (28-87-7)
22 Days in Japan by David Old (28-73-7)
22 Days in Mexico by S. Rogers and T. Rosa (65-41-6)
22 Days in New England by Anne Wright (28-96-6)
22 Days in New Zealand by Arnold Schuchter (28-86-9)
22 Days in Norway, Denmark & Sweden by R. Steves (28-83-4)
22 Days in the Pacific Northwest by R. Harris (28-97-4)
22 Days in Spain & Portugal by Rick Steves (65-06-8)
22 Days in the West Indies by C. & S. Morreale (28-74-5)

All 22 Days titles are 128 to 152 pages and $7.95 each, except *22 Days Around the World* and *22 Days in Europe*, which are 192 pages and $9.95.

"Kidding Around"
Travel Guides for Children
Written for kids eight years of age and older. Generously illustrated in two colors with imaginative

characters and images. An adventure to read and a treasure to keep.

Kidding Around Atlanta, Anne Pedersen (65-35-1) 64 pp. $9.95
Kidding Around Boston, Helen Byers (65-36-X) 64 pp. $9.95
Kidding Around the Hawaiian Islands, Sarah Lovett (65-37-8) 64 pp. $9.95
Kidding Around London, Sarah Lovett (65-24-6) 64 pp. $9.95
Kidding Around Los Angeles, Judy Cash (65-34-3) 64 pp. $9.95
Kidding Around New York City, Sarah Lovett (65-33-5) 64 pp. $9.95
Kidding Around San Francisco, Rosemary Zibart (65-23-8) 64 pp. $9.95
Kidding Around Washington, D.C., Anne Pedersen (65-25-4) 64 pp. $9.95

Automotive Books

The Greaseless Guide to Car Care Confidence: Take the Terror Out of Talking to Your Mechanic, Mary Jackson (65-19-X) 224 pp. $14.95
How to Keep Your VW Alive (65-12-2) 424 pp. $19.95
How to Keep Your Subaru Alive (65-11-4) 480 pp. $19.95
How to Keep Your Toyota Pickup Alive (28-89-3) 392 pp. $19.95
How to Keep Your Datsun/ Nissan Alive (28-65-6) 544 pp. $19.95
Off-Road Emergency Repair & Survival, James Ristow (65-26-2) 160 pp. $9.95
Road & Track's Used Car Classics, edited by Peter Bohr (28-69-9) 272 pp. $12.95

Ordering Information

If you cannot find our books in your local bookstore, you can order directly from us. Your books will be sent to you via UPS (for U.S. destinations), and you will receive them approximately 10 days from the time that we receive your order. Include $2.75 for the first item ordered and $.50 for each additional item to cover shipping and handling costs. UPS will not deliver to a P.O. Box; please give us a street address. For airmail within the U.S., enclose $4.00 per book for shipping and handling. All foreign orders will be shipped surface rate; please enclose $3.00 for the first item and $1.00 for each additional item. Please inquire about foreign airmail rates.

Method of Payment

Your order may be paid by check, money order, or credit card. We cannot be responsible for cash sent through the mail. All payments must be made in U.S. dollars drawn on a U.S. bank. Canadian postal money orders in U.S. dollars are also acceptable. For VISA, MasterCard, or American Express orders, include your card number, expiration date, and your signature, or call (505)982-4078. Books ordered on American Express cards can be shipped only to the billing address of the cardholder. Sorry, no C.O.D.'s. Residents of sunny New Mexico, add 5.625% tax to the total.

Address all orders and inquiries to:
John Muir Publications
P.O. Box 613
Santa Fe, NM 87504
(505) 982-4078
(505) 988-1680 FAX